Good Dividends

This book seeks to answer the question 'leadership for what?' We shall outline an answer by focusing on responsible leadership of business purpose through an inter-disciplinary perspective. Responsible leadership moves the axis of leadership from leader-followers to leader-stakeholders; away from looking at leadership as person-centric—the qualities, abilities, and effectiveness of the leader—to a focus on the purposes, responsibilities, and activities of leadership. Leadership orientation is about realising value for a range of constituencies, not just the shareholders of a business. In this way this book offers up an alternative business model to that of dominant neo-liberal approaches to capitalism and its flow-on effect to the leadership project. This is a model that draws on a most obvious assumption—if leaders maximise the use of all the capitals of their business they will maximise their dividends, and thus deliver their responsibility to the shareholders as well as other relevant stakeholders.

This book explores how five dividends (based on five capitals) can be developed through attention to a sixth dividend (and sixth capital)—the dividend from our planet and communities. The planetary dividend is the flourishing of humanity—but it is also a significant dividend to a business. For example, by engaging a business in a purpose-led orientation to enhance the planetary dividend, the dividend from human resourcefulness becomes manifest—employee sense of purpose, commitment, passion, and energy. The realisation of such can also connect with dividends from innovation, operations, and brands. For example, the business benefits from a purpose-driven brand.

In short, responsible leadership of business purpose outlines a case for leadership to focus on a connected portfolio of 'good' dividends as an answer to the question 'leadership for what?' The book is written by academics and organisational leaders. It draws on a range of research with leaders from a variety of contexts to illustrate the challenges but also the benefits of this argument. It is an ambitious book: ambitious, in terms of moving leadership towards realising purpose; ambitious by seeking to align a range of business disciplines around responsible leadership; and ambitious because it challenges the dominant assumptions that shape business leadership. However, it is based on a simple question: why would a business not wish to generate good dividends for all its stakeholders?

Steve Kempster is Professor of Leadership Learning and Development at Lancaster University Management School, UK.

Thomas Maak is Professor of Leadership and Director of the Centre for Workplace Leadership at the University of Melbourne, Australia.

Ken Parry was Professor of Leadership Studies at Deakin Business School, in Melbourne, Australia.

Routledge Studies in Leadership Research

Revitalising Leadership
Putting Theory and Practice into Context
*Suze Wilson, Stephen Cummings, Brad Jackson, and
Sarah Proctor-Thomson*

Women, Religion and Leadership
Female Saints as Unexpected Leaders
Edited by Barbara Denison

"Leadership Matters?"
Finding Voice, Connection and Meaning in the 21st Century
Edited by Chris Mabey and David Knights

Innovation in Environmental Leadership
Critical Perspectives
*Edited by Benjamin W. Redekop, Deborah Rigling Gallagher,
and Rian Satterwhite*

After Leadership
Edited by Brigid Carroll, Suze Wilson, and Josh Firth

Creative Leadership
Contexts and Prospects
Edited by Charalampos Mainemelis, Olga Epitropaki, and Ronit Kark

Theoretical Perspectives of Strategic Followership
David Zoogah

Good Dividends
Responsible Leadership of Business Purpose
Edited by Steve Kempster, Thomas Maak, and Ken Parry

For more information about this series, please visit: www.routledge.com/
Routledge-Studies-in-Leadership-Research/book-series/RSLR

Good Dividends

Responsible Leadership of Business Purpose

Edited by Steve Kempster,
Thomas Maak, and Ken Parry

LONDON AND NEW YORK

First published 2019 by Routledge

2 Park Square, Milton Park, Abingdon, Oxfordshire OX14 4RN

52 Vanderbilt Avenue, New York, NY 10017

*Routledge is an imprint of the Taylor & Francis Group, an
informa business*

First issued in paperback 2020

Library of Congress Cataloging-in-Publication Data
A catalog record for this title has been requested

ISBN: 978-1-138-10352-8 (hbk)
ISBN: 978-0-367-49735-4 (pbk)

Typeset in Sabon
by Apex CoVantage, LLC

This book is dedicated to the work and memory of our dear friend and colleague Professor Ken Parry. With great sadness Ken died in February, 2018 after a long illness with pancreatic cancer. He was the spark of energy that ignited this project. His work in the field of leadership studies has left a lasting legacy. Ken was one of the earliest to argue that leadership should be reframed away from the leader and towards a broader notion of leadership as a process of social influence (Parry, 1998). In the last decade his energy was oriented to the discourses of leadership twinned with the morality of the leadership influence. He had many misgivings that leadership studies too often pursued a narrow scientific endeavour that was disconnected to the social challenges that leadership should address. Conversations with a glass (or two) of good German beer followed a journey of practical idealism. What if the forces of capitalism that capture and so often corrupt leadership could be used to address the challenges that face humanity? Could leadership studies give more back than the relatively futile efforts thus far? It is the answer to these two questions that this book seeks to address. We hope it is a catalyst to engage debate and action. That would be a fitting legacy for a great scholar and a great bloke.

Contents

About the Contributors

Stewart Barnes is founder and Managing Director of QuoLux, which is a privately owned company that are specialists in leadership and strategic development working closely with small-medium sized enterprises (SMEs) to improve their productivity and profitability. Stewart has over 30 years' experience of leading, growing and developing a variety of private businesses in different markets in different countries, transforming organisations and their performance. He has created a Work Based Learning MBA (Leading Business) with the University of Gloucestershire and the fully online Leading MBA. Stewart is a Board Director and trusted advisor to a number of SMEs. He is researching his PhD in Leadership Learning, is a co-author of Leading Small Business (Edward Elgar) and has been published over a dozen times on the subjects of leadership, business planning, employee engagement, innovation and productivity.

Steve Eldridge is a Chartered Engineer and Senior Fellow of the HEA. In his early career he was the director responsible for quality, manufacturing and logistics systems in the European division of an American automotive systems supplier. He became an academic following completion of an Engineering Doctorate at the University of Manchester. As a Senior Teaching Fellow at Lancaster University Management School, he specialises in teaching Operations Management to non-specialist managers. He is the director of the MSc in Manufacturing Leadership Programme and a member of the LUMS Centre for Productivity and Efficiency. His current research portfolio encompasses a range of projects in both the manufacturing and service sectors that focus on the deployment of systems (e.g., sales and operations planning (S&OP)) and technology (e.g., agent-based simulation (ABS), Industry 4.0, innovation strategy) and how they contribute to sustainable value creation.

Luke Freeman is Joint Chief Executive of M F Freeman Group, which is a privately-owned SME with 100 employees and £25 million turnover with plans to grow to £50 million. They specialise in Property Development, Construction, Plant Hire, Leisure and Farming. Luke has been instrumental in successfully diversifying and growing the group of companies and they have won many awards for business and design. Luke has recently completed a Work Based Learning MBA (Leading Business) with the University of Gloucestershire. Luke is currently applying the concept of Good Dividends within his organisation.

Minna Halme is Professor of Sustainability Management at Aalto University School of Business and Director of Aalto Sustainability Hub (www.aalto.fi/sustainability). Her research focuses on sustainability innovations and co-creation of sustainable business models. She has participated in several European research projects and heads a number of national ones. She has published in several refereed journals and authored a number of books and reports. Her work has also been featured by *The Ecologist* and *The Newsweek*. She is a member of the Advisory Board of Finland's largest retailer SOK and has held memberships in UN Secretary-General's High-level Panel on Global Sustainability, the Finnish Government Foresight2030 group and the Administrative Board of WWF Finland. She is co-founder of Aalto University's cross-disciplinary Creative Sustainability master programme and Aalto Global Impact, and has received the Academy of Finland award for the social impact of her research.

Anthony Hesketh is Senior Lecturer in the Department of Work and Technology at Lancaster University Management School. Ant's research focuses on exploring how we understand, develop and articulate value in organisations. Work to date has examined the socially constructed nature of human capital theory, which evolved into a critique of first normative political economy, then a meta-theoretical critique of how value is understood in organisational settings. Frustration with the strangely enduring Cartesian Divide has led to recent work carving out a new theory of value. Achieving this has meant extending scholarship in the accounting and leadership fields to understand the daily challenges faced by senior executives. The new theory of value is outlined in this book.

Luke Hildyard was appointed Director of the High Pay Centre in March 2018. Previously Luke worked as Policy Lead for Corporate Governance and Stewardship at the Pensions and Lifetime Savings Association (PLSA), the trade body for UK pension fund investors. He was Deputy Director of the High Pay Centre from 2012–2015. Luke has authored a number of reports on subjects including inequality, corporate governance, responsible investment and workforce reporting. He has also previously worked for a number of think tanks and in local government.

Katalin Illes is Head of Leadership and Professional Development in the Business School at the University of Westminster, UK. Her early career included successful entrepreneurial and consulting initiatives. As an academic, Katalin led and developed collaborations between UK universities and higher education institutions in Denmark, Finland, Hungary and India. She also worked as Director of International Development of China's first liberal arts college. Katalin has led and developed innovative, creative, trust-based networks and partnerships to promote practice-based, life-long growth of individuals, communities and enterprises around the world.

Steve Kempster is Professor of Leadership Learning and Development at Lancaster University Management School, UK. He has authored the books *LEADing Small Business* (Edward Elgar) and *How Managers Have Learnt to Lead* (Palgrave Macmillan), and has co-edited (with Brigid Carrol) *Responsible Leadership: Realism and Romanticism* (Routledge), *Field Guide to Leadership Development* (Edward Elgar) and he has published widely in *The Leadership Quarterly*, *Management Learning*, *Leadership*, and other top-ranking journals. Steve's first career was as a chartered surveyor, during which time he ran his own practice. In his second career, his research and engagement interests span leadership learning, responsible leadership, and through addressing the question 'leadership for what?' examines the contexts, purposes, actions and outcomes of those who lead.

Malcolm Kirkup is Professor of Strategic Marketing, Pro-Vice Chancellor and Head of the Business School at the University of Westminster, UK. His early career included a strategic marketing role at Sears PLC, but he has since risen through the academic ranks in UK business schools including Cranfield, Loughborough, Birmingham, Lancaster, Exeter, Edinburgh and now Westminster. He has a passion for innovation and is particularly proud of his achievements in launching educational programmes that combine close working relationships with business, a practical and applied focus, an emphasis on sustainability and those which challenge conventional thinking. He is most proud of his role in the development of the ground-breaking One Planet MBA at the University of Exeter, in association with WWF and a range of corporates, and taking the University of Edinburgh's MBA to global recognition in terms of female participation.

Thomas Maak is Professor of Leadership and Director of the Centre for Workplace Leadership at the University of Melbourne. A graduate from the University of St Gallen, he held appointments at St Gallen, INSEAD, ESADE Business School and was formerly Head, School of Management and founding Director of the Centre for Business Ethics and Responsible Leadership at the University of South Australia. Thomas is a leading scholar in the field of responsible leadership and uses a multi-level lens to research leadership at the individual, group and organisational level, linking ethical theory, political philosophy, relational thinking and stakeholder theory. Thomas has extensive experience in leadership development and has worked for several years with PricewaterhouseCoopers on their award-winning senior executive programme 'Ulysses'. Beyond leadership research his interests include ethical decision-making, political CSR and organisational neuroscience. Through his work with leading social entrepreneurs in South Asia and South America he is also interested in social innovation and the advancement of human dignity in a connected world.

Ken Parry was Professor of Leadership Studies at Deakin Business School, in Melbourne, Australia. His research interests focused on all methodologies that are associated with the study of leadership. He brought auto-ethnography to management/business studies early in the century. He is co-author, with Brad Jackson, of the Sage *Short, Interesting and Cheap Book* about studying leadership—the No.1 selling leadership text. Most of his publications focused on grounded theory and other qualitative methods. He was widely asked to be a keynote speaker in industry and academic conferences.

Nicola M. Pless is Chair in Positive Business and Professor of Management at University of South Australia Business School and holds the 2011 Honorary Jef Van Gerwen Chair from the University of Antwerp for her work in the field of Responsible Leadership. She has served on the faculties of the University of St Gallen, INSEAD and ESADE Business School, and is a former Vice President of the International Leadership Development.

Her research has a global and strategic perspective and sits at the interface of leadership, stakeholder management, sustainability and innovation. She also explores the role of mindfulness and virtues such as empathy, compassion and dignity in processes of responsible leadership and ethical decision making. She has published more than 60 papers in books and academic journals such *Academy of Management Learning & Education, Human Resource Management, Journal of Business Ethics, Journal of Management Studies*. She sits on the board of the Academy of Business in Society (ABIS) and is an Associate of the Globally Responsible Leadership Initiative.

Sam Rawsthorne is a PhD student at Lancaster University Management School. He holds a BSc in Accounting and Finance and an MSc in Advanced Financial Analysis from Lancaster. He has also completed Levels 1 and 2 of the CFA© programme. He was awarded the Chancellor's Medal by Lancaster University in recognition of his exceptional undergraduate performance. He has provided research assistance on projects for the Pensions and Lifetime Savings Association and the Financial Reporting Council. Sam's PhD examines the properties and impact of narrative reporting on strategy and business models by UK firms.

Robyn Remke is a Lecturer in Leadership and Organisational communication at Lancaster University Management School, UK. Her research combines interdisciplinary interests in communication, gender and organisational studies to examine the role of, and potential for, leadership in specific organisational contexts. Robyn's current research projects focus on diversity and inclusion practices in the public sector, women in enterprise in West Africa and gender inclusivity and women's leadership in European business schools. Robyn has taught and conducted research in the United States, Europe, Africa and Asia, and she is a past president of the Organization for the Study of Communication, Language, and Gender (OSCLG).

Andy Webster is Detective Chief Superintendent and 'Head of Serious Crime and Specialist Capability' at Lancashire Constabulary. He joined Lancashire Constabulary over 25 years ago and spent most of his career as a detective specialising in homicide investigation. Andy has led high profile enquiries, including cold cases and investigations where the victim's body has not been recovered. He has also led the Constabulary's Public Protection Unit and as an Operations Manager, had the responsibility for delivering policing for the north of Lancashire. He describes his life watershed moment as completing the Executive MBA at Lancaster University, where he explored the application of Toyota production principles to the murder investigation process.

Steve Young is Professor of Accounting at Lancaster University Management School. His teaching and research interests include financial reporting, valuation and corporate governance. His current research priorities involve automated analysis of financial market text. He is associate editor of *Journal of Business Finance and Accounting* and his research has been published in leading international journals. He is a member of the Research Advisory Board of the Institute of Chartered Accountants in England and Wales, and has recently worked on annual report disclosure projects with stakeholders including the Financial Conduct Authority, Financial Reporting Council, Chartered Financial Analyst (CFA©) Society UK and the Pensions and Lifetime Savings Association.

Randall Zindler is a member of faculty at Lancaster University Management School. His lectures and research encompass governance, strategy and leadership. Randall is former group CEO of the international disaster relief organisation, Medair, and in that time Chaired EU-CORD, a network of similar organisations. He is currently an international board member of Mercy Ships and Chairman of the Swiss entity.

His background also includes humanitarian intervention in Africa, corporate roles within the Credit Suisse Group and Swiss Air Group. He has been a delegate at the World Economic Forum, in Davos and as a member of YPO has chaired several sub-networks of YPO and championed events that draw together the themes of purpose, people, profit and plant.

Part 1

1 Leadership of Purpose

In Search of *Good Dividends*

Steve Kempster, Ken Parry and Thomas Maak

Business has the very real potential to be the greatest mechanism on the planet to enhance humanity, if it can do this profitably and generate *dividends* for all its stakeholders.

All businesses seek to generate profits or dividends—how could it be otherwise? But let's go further. All businesses **should** generate good dividends. By good dividends we mean four things: that bigger dividends are good; that dividends are sustainable over the medium- to long-term; that dividends are connected to a good purpose and that dividends are realised through ethically good activities. And here's the thing . . . all four are interconnected and depend on each other. Research shows us that when businesses combine all four, these businesses outperform the market over the medium- to long-term (Hesketh in Chapter 11). However, for these good dividends to be realised it requires leadership commitment and action to align purpose and business. This seems straightforward, but again research shows us that this is far from the norm. It is not that there are few purposes to align a business to, but rather limited leadership awareness and understanding of how value is generated from such alignment. There is a fundamental need to move beyond philanthropy (fund raising for a local charity, or an employee volunteer day off once a month scheme) and make purpose central to the business model—enhancing society and realising good dividends. In this book we seek to outline how this can occur. We do this because business has the very real potential to use its assets (or capitals) to enhance, communities, society and humanity. It just needs leadership commitment and some ideas to move that commitment into action. But first, let's start with the much-abused term of 'dividend.'

A dividend is more than simply the term for a payment. It is an ownership in something to which a return today or in the future is anticipated. That return is typically divided up between the owners. It is of course a term we closely associate with business where shares are bought and sold on the basis of success and anticipated future performance. Yet it does apply to all organisations and institutions that have owners who can anticipate receiving dividends—hopefully good ones. Employees have a stake in the success of their organisations. We have a stake in our governments. Further, we all have a stake in the well-being of our communities and indeed the planet. So, it should be considered a much more encompassing term. And that's how we frame it within this book. Good dividends matter to all of us.

Good dividends are drawn from the use of capital. Capital (or stock—from the old English term for a tree stump) is something that can be increased by human endeavour. It is of course financial, and good dividends usually translate to an increase in financial capital. But the conflation is unhelpful. Financial is but one of six capitals: in addition to financial there is human capital, social capital (networks, relationships, communities), reputational capital (brand value), operational capital (transforming capability) and natural capital (planetary). All of the six capitals relate to all institutions—including but not limited to businesses, charities, NGOs, local and central governments.

And here's the thing . . .

If you maximise the capitals you maximise the good dividends—including financial. All can be systemically interconnected and we provide an example further on in this chapter to amplify this point. But it is rare for institutions—notably for-profit businesses—to overtly pursue the maximisation of all capitals. The preoccupation is with financial capital and financial dividends, and ironically, this preoccupation limits the potential financial dividend over the medium- and long-term. We explain why this is so in Chapter 2 and Chapter 4. Thus, the premise of this book is simple—it is about the role of leadership (arguably the most dominant social influence mechanism on the planet!) with a focus on purpose to maximise the six capitals and maximise the six good dividends.

This book is ambitious. We have sought to bring together academics and senior managers to address what we think is the fundamental question that the leadership field (and perhaps leadership practitioners) has not addressed: leadership for what? The answer we offer is leadership of business purpose through the notion of achieving good dividends. We will explore this answer in depth in this chapter and throughout the book. The ambitious nature of the book is related to the interdisciplinary approach. Too often, arguably invariably, discussions on leadership are delineated to an examination of the leader, the person, the role and to a lesser extent the leadership relationship. Here we examine the purposes, responsibilities and orientations of the activities of leadership with regard to the fiduciary duty and the generation of value. Our ambitions seek to reframe discourses on the role of business. We outline in Chapter 2 a set of four interdisciplinary cornerstones that have not been drawn together to date, yet we contend that it is prescient that we do. These are: moral capitalism, virtue ethics, responsible leadership and the grand societal challenges to humanity (alternatively described as the sustainable development goals [SDGs]). The four cornerstones form the philosophical foundation that underpins the arguments within the book, notably the necessity for leadership to influence organisational activity to generate good dividends, for shareholders, for communities and indeed for humanity.

It was estimated in 2007 that there were well in excess of 20,000 books on leadership (Grint, 2007). This number will have grown considerably since then. Although we have not read more than perhaps 5 per cent of these between all of us in this volume, we draw on this sample to assert that very few explore the theme of leadership of purpose (save for Robinson, Hickman and Sorenson, 2014). Purpose plays an important, if implicit, role in the growing body of research on the notion of responsible leadership (Maak and Pless, 2006a; Pless and Maak, 2011; Fernando, 2016; Kempster and Carroll, 2016). But because it is mostly implicit we believe that it is time to bring it to the fore.

Overwhelmingly, most leadership books can be classified under Grint's (2005) heuristic: leadership as person; leadership as position and leadership as process. Grint offers a fourth, that of leadership as results. The notion of results provides a sense of trajectory towards purpose—as an outcome orientation. But purpose is so much more than simply results. Purpose can be seen to be a journey of investment towards the achievement of outcomes to which a person can gain fulfilment. Societal purposes enrich such fulfilment through being achieved for others. Societal purpose becomes 'an aim that guides action in a broader societal realm' (Kempster, Jackson and Conroy, 2011). Howie, drawing on the writings of Aristotle, suggested a 'being [realizes] a purpose outside that "being", for the utility and welfare of other beings' (1968: 41). Aristotle was framing purpose as 'telos'—a quest in which people gain contentment from the commitment and investment of their talents to this journey. In this way purpose has a strong moral base. Moral orientation to purposes of everyday activity is the central theme that runs throughout this book.

Let us offer a challenge at the outset. The Young Presidents Organization (YPO) is made up of 25,000 members—one of whom is a chapter author (Randall Zindler). It is a global network of CEOs, Presidents and Chairs of organisations of a minimum size and complexity. The total combined revenue of members-run companies is in the region of six trillion dollars—reflecting an estimated 7 per cent of the world's output. If the supply chain and customer engagement are included in this reckoning the capability for change is most real. Imagine all of this interconnected dynamic of YPO and other networks being put toward more engagement at realising positive societal impact. What might be the result? Would there be progress towards the elimination of modern slavery, or disease eradication, enhanced food and water security, reductions in poverty, or perhaps a sizeable step towards addressing climate change? Or would shareholders be less well off? Would the executive leadership of these organisations have failed to serve their fiduciary duty to the shareholders and be out of jobs? Would share capital have fled these organisations to find traditional 'safe' harbours? It seems highly likely that the latter set of questions would form an understandable refrain of neo-liberal capitalism. There is the need to work with such a refrain and engage within the norms of the existing system. In a sense, use capitalism to change itself. Drawing on a metaphor from judo, use your opponent's strength against his/her self. This, then, is the necessity of the notion of the good dividends. We use the notion of dividends—a very real symbol and discourse of capitalism—as the focus of organisational leadership of purpose.

We offer a brief vignette as a means of introducing the good dividends. Steve had collected his youngest son from university and journeying home in the car Rob explained what his Masters in research was on. Over the next 90 minutes or so the intricacies of bioinformatics were explained. It seemed that society, over the next few decades, was on the cusp of considerable change in terms of breakthrough health research. The ability to run thousands of experiments in a week through software, which would have taken years in traditional laboratory experiments, would revolutionise biological research. Rob's research was working on protein refinements (Shuid, Kempster and McGuffin, 2017). All seemed most exciting, certainly his dad thought so with regards to gaining fulfilling employment. But no, seemingly bioinformatics is too distant from market value at present and there is a dearth of jobs.

As they pulled off the motorway for a coffee at a service station, Rob asked 'what's happening with your research.' 'Well let me tell you about the good dividends' was Steve's response. Between parking up and getting into the queue for coffee all was explained. There are six good dividends. The word *good* is used in three ways with regard to the financial dividend: good in the sense of quantity; good in a sustainable sense of how it has been derived—a medium- to long-term orientation; and good in terms of how it has come about—the virtuous conduct of the organisation and related partners. The good financial dividend is the result of an organisation's attention to maximising all its capitals. In this way the output of the capitals as a financial dividend is interrelated within a systemic web of five other good dividends: good brands, good human resources, good innovation, good operations and a good 'one-planet' community (the idea of one planet as a symbol of humanity and nature being as one unity comes from the World Wildlife Fund and we acknowledge their contribution here; when we speak of 'planetary' in this book we refer to this unity). Each draws on the other as a consequence of leadership attention to each and to the whole. For example, appropriate leadership will yield greater returns from employees (the human resource dividend), including increased commitment, curiosity, engagement and responsibility—realising human resourcefulness.

Further, positive outcomes of this flourishing human resourcefulness include reduced sickness, lower attrition and greater well-being. This dividend enables enhanced innovation and utilisation of resources. With leadership aligned with societal needs, social innovations will inform organisational innovation and become a fertile ground for new products and services, alongside process improvements reducing waste and enhancing productivity. The overt dividend to our planet and to our communities reinforces the meaning and purposes of work. With the organisation aligned, the authentic marketing narrative strengthens the customer relationship, particularly through purpose-driven brands. The deepening of attachment, engagement and sense of collective community with customers enhances the value of the products and services. The dividend becomes manifest as increased brand equity and related brand value. For employees, there is further benefit from working for an organisation with a high customer reputation that is valued by communities for its approach and engagement with societal needs. The strength of this reputation feeds back to greater identification with the organisation and its purposes that inter alia reinforces attention to innovation and good use of resources. Ultimately, of course, all these dividends feed back to greater returns for owners/shareholders. The shareholders are investing in a 'good' organisation with good dividends. The good financial dividend invests back to encourage and reinforce human resourcefulness creating a virtuous cycle replenishing the six capitals that become further utilised for on-going good dividends. The essence of the good dividends is that it is a business model based on capitalism rather than a bolt-on initiative to pursue sustainability.

This was not quite how a father and son chat actually occurred, but it captures a flavour of the conversation. Rob's direct comment [that perhaps only a son can give] was: 'Surely this is common sense . . . why would a business not do this? It does seem strikingly obvious.'

Why indeed would organisations not seek to maximise their dividends by drawing these six good dividends together? Why do organisations underutilise the available six capitals? Why is there the need to write a book on such obvious common sense? The answer to these questions lies within the four cornerstone themes of the book that are outlined in Chapter 2. In short, the complexity lies with our neo-liberal capitalistic assumptions that have captured leadership orientation. By giving prominence to purpose and responsibilities of leadership, by embracing the grand challenges that face communities and the planet, and by reframing the business model around moral capitalism, the power of leadership has the chance to realise good dividends for society at a time when it has never been more required; and at the same time realise good dividends for the organisation, employees, customers and suppliers, and of course the share-owners. This book then is a journey that seeks to reclaim this virtuous common sense.

We next provide a brief journey through the structure of the book and the chapters. The book is organised into three parts:

Part 1 comprises three chapters. Chapter 2 lays out the four cornerstones of the book: namely: the capitalism cornerstone—Neo-liberal assumptions versus moral aspirations; the philosophical cornerstone—MacIntyre's (1985) virtue ethics; the leadership cornerstone—purposes and responsibilities; the systemic cornerstone—the societal grand challenges. In Chapter 3 Thomas and Nicola Pless explore responsible leadership through examining leadership and values creation in a systemic world. The chapter situates the role of leadership within current events and future challenges. In Chapter 4 Steve, Ken and Thomas explore the systemic nature of responsible leadership through the good dividends and introduce each of the six good dividends.

Part 2 is formed by an examination of each of the six dividends—indeed each dividend forms a chapter. The chapters give attention to the stakeholders who receive and generate the dividends. It has been the aim that the chapters are written as an interdisciplinary partnership between leadership and the respective discipline of the dividend. Part 2 is opened and closed by two examinations of the financial dividend. In Chapter 5 Steve Young, Sam Rawsthorne and Luke Hildyard explore the financial dividend through published stakeholder communications that illustrate the low salience of the value anticipated from employees with financial statements. In Chapter 6 Robyn Remke and Steve examine the human resource dividend and the leadership challenges for realising this dividend that has been so long anticipated—they argue for the need to give attention to human resourcefulness developed out from what they describe as responsible human resource management. Steve and Minna Halme unpack the notion of the social innovation dividend and give insight to the opportunity it offers through three case studies. The chapter highlights the need for understanding and working with stakeholders and the importance of an organisation learning its way into realising value to the business and society through social innovation. In Chapter 8 Steve Eldridge and Steve offer us a new way of understanding operational management through a focus on realising value across a range of connected stakeholders. By connecting behavioural operations and sustainable operations with traditional approaches to operations management they utilise a case study of a homicide investigation that applies lean thinking to illustrate the gains from operational dividend for the organisation and society. In Chapter 9 Malcolm Kirkup and Katalin Isles address the brand dividend through a leadership case study of Kresse, co-owner of Elvis & Kresse, a business established by the reclamation of decommissioned fire hoses from the London Fire Brigade, and the transformation of the hoses into affordable luxury fashion accessories. They outline a set of key elements that enable a purpose-driven brand dividend to be realised. In Chapter 10 Thomas and Nicola Pless outline the leadership role of stewardship for the realisation of the planetary dividend. They give particular attention to the challenge of climate change to illustrate the moral agenda of such leadership in addressing matters of intra and intergenerational justice. The final chapter of Part 2 returns to the finance dividend. Drawing on the discussion and arguments of the preceding chapters Anthony Hesketh will explore the need for leadership to rethink value and the utilisation of capital from maximising all dividends. Measuring the dividends involves the natty problem of addressing what constitutes value in the dividends. How, for example, can a balance sheet make sense of the intangible values of innovations, community engagement and support, customer loyalty and brand values, or human resources? Anthony outlines an argument for how these intangibles, the six capitals we mentioned in the opening of the chapter and the six dividends, can be measured.

In the final part, Part 3, there are three chapters associated with three questions: How does governance enable the realisation of the good dividends? How might action start with regard to pursuing the six good dividends? And how do we generate an evidence base for realising the good dividends and the notion of responsible leadership of business purpose in a variety of contexts? In the first chapter, Chapter 12, Randall Zindler will lay out the case for leaders (re) considering governance if the good dividends are to be realised. The chapter considers the two dominant governance models—the Anglo Saxon and the European Continental—and draws on discussions with various leaders to highlight key principles that may be considered as most salient for leadership in overseeing the realisation of the good dividends. In Chapter 13, Steve and Stewart Barnes explore how action might start in partnership with an owner-manager, Luke Freeman. Attention is given to why Luke adopted the good dividends and how he has started to utilise these across his portfolio of businesses. His starting point was to explore how to realise the planetary dividend. The chapter outlines a method Luke has used to see how the Sustainable Development Goals can be mapped to his business in a manner that adds value to his business, to his stakeholders, his immediate community and to the planet. In the final chapter of the book Steve and Thomas outline an agenda for research—a longitudinal research project that seeks to develop an interdisciplinary community of researchers and organisations working in a 'collaboratory' fashion (Kempster et al., 2017): how a strong evidence base for the good dividends could be developed.

Conclusion

The central thesis of the book then is to explore how responsible leadership can be developed within an organisational context. Such leadership seeks to pursue purpose through a systemic set of six good dividends. The book is not about the people who lead—their qualities, personalities, traits and styles—as with most leadership books. Rather, it is focused on the responsibilities of leadership, the purposes of leadership and what these people seek to achieve. The book is undertaken in a unique interdisciplinary way. The systemic and interdisciplinary orientations are challenges for all chapter authors in terms of reaching beyond disciplinary boundaries. For leadership studies this has not been conducted before with regard to a focus on purposes and responsibilities; but the necessity to reach beyond the norms is necessitated by the prescient circumstances the world is facing.

Despite the complexity of the challenge we are seeking to address we still hold to the common sense nature of what we are exploring. Common in the sense that we hope the central idea seems most obvious and simple; and common in terms of resonance that the ideas connect to peoples' lived experience of the world, which echoes the prophetic question of a 23-year-old biologist—'why would a business not do this?'

2 Four Cornerstones That Underpin the Good Dividends

Steve Kempster, Thomas Maak and Ken Parry

The metaphor of the cornerstone seems most apt. Traditionally the cornerstone was the first stone laid from which all other stones would take as the reference point. We have greatly abused the metaphor by having four cornerstones. However, the rituals and rites, including burials, which often go hand in hand with the laying of the cornerstone, have some sad resonance here. We very sadly have to report Ken Parry passed away during the writing of the book. The four cornerstones were most important to Ken conceptually. He was impassioned about the necessity for the leadership dividend to realise its necessary contribution to humanity and to address the grand challenges that gather around us like the 'perfect storm.' The essence of Ken is thus buried within the writing of these four cornerstones.

The four cornerstones form the foundations for the book. In this way they provide the reference point for all the subsequent chapters. We start with capitalism and the necessity to consider reframing this towards the original ideas imagined by Adam Smith where there would be an 'invisible guiding hand'; a sense of capitalism being imbued with moral expectations (Ulrich, 2008).

#1: The Capitalism Cornerstone—Neo-Liberal Versus Moral Capitalism

Capitalism has been a force for tremendous good. Rand, for example argues most persuasively that in human history capitalism is the only social system that gives freedom, is based on voluntary action and confers individual rights (1967: 27). The moral justification for capitalism is extensive. But Rand (1967: 29) suggests it does not lie with altruism in terms of the best way to achieve the common good. He asserts that capitalism does create a common good associated with the primary purpose to protect freedom and individual rights. Rand suggests that capitalism is not about tribes or about altruism—where a view is taken about the intrinsic good or subjective good. It is a self-centred doctrine—a person works to support her life, guided by her rational self-interest, enabled by her own mind. 'Growth of societies is not a consequence of sacrifice for the common good but a result of the productive genus of free men [and women] who pursued their own personal interests' (1967: 33). There is thus an asserted moral basis of capitalism associated with freedom of choice. Markets are self-controlling mechanisms not at the will of tribes or dictators—who often abuse the notion of common good to meet certain ends. Capitalism is also seen to enable flourishing of humanity through such freedom as a consequence of innovations that compete to satisfy human needs and generate wealth as a consequence.

Neo-liberal capitalism follows on from these ideas. It assumes the market makes the most sense in terms of satisfying personal and collective aspirations. Neo-liberal capitalism emerged in the 1980s as a response to the Keynesian economic era of post war up to the late 1970s. The criticisms were that the 1970s era was one of reduced influence of markets (because of views of the *subjective and politicised common good*— pursued through government intervention) and this had led to low levels of innovation, productivity investment, and high levels of unemployment and high personal and corporate taxation. The prescription to these ills was seen as deregulation, reduction in trade barriers, centrality of the market and allowing freedom of capital and freedom to the labour markets. All then was apparently good as we spent and consumed through the 1990s and into the millennium. Indeed, the fall of the Berlin Wall signalled 'the end of history' (Fukuyama, 1993); there was no longer a competing economic system. Commensurate with such deregulation of markets was the marketisation of financial capital. The very loose regulation of the 1990s and the resulting globalisation 'on speed' at the turn of the millennium laid the seeds of the 2007 financial crisis (for a useful review and analysis of which see Engelen et al., 2011). The paradoxical solution to the crisis of such neo-liberal capitalist outcomes has been to lean on neo-liberal principles to solve the problem—that is, the post-crash period of austerity.

The question posed by du Gay and Morgan (2013) is why has there not been a general outrage against neo-liberalism. As Crouch (2011) comments, we have 'the strange non-death of neoliberal capitalism.' It has an extraordinary hold (some might say strangle hold) on many societies. Why is this? In part because of the great successes of capitalistic wealth in holding the fabric of society together in terms of taxes that support societal needs, and in terms of technological innovations, and in this way sustains the freedoms that Rand speaks of as a moral justification. But also the gathering momentum of the emerging and rapidly growing consumerism in Asian economies, pre-dominantly in China and India. While the global financial system imploded billions of dollars were spent on Western products.

A closer look at the developed economies in the West reveals that neo-liberal capitalism has arguably not fulfilled its quasi-moral purpose to maximise wealth, because it has not embraced the reciprocal embeddedness of any organisation (private or public) within society. Rand (1967: 32) spoke of the innovation and exchange of value being maximised when 'the free market is [led] by those who are able to see and plan long range—and the better the mind, the longer the range.' It is the short-termism along with an amoral concern with regard to communities that are significant structural weaknesses of neo-liberal capitalism. Adam Smith recognised this element with his notion of the 'invisible hand'—the morality in society framing capitalism. Indeed, throughout his lifetime Smith was deeply concerned about the moral foundations of society and the idea that markets should be cut loose would have appeared strange to him (perhaps horrified him with regard to societal consequences). The notion of the 'invisible hand' was conceived after he published his ground-breaking *Theory of Moral Sentiments* (1759) intended to work in tandem with the *Wealth of Nations* where he assumed that moral boundaries would prevent market actors, such as the baker or the butcher, from pursuing ruthless self-interest (1776). However, neo-liberal economists readily embraced the idea of de-coupled self-interest based on selective reading of Smith, or Milton Friedman for that matter. The latter famously viewed corporate social responsibility as 'socialism', but then his comments were made at the height of the Cold War and have to be put in the context of communist-driven totalitarianism. We suggest that 50 years later the weaknesses of neo-liberal capitalism and the ever-increasing evidence of astonishing levels of economic inequality that abound the globe necessitate a need to embrace moral capitalism that is rooted in a long-term orientation, which overtly embraces the societal 'invisible [guiding] hand.'

The long-term orientation is a part of a bundle of aspects that enable moral capitalism to become manifest. This bundle is most distinct from neo-liberal capitalism. It draws on virtue practices (more on this shortly in the next cornerstone). Fourcade and Healy speak of a distant history of capitalism in which markets had 'nurtured historic bourgeois virtues of integrity, honesty, trustworthiness, enterprise, respect, modesty, and responsibility' (2007: 4) – the influence of Quaker business leaders speaks prominently to these characteristics. Translating past virtues of capitalism to present needs Stephen Young in his book *Moral Capitalism* comments: 'To sustain our profits over time, we need to replenish the capital we invest in the business. That capital comes in different forms: social capital, reputational capital or "goodwill," finance capital, [natural/planetary] capital, and human capital [and we add operational capital]. These forms of capital are the essential factors of production' (2007: 2). These capitals readily translate to stakeholders: social capital—communities; reputational capital—customers; financial capital—owners/investors; natural—the environment; human capital—employees; as well as operational capital—organisations and their activities and practices that enable products and services to be generated. In Chapter 1 we described the relationship of these six capitals to the six good dividends. The connection of all capitals is a shared and reciprocal relationship anchored in notions of purpose and place. This is neatly captured by Yang (citing Confucius):

'Now the man of perfect virtue, wishing to be established himself, seeks also to establish others; wishing to be enlarged himself, he seeks

also to enlarge others.' Treating others with perfect virtue in dealing with the reciprocal relationship between a corporation and the
stakeholders is the basis for moral capitalism to replace [neo-liberal]
capitalism necessarily, making all corporations and their stakeholders benefit from market economy.

(2010: 81)

The argument of Yang is that the common good is achieved through
moral capitalism because the organisation's interest is maximised when
all capitals are maximised. A short-term orientation cannot maximise the
dividend from the utilisation of all the capitals (Ant Hesketh explores this
in Chapter 11). As a consequence, neo-liberal capitalism fails to serve the
fiduciary duty to the owners/investors of organisations by failing to invest
in all the capitals and draw on all the dividends from all of the capitals.
Put another way, maximising the value to all stakeholders maximises the
return to the owners/shareholders. But capitalism is more than exchanges
of value for stakeholders. We return to Rand's notion of freedom and
fairness. Meyer (2015) cites the story of the aftermath of Hurricane Fran
in 1996 and its impact on North Carolina, leaving more than a million
people without power in temperatures over 90F. People could not keep
ice. Four young entrepreneurs in part of the state with power brought
ice down and started to sell it at $8 a bag (when normal prices reflect $1
a bag). A queue developed and people paid this amount, until the police
turned up and arrested the entrepreneurs. The queue broke into applause
as the entrepreneurs were led away in handcuffs. Despite losing out on
their ability to obtain ice, fairness was a supererogatory moral principle.
In this way capitalism is more than economics; it is imbued with moral
expectations (Meyer, 2015; similar with Ulrich, 2008).

Indeed it could be argued that while Adam Smith was the visionary of
a balanced, highly productive, but morally embedded economy, the so
called 'ordo-liberal' school of thought—a group of German economists
who were partly influenced by Catholic social thinking, among them
Walter Eucken, Alexander Ruestow and Wilhelm Roepke, translated
Smith's ideas into the twentieth century. Their influence on the foundations of the German success model after World War II are visible to this
day: capitalism works best if its raw energy is embedded in a framework
of 'ordo-ethical standards' focused on the virtuous interaction of self-
interest and the common good (Enderle, 2016; Lütge, Armbrüster and
Müller, 2016).

Hence, the essence of our argument is that capitalism should be seen
to be a moral dynamic and that key market actors need to be conscious
that the pursuit of self-interest cannot come at the expense of the greater
common good. A balanced, embedded capitalism will be more effective:
more effective in terms of thoughtful use of the six capitals, and careful engagement with the associated stakeholders. Although Adam Smith

(in the Wealth of Nations, 1759) gave emphasis to self-interest-seeking behaviour as a means to efficient market systems he acknowledged that there were societal consequences 'when such behavior was not bound by virtuous behavior, such as compassion for others' (Newbert and Stouder, 2012: 247).

It is to the virtuous behaviour that our second cornerstone picks up next.

#2: The Philosophical Cornerstone—MacIntyre's Virtue Ethics

The philosophical cornerstone in this book is built on virtue ethics and in particular a reading of the same through the work of Alistair MacIntyre (1985). Virtue ethics is both an orientation and an interpretation of ethical behaviour. For example, it is different to moral behaviour associated with the decisions people make (deontological ethics) focused on doing the right thing—the means justifies the end; or decisions associated with serving the greatest good (utilitarian ethics)—the end justifies the means. Virtue ethics is towards the moral conduct of people through their intentions and everyday actions. It is how they live out their lives. For example, and with direct application to organisations, we are what we repeatedly do. Excellence is not an act but a habit, a virtue (drawn from Aristotle).

Virtue is a behavioural disposition (or acquired habit) to act towards moral excellence in a persistent way in a variety of situations. From an Aristotelian perspective virtue is the mid-point behaviour between excess and deficiency. For example, the virtue of courage sits between the shyness to act and aggressive risk-taking. A person's virtues disposition draws upon a deep rooted and complex multi-level relationship with values, emotions, interests, attitudes and expectations—drawn together to reflect the notion of 'character.' Character does not sit alone but is connected with others through the notion of disposition. Disposition captures a sense of a person's education and development with others, the place they work, the people they work with, the work they collectively do together, the interests, the orientations and attitudes that are shared amongst colleagues. A disposition then is a dynamic that manifests as collective persistent behaviour. A virtues disposition in for example the health context might be a persistent collective behaviour to pursue societal well-being and prudence in their everyday activities, commitments, interests, attitudes and purpose of their collective work. An alternative disposition (and potentially non-virtuous) might be to pursue profit maximisation and efficiency in self interest and to the exclusion of other needs. In this context well-being is secondary to the purposes of profit. With profit as the primary and dominant goal it is possible that well-being becomes removed from everyday concerns. This is not to say profit or efficiency is unimportant—it is just as important in moral capitalism—but such an orientation has many unfortunate consequences, notably an increasing propensity towards amoral conduct and disconnect from society. To help make sense of this argument we need to unpack MacIntyean virtue ethics.

In MacIntyrean language societal well-being and prudence are derived out from the practice virtues of the organisation. Virtues are categorised as follows: first, a concern with the achievement of internal goods—outcomes that have benefit for society and are derived from the practice virtues of organisational activity (for example, drugs generated from the practices within a pharma organisation to generate well-being for people, along with prudent management of resources that sustains this ability to generate well-being); second, the practice virtues have qualities contributing to the good of a whole life (people feeling fulfilled in their work and that such work has meaning connected to a worthy purpose—individual and collective); and third, practice virtues can only be possessed by people within an ongoing social tradition—the practice virtues draw from a history of meaning associated within the specific organisation (MacIntyre, 1985: 273).

The distinction between internal goods and external goods is most significant. Goods that are internal relate to the practices that occur within an organisation in generating services or products that produce benefit beyond the organisation. Examples of such internal goods would reflect quality or customer care—the customers' satisfaction of a cappuccino prepared and presented to a customer along with consideration for the well-being of the customer—the need the customer might have for the drink, or indeed care that the lid of the takeaway cup is firmly on. External goods are such aspects as money, status or power (MacIntyre, 1985: 190)—the payment for producing the cappuccino. When people participate in practices (activities) primarily for external goods, the standards of excellence of these practices are valued in a transactional manner—what the transaction will generate in terms of profit or remuneration. In contrast an employee's participation in practice virtues that create internal goods (benefits for the customer or society) are intrinsically valued by an employee for its contribution to others. Again using the examples of excellence of quality or excellence of customer service (both internal goods), are undertaken because they are valued by an employee and are part of their everyday practice—it occurs as a habit, it is their virtue disposition. External goods (the profit from the excellence of quality and excellence of service) enable the investment in sustaining and developing the internal goods.

It has become most common for external goods to dominate discourses in organisation to the exclusion of internal goods—even in public and health sectors. In major part this reflects the hegemony of the neoliberal orientation. We outline a case where external goods have become the primary purpose. The case is in the UK health sector, and that of Mid-Staffordshire Hospital. The Francis Inquiry (Francis, 2013) looked into the severe deficiencies of the hospital. It examined the incidents of major patient distress (and fatalities), for example, suffering from dehydration. The report highlighted that the ward nurses had to prioritise ward efficiency rather than attend to the distressed patients' immediate needs. The inquiry commented on fatalities that occurred as a consequence of such prioritisation. So, even in a quintessential context where virtue disposition of care-giving would seem so overwhelmingly central to the organisation's sense of purpose, the internal good in the form of excellence of care, with the practice virtue as the giving of care, was overwhelmed by the pursuit of external goods—the quantum of resource consumed per patient.

MacIntyre's (1985) rather bleak thesis in *After Virtue* suggested that such an example would become inevitable in a neo-liberal capitalist world. He argued managers would seek to maximise external goods and minimise, even eliminate internal goods:

> Institutions are characteristically and necessarily concerned with . . .
> external goods. They are involved in acquiring money and other
> material goods; they are structured in terms of power and status, and
> they distribute money, power and status as rewards. Nor could they
> do otherwise if they are to sustain not only themselves, but also the
> practices of which they are the bearers. For no practices can survive
> for any length of time unsustained by institutions. [. . .] In this con-
> text the essential feature of the virtues is clear. Without them, without
> justice, courage and truthfulness, practices could not resist the cor-
> rupting power of institutions.
>
> (MacIntyre, 1985: 194)

The overt instrumental and transactional attention to external goods would become aligned with an institutional sense of purpose focused on neo-liberal expectations. A consequence of such a purpose, and the dominance of external goods over internal goods, is the loss of *eudaimonia* (eudaimonia being a state of well-being that occurs through enactment of virtuous activity providing intrinsic satisfaction, and human flourishing (Park and Peterson, 2006, cited in Fernando, 2016). The loss of such eudaimonia is related to loss in employee performance, commitment and well-being. We think it is highly plausible that issues of weak productivity would relate to low eudaimonia, low sense of purpose, low level of internal goods and low level of virtue practices.

The central question then arises: Who in the institution takes on the 'essential' role of protecting the practice virtues and associated eudaimonia from such corruption? It is undoubtedly the senior managers (Moore and Beadle, 2006: 373): there is the need for courage and character from managers to sustain a virtuous business organisation 'in order to resist the corrupting power of institutions' (MacIntyre, 1985: 375).

The influence, power and role modelling of senior managers has been shown to be most central to the ethical conduct of organisations and in particular on the influence of middle manager ethical behaviour (see for example the similar findings in: Trevino, Brown and Hartman, 2003; Brown and Mitchell, 2010; Schaubroeck et al., 2012). Notable is the research of Brown and Trevino (2014). Their research shows the dearth of reported senior managers as perceived ethical role models. The highest occurrence of ethical role models is at the level of supervisor/first manager. Why might this be so? Why is there a decreasing perceived sense of ethical leadership as someone progresses up the organisational hierarchy? Why do Buchholtz and Carroll (2012) assert that organisations are dominated by amoral behaviour (amorality is an assumption that ethics is outside of the realm of business)? Why is there a high level of moral disengagement (Detert, Trevino and Sweitzer, 2008) and a lowering of an individual's moral impulse and diluted sense of moral identity (Shao, Aquino and Freeman, 2008) in organisations? A most persuasive piece of research undertaken by Anand, Ashforth and Joshi (2004) gives a possible answer to these questions. They highlight the powerful and connected dynamic of socialisation and rationalisation. 'In terms of socialisation, managers and employees engage in activities with historic cultural antecedents reinforced by role modelling behaviour, the outcome of which is that conduct is perceived as normal' (Kempster and Gregory, 2017: 498). The rationalisations draw from socialisation and in turn reinforce expectations of everyday norms and practice. Anand et al. offer a range of rationalisations such as a 'denial of responsibility'—what can I do I have no other choice but to engage in such activities, or a 'denial of harm'—no one is harmed so nothing is ethically wrong, or perhaps a 'denial of victims'—they had it coming to them, or by 'social comparison'—others are worse than us, or indeed an 'appeal to higher loyalties'—we do this to satisfy a greater cause, or through loyalty to a boss (Anand et al., 2004: 11). This does not mean, necessarily, that managers in organisations are immoral, or amoral people. Outside of the business context people separate their business identity from their sense of personal moral identity (Brown and Trevino, 2014). But because the price of their moral failure is so much greater—Enron comes to mind—we must make sure that business and personal moral identity operate in sync, not against each other.

The academic evidence, and the seemingly never-ending business scandals, point to MacIntyre's (1985) thesis as being sadly prophetic. The neo-liberal capitalistic context has much influence on the prevalent corrosion in virtue practices. It seems fair to assert that without a mechanism of substantial social influence MacIntyre's prediction that management will eradicate internal goods in order to maximise external goods would be the norm. In relation to the notion of internal and external goods, amorality is the sole pursuance of external goods (profit, power, titles, rewards) with no regard or pursuance to internal goods (societal needs). In this sense moral activity (indeed moral capitalism) becomes manifest when leadership orientation and attention is to linking the production of external goods (profit) with protecting and enhancing internal goods (quality and service) through nurturing and seeking excellence of virtue practices connected to realisation of purposes.

MacIntyre's argument that it is all the fault of management is paradoxically the solution through the significant social influence mechanism that is leadership. More specifically the quintessential essence of leadership to the purposes and responsibilities it seeks to achieve.

#3: The Leadership Cornerstone—Purposes and Responsibilities

Leadership scholars have estimated the spend by organisations in the United States to exceed $12.5 billion per annum on leadership development training (Sowcik and Allen, 2013: 56) and in excess of $40 billion globally (see discussions on spending in DeRue, Sitkin and Podolny, 2011). Yet we contend that there has thus far been limited returns on this investment. We have still to reap the leadership dividend. To [miss]quote Dr Martin Luther King (with edits):

> It is obvious today that [leaders] have defaulted on [their] promissory note insofar as [society] is concerned. Instead of honouring this sacred obligation, [leaders] have given people a bad cheque; a cheque which has come back marked 'insufficient funds.' But we refuse to believe that the bank of justice is bankrupt. We refuse to believe that there are insufficient funds in the great vaults of opportunity of [our societies].
>
> (King, 1963, in Alvarez, 1988)

To continue in this spirit—never has there been a greater time for responsible leadership to address the grand challenges that threaten humanity. It is encouraging that there are examples of leaders who prioritise internal goods through a clear sense of purpose. What unites them is not so much a common purpose—that may differ according to underlying virtues and motivational drivers (Pless, 2007) but the core idea that profit must follow purpose. Take the well-known example of the late Ray Anderson, CEO of Interface, the world's largest carpet manufacturer (and by 2020 a zero-emission company); his view was that business needs profit to exist but that every business must exist for a higher, nobler purpose than profit—whether this is the preservation of our planet or advancing humanity through products and services, or software, as it is the case with Atlassian, Australia's most admired company. Still, these examples are the exception, not the rule. Over the last decade the disquiet with the high level of moral disengagement across our institutions in tandem with the worst excesses and effects of neo-liberal capitalism has led to increasing attention to the responsibilities of leadership (see for example: Maak and Pless, 2006a; Waldman and Balven, 2014; Maak, Pless and Voegtlin, 2016; Kempster and Carroll, 2016). Pless and Maak offer up a helpful definition:

> Responsible leadership is a multilevel response to deficiencies in existing leadership frameworks and theories; to high-profile scandals on individual, organizational, and systemic levels; and to new and emerging social, ethical, and environmental challenges in an increasingly connected world. The scope and complexity of these challenges calls for responsible leadership and responsible leaders who acknowledge their shared, significant responsibility in tackling problems and challenges.
>
> (Pless and Maak, 2011: 4)

In its simplest form the question that orientates responsible leadership is 'for what and to whom are leaders responsible?' (2011: 4). This orientation extends the leadership relationship from the unit of leader-follower, to leader-stakeholder (Maak and Pless, 2006b). In Chapter 3 Thomas and Nicola offer up a re-examination of responsible leadership in terms of this critical re-orientation and its implications for organisational leadership and the pursuance of good dividends.

Within this chapter we link the leader-stakeholder orientation to the previous cornerstone on practice virtues. Cameron (2011) helpfully elaborates on the link between the reframed leadership relationship and virtues by considering responsibility in terms 'of what is right, correct and best' (2011: 26). He draws on extensive evidence of the increased organisational performance as a result of virtues orientation within leadership. Further the extended leader-stakeholder relationships centred on such a virtuous disposition generates desirable ends. 'These ends can provide advantages for all constituencies—rather than benefiting some at the expense of others—by focusing on virtuous outcomes' (2011: 32). In essence, leadership that focuses on the virtuous outcomes, the internal goods, that benefits all, generates the external goods of profit. In this way profit is a morally good outcome through its embedded relationship with virtuous outcomes. It is most important though that we set this into context with regard to senior organisational leaders' primary duty—the care to owners/shareholders with respect to fiduciary duty.

An Institution's Responsibility—The Fiduciary Duty

Fiduciary duty is in essence a set of practice virtues—virtues of care, loyalty and prudence. The origins of fiduciary duty stem from Roman *Fideicommissum*, the Germanic *Salmannus* and the Islamic *Waqf* (Avini, 1995/1996, cited in Eccles, 2017) that are associated with trust to undertake a duty of care. Although dominated in contemporary discourse in the business realm, fiduciary duty is applicable to many relationships such as: ward/guardian, attorney/client and counsellor/client.

> If a person in a particular relationship with another is subject to a fiduciary obligation, that person (the fiduciary) must be loyal to the interests of the other person (the beneficiary). The fiduciary's duties go beyond mere fairness and honesty; they oblige him[/her] to act to further the beneficiary's best interests.
>
> (DeMott, 1988: 882)

Those in organisational leadership positions of responsibility are the *fiduciaries*. The duty of care is owed to *beneficiaries*. With regard to corporations, often national company law identifies the beneficiaries as the owners/shareholders and thus a legal duty of care to such owners is a superordinate responsibility. Perhaps the key is the interpretation of 'loyalty to the *interests* of the other person.' Is the interest over the short-, medium- or the long-term? Recent debates on executive pay open up an interesting insight on the purity of the duty of care relationship. For example, the process of linking 'managerial remuneration practices [with] the almost ubiquitous share option schemes to align the interests of managers with those of shareholders' is perhaps an indication of a lack of trust in the relationship where this overt mechanism is required' (Eccles, 2017: 12).

The fiduciary relationship has been closely coupled with neo-liberal capitalistic expectations. The essence of which is a very narrow orientation that excludes consideration of other relationships unless they have a direct short-term impact on the financial bottom line. A prevailing assumption is that the fiduciary duty would be maximised through neo-liberal principles. It is questioning this assumption that has in part catalysed this book. Is the fiduciary duty that focuses on neo-liberal assumptions being under-served? Would moral capitalistic assumptions enrich this duty of care? Would a leader-stakeholder orientation provide a necessary mechanism for such maximisation? Connected to these three questions is a link between capitalism, duty of care, responsibilities of leadership and the notion of justice. Let us explain by drawing on the early Adam Smith from his Theory of Moral Sentiments:

> Justice [. . . .] is the main pillar that upholds the whole edifice. If it is removed, the great, the immense fabric of human society, the fabric which to raise and support seems in this world, if I may say so, to have been the peculiar darling care of Nature, must in a moment crumble into atoms.
>
> (Smith, 1759: 45, cited in Eccles, 2017)

If business leaders act in the narrow confines of setting aside value generation associated with other stakeholders there is the very real risk that decisions and acts will eventually harm the shareholders as their interests are inextricably linked to society, and indeed, humanity. We shall explore the risks impacting on humanity in cornerstone #4. But before we do, we offer here a simple and obvious proposition: Maximising the six capitals (financial, social, natural/planetary, reputational, human and operational) would maximise the fiduciary duty over the medium- to long-term. This in fact is the core belief on which more enlightened business leaders such as Aaron Feuerstein (Malden Mills) or Ray Anderson (Interface) operate: doing the right thing might not 'pay off' in the short run, but it will always be rewarded in the long run.

Our proposition is not new to scholars within the field of corporate and social responsibility (CSR). Businesses violating this proposition risk their licence to operate. That licence is based on, and the result of it, a social contract with society, represented through a wide array of stakeholders. A social contract 'is formed when rules and assumptions are developed on behaviour patterns within [societies]' (Fernando, 2016: 11). Business institutions can only survive with the commitment and good will of society (Donaldson, 1982). On one level, the most common level, corporations are obligated to report on CSR activity. A lack of attention to this is a breach of fiduciary duty. The consequence can be executive leadership responding to this responsibility to embrace stakeholder needs, observe legal requirements and generate a CSR policy within annual reporting. Framed this way CSR is a cost rather than a process of value generation. However, recent research has helpfully offered up useful evidence to suggest value is generated when corporate responsibility moves beyond the reporting process or philanthropic orientations and becomes an integrated aspect of the business model (Orlitzky, Schmidt and Rynes, 2003; Porter and Kramer, 2006; Nakao et al., 2007; Halme and Laurila, 2009)—often referred to as strategic CSR (see McWilliams, Siegel and Wright, 2006). An assumption that this is an amoral, cynical and instrumental approach fails to appreciate the moral argument (Fernando, 2016). First, executive leadership must attend to the institutions' fiduciary duty—to give priority to the owners' capital. If an altruistic approach was adopted shareholders' capital might be depleted. But not only shareholder capital; human capital may be reduced—for example employees' remuneration could be impacted. Second, altruistic or philanthropic gifts are moral decisions of individuals. If executive leadership acts in such a manner then how do they arbitrate between possible beneficiaries? Which stakeholders benefit from such altruism and why? Milton Friedman (1970) was adamant that the company's profit is not the managers to give away. Third, and perhaps most fundamental, there is a case that such altruistic approaches may reflect a form of displacement from the moral purpose of the institution—in part limiting the moral potential of capitalism. In a sense, philanthropic engagements perpetuate CSR as a 'nice' thing to do, and is not central to the institution's business model.

Perhaps CSR governance and associated activities have become the problem: CSR exists as another aspect that a business needs to manage, and as such becomes manifest as a cost. Reframing CSR as value generation for many stakeholders, and in particular shareholders/owners is an essential step. How this may occur is a central concern of this book, and is elaborated in detail in subsequent chapters. However, such reframing alone is not sufficient. Recent research by Hafenbrädl and Waeger has shown that senior executive belief in the link between CSR and profitability is only part of the equation. There is the need for a sense of 'moral outrage' (2017: 3)—where business as normal (neo-liberal assumption) is not acceptable.

Moreover, what may be required is to revisit the actual purpose of the firm through the development of a theory of business, and not a theory of the firm. Donaldson and Walsh (2015) have stressed that the latter is ill equipped to handle the many expectations we hold for business practice. A broader theory of business that is both empirical and normative would start from purpose and thus the place of business in society to determine accountability, control and outcomes (Donaldson and Walsh, 2015: 195). Such a theory would also overcome the so-called 'separation thesis'—the view that a firms' economic activities are somehow detached from ethical considerations and instead recognise that such activities are integrative in nature (Harris and Freeman, 2008; Donaldson and Walsh, 2015).

#4: The Systemic Cornerstone—The Societal Grand Challenges

In Search of Moral Outrage

If a meteor was heading towards the planet, due to hit earth in 30 years' time, this would be the topic of conversation on everyone's lips. People would explore, discuss and demand what action is going to take place. The details would be known in exacting depth, like a football fan who understands his team's results and performances and can recount who scored and in which game from a match 20 years ago. Yet in putting together this section, to examine the systemic nature of the grand challenges that impact on our local communities and globally, it has been a most painful struggle to gather together the necessary detail. In a sense the biggest moral outrage is that this detail is not to hand and not known to all, and of course not part of everyday discourse—especially leadership discourse. In part the 2007/2008 credit crunch is to blame. It caused governments, organisations and societies to take our collective eyes understandably 'off the ball.' There is a certain paradox that never has humanity had a greater need and greater capability to collectively know the details of the grand challenges, but had such little awareness and understanding of the grand challenges despite the abundance of data.

The grand challenges are systemically connected. In broad terms, humanity has always faced some of the challenges: poverty, human rights, inequality, diseases, famine and water security. However, the impact of the Anthropocene—humanities impact on the planet—that commenced with the first industrial revolution in the 1800s has distorted and exaggerated these challenges. Climate change is gathering pace. It is overwhelmingly accepted that the climb in average temperatures is related to increased carbon, nitrous oxide and methane utilisation in our everyday living (intergovernmental panel on climate change, 2013). In particular, it is acknowledged that there has been what is known as 'the great acceleration' since the end of the Second World War (Steffen et al., 2015). Steffen and colleagues succinctly capture the essence of the increasing pace of change with regard to the impact on the 'earth system' with a set of unsettling indicators (2015: 84–88). The socio-economic indicators paint a picture of sharp increases in such aspects as water consumption, fertiliser consumption, transportation and urban population. With regards to urbanisation, it is estimated that over the next three decades the quantity of urbanisation will equal all of the urbanisation to date. The earth system indicators are rather disturbing, illustrating a sharp and continuous rise over the last 50 years with all indicators save for a stabilisation of methane, fish capture (because we have reached limits of what can be caught) and ozone. The latter has impacted Southern Australasia like no other part of the world with New Zealand having the highest skin cancer rate per capita. Methane is an unexplained (good) surprise while ozone shows the scope of what is possible through concerted intervention. The other indicators are carbon dioxide, notorious-oxide, surface temperature, ocean acidification, biosphere degradation, tropical forest loss and nitrogen to coastal zone. Surface temperatures have risen 0.5 degrees in the last 30 years. Estimations of keeping surface temperatures to no more than an increase of 2 degrees seem under severe threat. Indeed Berners-Lee and Clark (2013) have persuasively estimated that the carbon assets already known and capitalised in the assets of the energy industry (in which our pension funds are inextricably entwined and thus necessitate turning such assets into future pensions!) will lead to a temperature rise in excess of 4 degrees. (These temperatures are planet averages—over land and in different parts of the globe these are conservative numbers). Sea levels have risen by 10mm since 1994 (Albert et al., 2016). Already islands are under threat. Five of the Solomon Islands have disappeared and people have been moved off these. As temperature rise exceeds 2 degrees the global picture is one of most ocean-facing cities of the world under severe threat from the combination of sea level rise of approximately 50cm by 2050 (and probably over 100 cm by 2100) and more severe and more frequent cyclones (Schaeffer, Hare, Rahmstorf and Vermeer, 2012). The global GDP impact is estimated to be 10 per cent (Hanson et al., 2011).

Some more disturbing data. The impact of humanity has led to 20 per cent of the fish in the Mediterranean having micro plastic particles in their bodies (we wonder how much micro-plastics are now in humans). About a quarter of the carbon dioxide in the atmosphere is absorbed into the oceans. The impact is ocean acidification, which leads to changes in marine ecosystems and biodiversity. For example, many coral reefs are under severe threat including the Great Barrier Reef, which has experienced unseen coral bleaching in 2016 and this threatens the long-term survival of one of the earth's most precious ecosystems. 'Ocean carbonate chemistry is likely [sic] changing faster than at any other time in the last 300 million years' (Hönisch et al., 2012) and 'biodiversity loss may be approaching mass extinction rates (Barnosky et al., 2012)' (Steffen et al., 2015: 92). With current extrapolations of climate change, urbanisation and population growth, it is estimated that by 2050 there might have been a 50 per cent extinction of plant species (Stork, 2010). A recent paper in the journal *Nature* rather underscores this point. The tropics, that are home to more than 75 per cent of all species on earth, are under great threat (Barlow et al., 2018). The authors highlight that global biodiversity is close to collapse: 'The fate of the tropics will be largely determined by what happens elsewhere in the planet. While most of us are familiar with the impact of climate change on the polar regions, it is also having devastating consequences across the tropics' (Barlow, 2018).

As mentioned earlier the surface temperature estimates are global averages. Particular areas of the world will suffer dramatically and patterns of weather are predicted to become more extreme. Indeed this is the case at the time of writing. The countries of Nigeria, Somalia, Sudan and Ethiopia are suffering extreme drought. Estimates of children at risk of death have been offered in the region of 1.4 million at the time of writing (UNICEF, 2017).

Connected to earth system changes are geo-socio and related geo-political impacts. The severe disruption because of climate change leads to water and food security crises, accentuating poor diets and malnutrition, which gives diseases plentiful opportunity to devastate communities. Interlinked with severe limited levels of income and wealth, often associated with most fragile geo-political contexts, this leads to displacement and migration. The UNHCR currently estimate that at present on earth 1: 120 people are migrants or displaced people through geo-political conflict and natural disasters (68.8 million people)—greater than the UK population. Over the next 50 years the impact of climate change within a combined socio-ecological and geo-political dynamic will greatly exasperate this when understood as a systemic wicked problem (see Chapter 4 for an examination of systems thinking and Chapter 10 for an application in the context of climate change). We capture this dynamic in Figure 2.1.

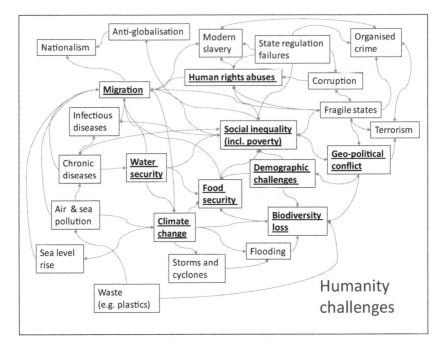

Figure 2.1 A Systemic View of the Grand Challenges
Source: Adapted from Helbing, 2013

Such a system operates in a non-linear fashion. That is, the system seeks to be resilient to change (absorbing shocks and still functioning). However, non-linear complexity points to systems adapting and potentially flipping into a very new and different (for us dangerous) state. It is suggested that this will occur at some point systemically as a consequence of breaching Earth's boundary conditions. There are nine of these and we have presently exceeded three (biodiversity loss, nitrogen cycle and climate change). 'The others are under intense pressure, directly from the ongoing environmental degradation of land and sea and air masses, and indirectly from the cascading systemic effects from changes to other processes' (Whiteman, Walker and Perego, 2013: 313). Recently Steffen et al. (2015) have reported that the situation has become much more pressing.

The impact of such socio-ecological issues runs alongside many other major challenges of our time. For example, the growth of modern slavery is directly connected to the extraordinary levels of migration and displacement. The United Nations International Labor Organization suggests 21 million people are captured in modern slavery globally—where the majority are women and girls—from which human traffickers make

$150 billion each year from the extreme abuse of these millions of people migrating (UNICEF and Amnesty International, 2017—more people in slavery today than there has ever been in the history of humanity). It is the vulnerability of such people as a consequence of socio-political and socio-ecological changes that creates such disturbing abuse of human rights. This vulnerability is connected to local and global inequalities of resources and income. Amongst the many moral outrages inequality is a big one and impacts on many (arguably all of the others). In 1960 20 per cent of the world's richest countries had 30 times the wealth of the poorest 20 per cent; by 1995 this had grown to 79 times (Economist, 2002). A recent report by Oxfam (2017) reported that:

> nine billionaires owned the same wealth as the poorest half of the planet. It is obscene for so much wealth to be held in the hands of so few when 1 in 10 people survive on less than $2 a day. Inequality is trapping hundreds of millions in poverty; it is fracturing our societies and undermining democracy.

Inequality is a broad theme. It not only includes poverty, but is also related to education, to food and malnutrition, to health and to employment—developed and developing nations have a common challenge of unemployment and inequalities. But the challenges of the developed world are of course most relative. On one level, and led by the intervention of notable foundations, the number of polio-endemic countries has reduced from 125 to 3 since 1998, and since 2000, 440 million children have been immunised against vaccine preventable diseases (Gates Foundation, 2014). However, on another level the in-depth picture is most arresting. About 2.5 billion people lack basic sanitation, just under 2 billion have to walk a kilometre for water, resulting in approximately 2 million children a year dying of diarrhoea; biomass heating in homes kills about 1.5 million people a year of which half are under 5 years old (Shah, 2013)—every 90 seconds a child dies from a water-related disease. In light of these numbers the highly admirable work of Gram Vikas under the leadership of Joe Madiath sends a shining light over an ocean of darkness (see Pless and Appel, 2012). The areas of highest population growth are in the areas of greatest poverty and of lowest agricultural productivity and these areas are at greatest impact from climate change.

Indeed the notion of inequality is a binding challenge that sits alongside that of climate change—more on this in Chapter 10. The fracturing aspects of societies as a consequence of many of these elements coming together reflect the increase in nationalism in Europe and the US and the turning away from the global picture. This is perhaps an understandable reaction if there is the absence of active, plausible and attractive alternatives. The Brexit vote was a striking example of leadership of purpose gone AWOL (absence without leave, Kempster 2018). Yet there are green shoots of change. Steps forward have been much articulated over the last two decades. The United Nations with the Millennium Goals and now translated into the Sustainable Development Goals (SDGs) is a useful global pathway. With 169 targets these have been helpfully summarised into 17 goals (United Nations General Assembly, 2014). Recently the World Business Council for Sustainable Development have released an online report with tools guiding business to take action to implement the SDGs (2017). We will say more about the SDGs in Chapters 10 and 13, which explore the planetary dividend and how these SDGs can be translated into everyday activity and add value for small, medium and large organisations. At this point we wish to emphasise that the approaches to taking action with the SDGs (the various reports and statements) for the most part have been crafted for government or inter-governmental engagement. There still remains a dearth of attention to how organisations can become engaged in this critical agenda (Hajer et al., 2015) as part of everyday activity, which adds value to stakeholders and serves the fiduciary duty, rather than (or perhaps additional to), philanthropy. It is to this agenda—linking business value with social impact—that this book seeks to make a contribution.

We have provided but a glimpse of the complex systemic web of challenges that face humanity. We have offered this narrative, not to depress people, but instead to offer this 'perfect storm' of grand challenges to galvanise a 'moral outrage.' This moral outrage needs to become a central purpose on which leaders and their organisations can and will make a significant impact. It is both enlightened self-interest and fundamental purpose of moral capitalism to address these grand challenges. Indeed the ability of governments to address these challenges is only possible in partnership—a grand partnership with businesses, NGO's, social enterprises and the voluntary sector. The agency of leadership is key (Hajer et al., 2015). As Thomas with Nicola (Maak and Pless, 2009b: 539) suggested:

> Given the power, potential, and abilities of business leaders to make this world a better place the least we can expect from business leaders is that they recognize their co-responsibility for addressing some of the world's most pressing problems; not as one-dimensional agents of shareholder interests, but as active and reflective citizens of the world who happen to be managers and leaders in a corporation.

The need for societal purpose in organisational leadership is pivotal. It has been argued (Kempster, Jackson and Conroy, 2011) that within the leadership relationship there is typically the absence of a societal purposeful discourse. It is a sad irony that the grand challenges are 'the gift that keeps giving' in terms of the choices for businesses to engage with. Translations of the business's purpose and activities need to be reframed to embrace the grand challenges relevant to the business; the question that must be addressed is' —how can the business engage with the grand challenges in manner that is aligned and adds value to the business and advances the fiduciary duty of leadership? Leadership of purpose needs to be infused into the DNA of the business model, into everyday conversations, and into how value and purpose are interconnected. It is for the remainder of the book to give insight into how this can occur for the leadership of organisations of all sizes and in all contexts. A relevant quote that captures the essence of the challenge to those who lead: 'If not you, who? If not now, when?' (Sir Frank Dick).

3 Responsible Leadership
Reconciling People, Purpose, and Profit

Thomas Maak and Nicola M. Pless

While the research domain of responsible leadership is a fairly recent development, the term as such is not new. Responsible leadership was first used by Harvard professor George Smith in the subtitle of his 1962 textbook *Business, Society, and the Individual: Problems in responsible leadership of private enterprise organizations operating in a free society.* The author's objective was to help readers to get acquainted with 'real business life [that] for the responsible business leader involves keeping in perspective all the economic facts and all the human and political facts that are inside his/[her] enterprise, as well as those that are outside' (p. xiii). Smith's perspective was advanced and far-sighted, but also representative of the individual focus in the CSR debate of the time. Indeed, the early debate on CSR was mostly a debate on responsible leadership in the "free world" and the attitudes and behaviors pertaining to the "responsible business leader" (Smith, 1962).

Zooming forward more than half a century it is fair to say that responsible leadership in business and society has never been more important, but at the same time it seems more distant than ever: we live in a connected world and are witnessing the growth of a sharing economy but social cohesion and well-being are declining. Digital futures are here, or so it seems, but the price is disruption and unsettlement through a largely ungoverned digital universe in which truth has become an ancient concept and moral boundaries no longer exist. Narcissistic and power-hungry "leaders" conduct politics as "deal-making" and seem to have annihilated 40 years of diplomacy and progress through the ruthless pursuit of self-interest and pseudo-nationalism, blurring the lines between dictators and so-called leaders of the free world, and those between fiction and reality: "*Power* is power" concludes an intriguing self-referential dialogue on what constitutes power in the TV adaptation of "Game of Thrones". Indeed the computer-generated masses of Game of Thrones look not so different from masses at the doorsteps of Europe seeking access to the promised lands of free health care, flat-screen TVs and German appliances. Far-right parties in Europe are surging and humane ideals of a global civil society seem to have evaporated in the post-truth boiler rooms of interest driven tweets. Humanity is at a crossroad, faced with profound ethical tragedies: migration, extremism, climate change, and destructive leadership.

Our point here is not to dwell in apocalyptical skepticism; rather, we would like to stress the fundamental importance of responsible leadership in what is simultaneously a connected and disrupted world. This book is an attempt to overcome the paradoxical state of leadership in the twenty-first century and the concomitant retreat of values and virtues—through a renewed sense of purpose. In the following we will therefore discuss some of the core features of responsible leadership and suggest areas for future research—in the hope for better futures and convinced that once we make the pragmatic turn towards a clearer conceptualization of responsible leadership and a greater awareness of what it means and implies, and unpack what needs to be done—then such practice can be enacted and reinforced in the pursuit of a more dignified world.

More specifically, we will discuss three questions: *Why? What?* and *How?*—*Why* do we need to focus on responsible leadership in particular? *What* constitutes responsible leadership, in other words what are its key features? And finally, *how* can we make sure that it is developed—in theory *and* in practice?

Why Responsible Leadership?

Similar to the question Steve's son raised in Chapter 1 we could simply ask: isn't *responsible* leadership the obvious way to lead? How could any reasonable person in such a position lead differently? Indeed, in an ideal world this question seems superficial and redundant—we would hope that leaders are aware that with power comes responsibility, that leadership is a calling to help others to grow as individuals, and that ethical qualities are indispensable for a leader to be respected and effective. However, if this was a staged monologue the instructions would read: 'followed by sarcastic laughter' . . .

Leadership observers have long realized that we neither live in an ideal world where our leaders are inherently responsible—'saints rarely seek appointed office' (Lipman-Blumen, 2005)—nor should we hope that leaders act to higher standards. Indeed, we can be grateful if leaders comply with standards of common decency and act in line with values we all consider important rather than considering themselves exempt from them. The temptations of leadership are such that all too often leaders feel elevated and exceptional and subsequently no longer adhere to important norms and values. Again, this is a pragmatic, not a negative assessment. It reflects a reflexive view of the world as it is: imperfect, crowded, and when it comes to leadership, often selfish and messy.

So when it comes to the *Why?* there are a number of reasons to consider: first, the state of the world in general and the lack of responsible leadership we observe. Second, the state of the business world in particular—the annually published Edelman trust barometer, which measures the level of trust in business leaders through a large-scale survey of the informed public, makes for some depressing reading: year after year the Edelman group reports that trust in business leaders is at an all-time low—on average it sits at 20 plus per cent in most of the developed economies. This means that only 1 in 5 informed citizens trust business leaders to do the right thing and to tell the truth. This is not only a reflection of a persistent credibility crisis but puts in question the legitimacy of business leaders and subsequently the license to operate for organizations in the respective countries. That crisis was triggered by high-level business scandals and individual leadership failures at the start of the millennium—most prominently the demise of Enron and Arthur Andersen—carried forward by the global financial crisis, and has been reinforced by recent scandals in the car industry and banking sector. Third, this means in essence that stakeholders at home and abroad expect leaders to do better, and more: generate more of the six dividends we highlight in this book and accept responsibility in areas such as human rights, distributive justice, and global warming. More specifically, stakeholders pay increasing attention to the political role and responsibility of business leaders in the pursuit of a global common good, they ask probing questions about business's role in the fight against poverty and as 'secondary agents of justice' (Young, 2011). Lastly, perhaps because we all assume that leaders have an inherent sense of responsibility, the latter plays only a very minor role in leadership research. In fact, Waldman and Galvin (2008) suggest that responsibility is missing from established key leadership descriptors, such as transformational, charismatic, authentic, servant, shared, or even spiritual and ethical leadership, 'and that it is actually this element that is at the heart of what effective leadership is all about. In a nutshell, to not be responsible is not to be effective as a leader' (Waldman and Galvin, 2008: 327). They are right, of course; in a world of contested values in which responsibility in all its forms—individual, organizational, and at societal level—matters in the marketplace, leaders cannot afford to ignore the challenges to their legitimacy.

What Constitutes Responsible Leadership?

Responsible leadership thus responds to existing gaps in leadership theory *and* the practical challenges facing leadership including expectations to do better and more. Naturally, it focuses on questions of *responsibility*— including accountability, appropriate moral decision making, legitimacy, and trust. In other words, responsible leadership seeks to first define what "responsible" means in the context of leadership. Second, being accountable for one's actions, acting with one's constituencies in mind, and being a good citizen, are not just semantic variations on the term "responsibility"; they are inherently *relational* concepts. By definition, responsible leadership is geared toward the concerns of others and seeks to clarify who the "others" are and what responding to their concerns entails. Hence, our original definition describes responsible leadership as 'a relational and ethical phenomenon, which occurs in social processes of interaction with those who affect or are affected by leadership and have a stake in the purpose and vision of the leadership relationship' (Maak and Pless, 2006a: 103).

We broadened the traditional view of leader—subordinate relationships to leader—stakeholder relationships in response to the dramatic changes of leadership work over the past decades. We stressed that not just direct reports, but numerous stakeholder groups, are part of the leadership project and that accordingly diverse relationships are at the heart of leadership such that 'building and cultivating . . . ethically sound relations towards different stakeholders is an important responsibility of leaders in an interconnected stakeholder society' (Maak and Pless, 2006b: 101). Obviously, the required level of regard for others varies with the nature of the leadership project. However, it requires from leaders distinct qualities, or what we have labelled *relational intelligence*: relational qualities driven by emotional, social, and ethical intelligence (Pless and Maak, 2005). In sum, responsible leadership seeks to define the role of leadership and the responsibilities of leaders in a stakeholder society centred on the belief that only a an authentic relational, values-centred approach will be effective.

Accordingly, responsible leadership cannot be captured and defined by focusing on the leader only—her relational qualities, values, and abilities to influence diverse constituencies—but must mirror the complexities of the leadership project and the context in which it happens. In other words, responsible leadership ought to be conceived as a multilevel concept, encompassing individual, team, organizational, and societal levels. This means that researchers have to push the boundaries of leadership research. Not to make a one size fits all theory but to make sure that all dimensions of responsibility are reflected. The essence of the afore-mentioned quote by Waldman and Galvin stresses that extant leadership research is myopic when it comes to issues pertaining to responsible leadership, a result of the micro-lens approach traditional research is taking, as well as paradigmatic shortcomings in traditional leadership research. Three shortcomings are most notable: first, the academic obsession with the *leader* and the traditional *leader-follower dyad*, both of which result in oversights when it comes to leader-stakeholder relationships and give emphasis to an individualized rather than a *socialized* conceptualization of leadership; second, a *limited view of leadership work*, mainly focused on influence and effectiveness in teams and organizations rather than the full scope of the leadership project involving internal *and* external constituencies—thereby "reducing" leadership complexity rather than mirroring it; and third, normative ignorance, or *ethical myopia*, by excluding moral motivation, virtues, and non-instrumental values from leadership research as if these drivers, resulting in responsibility mindsets, were a private matter rather than a key ingredient of the leadership project.

Hence, what is needed is a multilevel theory that connects individual, organizational, and institutional factors such that the full range of leadership responsibilities can be addressed. In this sense, researchers in the responsible leadership domain deal with: individual factors, such as values, virtues, and ethical decision making; organizational-level leadership, including the links among corporate social responsibility, stakeholder theory, and leadership; and consider institutional factors and their influence on responsible leadership, notably the societal or cultural context, as defined by factors such as power distance and humane orientation that indicate the extent to which social concerns are part of cultural practices. We are not suggesting here that all these dimensions are to be considered all the time. What we suggest is that leadership research must be conscious of these levels, how they interact, and what this means for responsible leadership.

What has become clear though is that effective responsible leadership requires leaders to focus on a compelling and credible purpose of their organization—a purpose that engages stakeholders and is geared towards legitimate and desirable objectives (Donaldson and Walsh 2015; Pless, Maak and Waldman, 2012). In this book we propose that the six dividends provide a compelling pathway to achieve just that on an aggregate level. At the actor level, that purpose may best be promoted through a clear role identity of the leader, encompassing sense-giving and the moral labour of responsible leadership. We have suggested elsewhere (Maak and Pless, 2006a) that a role model enables leaders to integrate responsibilities, relationship, and purpose. We propose four roles pertaining to the normative tasks of responsible leadership: the leader as visionary, servant, citizen, and steward.

Vision and purpose are closely connected and touch on the 'Why', the meaning and purposeful direction of the leadership project, however defined. Without a compelling vision, why would anyone follow?

Of course, there are the pragmatics of making a living or those who just want to follow direction within a given organizational context. However, as soon as we broaden the circle of influence to other stakeholders, especially those in non-reporting relationships, it becomes clear that leaders need to be able to provide a more compelling vision than, say, maximizing profit, beating the competition, or be a technology leader. Instead, a vision should encompass an aspirational, purposeful cause such as, 'Advancing humanity through software' (Atlassian), 'We exist as a business to help solve the environmental crisis' (Patagonia), or 'Making poverty history' (The World Bank). A spirited noble purpose is what gives individual life meaning and organizational life direction. As human beings we are on a constant quest for meaning (Frankl 1959/2004)—and it is the first responsibility of leaders to develop the courage to advance human dignity through other-regarding action (Pless, Maak and Harris, 2017).

Through its emphasis on other-regard responsible leadership echoes the idea that leadership is first and foremost about others—followers as stakeholders—not about the leader. Hence, it supports the idea of the leader as servant. This is not a new concept, but dates back to religious beliefs. In its current form it is largely based on Greenleaf (1977/2002), who in turn builds on Hesse's short novel *The Journey to the East*. The novel is about a group of travellers who, after breaking apart, discover that their servant Leo led the group and held it together. Servant leadership asks whether those whom the leader serves grow as persons. If the answer is yes, the leader was successful and effective. Thus, servant leadership turns the world of autocratic leadership upside down, reminding us that leadership ought to be about the leader's constituencies in the first instance such that the leader's task is to serve the needs and legitimate interests of others (Greenleaf, 1977/2002). The idea of a leader as servant in the context of responsible leadership implies that leaders serve others and a purpose nobler than themselves.

In Chapter 10 we elaborate in more detail on the other two core roles—the leader as citizen and steward—so that we will only mention them in passing here. The *citizen* depicts the basic expectations that leaders should behave like *good citizens*, active and caring members of communities and contributing to their well-being. But this role also suggests that leaders have to embrace the new political role expectations vis-à-vis global justice and active engagement in matters of human rights. Moreover, as *stewards* they should embrace long-term thinking bridging past, present, and future generations and not only aim at a positive legacy, but commit their organizations to leaving both communities and planet better off—by making sure that their organization produces a planetary dividend. Responsible leaders integrate these four roles not only at a cognitive level, but they practice these and lead by example, inspiring others to do the same.

Developing Responsible Leadership

Responsible leadership is a multilevel response to deficiencies in existing leadership frameworks and theories; a response to high-profile scandals on individual, organizational, and systemic levels; and a response to new and emerging social, ethical, and environmental challenges in an increasingly connected world. The scope and complexity of these challenges call for responsible leadership and leaders who acknowledge their shared responsibility in tackling these grand challenges. Responsibility means being responsible *for something* and *to someone*, implying accountability and trustworthiness. As for the former, one would expect action and direction in line with a logic of appropriateness; as for the latter, it should have become clear that responsible leadership is socially embedded and hence must be understood in its relational complexity. This in turn implies, of course, that responsible leaders are made, not born, and that responsible leadership needs to be nurtured and developed at the individual level, within teams, in organizations, and at the interface of business and society.

True responsibility in our view emerges when leaders develop the ability to *integrate* across these levels (Pless et al., 2012), displaying the motivational drivers and virtues of a responsible leader, sharing responsible leadership among team members, committing their organizations to sustainable futures in line with the six dividends, and building sustainable relationships—and trust—with all relevant stakeholders.

While the foundations for responsible leadership should effectively be laid throughout childhood and in schools, and reiterated at university level, we suggest that international service-learning programs are an effective tool to develop such qualities at executive level (Pless, Maak and Stahl, 2011). Hence, even if the competencies and qualities we highlighted here are absent, there are effective ways of developing them through service-learning programs embedded in a learning infrastructure focused on tackling some of the grand challenges we stressed above. Experience shows that the best results are achieved when development programs provide a holistic or 3-D experience triggering learning and reflection at the cognitive, affective, and behavioral level. This should come as no surprise as these levels reflect the *whole self*: responsible leader mindset, motivational drivers such as empathy and compassion, translated into responsible action and pro-social behavior. Hence, responsible leadership is a multilevel, whole person concept oriented towards a for the noble purpose of positive futures.

The notion of developing the whole person to enact responsible leadership is a useful segue towards the systemic orientation in which we next situate responsible leadership—the areas of responsibility associated with the six good dividends. The essence of Chapter 4 is towards the operationalization of responsible leadership as visionary, servant, citizen, and steward across these six areas (plus governance) through a particular attention to realizing value for the respective stakeholders.

4 The Good Dividends

A Systemic Framework of Value Creation

Steve Kempster, Thomas Maak and Ken Parry

It is the intention of this chapter to offer up a system of value generation centred on leadership of purpose that seeks to connect together and operationalise the four cornerstones of Chapter 2 and Chapter 3: moral capitalism, virtue ethics, responsible leadership and global systems thinking.

The original idea of the good dividends emerged in an excitable conversation between Steve and Ken in Steve's kitchen while making soup. In fact, it was not good dividends but rather *virtuous* dividends that so excited us and became the spark of energy that has catalysed this project. We had been depressing each other about a range of connected themes: the decline of virtue practices in organisations (please see Chapter 2 and the discussion on MacIntyre (1985), that explores virtue practices, the contribution they generate for society and why these have declined); the absence of societal purpose in for-profit and not-for-profit institutions; the problematic nature of engaging in societal purpose conversations in leadership relationships (Kempster, Jackson and Conroy, 2011); and the pressing need for such conversations with the ever-worsening situation regarding the grand challenges facing humanity. The concept behind the virtuous dividend formed as a consequence of addressing two interrelated questions: what would an organisation be doing if it overtly pursued virtue practices? Would this lead to societal purpose becoming prominent in everyday activity? With soup spoiling we sketched out an answer. If employees had a clear sense of purpose and applied their talents (practice virtues) and generated internal goods (outcomes valued by society) it would be hard to imagine the organisation would be worse off—surely there would be greater external goods (profits). Leadership then would seek to focus on creating an environment in which this was the norm—leadership of purpose would generate virtuous dividends. A few months later, sitting in a hotel lounge in Barcelona, Thomas joined the conversation and collectively we unpacked a greater sense of the earlier notion of virtuous dividends into a system of good dividends that connected moral capitalism with virtue ethics and responsible leadership.

A stimulating journey of conversations with an ever-growing group of colleagues followed—each extending and shaping the emerging system.

The conversations were no longer centred in the leadership field and on the leader. Purpose connected to the idea of what had emerged as the 'planetary dividend'—benefiting communities and the planet as a whole, at present and in the future—stimulated systemic and interdisciplinary conversations about good dividends. This journey of interdisciplinary conversations led to the emergence of a conceptual system. We speak here of system, rather than framework or model, as systems thinking is most critical to how we have come to conceive of the relationships and interactions between the good dividends, leadership of purpose and the grand challenges, and how such relationships and interactions are nested within a hierarchy of systems. We hope the language is not too indigestable. We think it is worth the effort as it to deliberately structure thinking.

Systems Thinking and Purposeful Human Activity

When we speak here of systems thinking we are in particular drawing on the work of Peter Checkland. A systemic perspective embraces an engagement with the whole system. It seeks to understand the complex whole by attention to particular elements that help construct the system. But importantly the particular elements are limited in value in terms of explaining the whole. The key is the integrative nature that creates an emergent property of a system. Checkland and Scholes (1999) offer the example of a bicycle. Its ability to be useful as a system for transportation is as a consequence of the integrative nature of the system. Other aspects of systemic thinking relate to the notion of hierarchy—levels of systems that generate emergent properties- and control—to manage how the system achieves its purposes.

The notion of purpose is most central to systems thinking—in particular to soft systems. Hard systems are associated with an orientation that assumes a world in which purposes are unambiguous, and systems can be designed and measured related to such clarity. Hard systems become problematic when considering purposeful human activity, because people comprehend the world differently and offer up different interpretations of the purpose of human activity. For example, is a prison a place of punishment, or a place of rehabilitation, or a warehouse to store people who would otherwise cause harm to society? Or perhaps a university for educating prisoners to become better at criminal activity (and not get caught). All four questions reflect different stakeholder perspectives. Ignoring the last one, all can be systems of purposeful activity that a prison governor may seek to make manifest. However, achieving all three may be mutually exclusive. Politically the governor may well have to be pursuing all three simultaneously and perhaps achieving none, yet satisficing various stakeholders at particular moments in time. Checkland and Scholes offer up the example of the Concord project (to build a supersonic plane). Peter Checkland was asked to work on the project to make sense of the lack of progress. Through the lens of soft systems thinking he offered the insight that there were at least two different purposes to the Concord project: the French to establish national prestige for technological advancement and the British as a way (ironically at this time of writing with Brexit) to demonstrate commitment to the European project of the EEC (now EU). The project became an endless journey of conflict between the partners as they pursued different purposes. For example, it was not in the British interest for expediency as negotiations proceeded on the greater project—entry into the EEC—whilst at the same time looking like good Europeans. The notion of purposeful activity assumes that we humans have intention with regard to what we do orientated to a purpose(s). Yet such purposes are rarely expressed and made explicit. In the Concord project team, the British engineers were not aware of the highest-level purpose with regard to EEC membership. Their purpose that shaped their activity was to build a plane. If this system succeeded in a timely fashion the higher system would not succeed. There were two systems in conflict. As a consequence conflict persisted between British engineers and British government officials, and between British and French engineers and British and French government officials. Yet all actors in this project were seeking purposeful activity. The focus of soft systems is on purposeful human activity that is embedded in problem situations, rather than problems (as with hard systems). It assumes people to be 'immersed in complex action which they [are] trying to make purposeful . . . to make a situation seen as problematical somehow better' (1999: 24).

In many respects organisations are caught in a hierarchy of soft systems; they are made up of human activity systems, and the organisation sits within greater systems (like with the Concord example). The grand challenges described in Chapter 2 reflect the emergent properties of these greater complex systems. Indeed, the various grand challenges form a system with the emergent property—that of leading to an environment that threatens humanity—as shown by Figure 2.1 in Chapter 2. Although the complexity of the system is at first glance messy and rather difficult to follow, such complexity must not be designed away for purposes of ease of understanding and elegance. As a whole it forms a rich picture of a situation that is super complex and not easy to tackle. It is a wicked problem that can only be addressed through multiple agencies working in collaboration through a process of collective learning, innovation and adaptation (Grint, 2005). In Chapter 2 we ran through many of these elements and touched on the notion of a systemic tipping point from which discontinuous change and cascade effects occur. Helbing helpfully examines the financial meltdown of 2007–2008 as just such an example:

> Everyone seemed to be doing their own job properly on its own merit. And according to standard measures of success, they were often doing it well. The failure was to see how collectively this added

up to a series of interconnected imbalances. Individual risks may rightly have been viewed as small, but the risk to the system as a whole was vast. For example, while risk diversification in a banking system is aimed at minimising risks, it can create systemic risks when the network density becomes too high.

(2013: 53)

Examining the systemic model shown in Figure 2.1 the density of inter-connections is very high. Modest increases in one or more areas can have significant effect on the whole system. This is anticipated to be the case for the planetary system. Models have been developed to try and anticipate when the tipping point may occur. 'The trajectories of human population, energy demand, economic development, and climate policy therefore create the very real possibility that over the coming century, atmospheric CO_2 concentrations will be the highest of the past 22 million years' (Diffenbaugh and Field, 2013: 489). They conclude that '[i]t is highly likely that those changes will intensify in the coming decades, unfolding at a rate that is at least an order of magnitude—and potentially several orders of magnitude—more rapid than the changes to which terrestrial ecosystems have been exposed during the past 65 million years' (2013: 490). In essence we are probably very close to systemic cascading and the tipping point of systemic change and the considerable impact to humanity. The anthropogenic system, described above, is interconnected to inter-organisational systems and intra-organisational systems, all of which are inextricably connected to the influences, decisions and actions of those who lead.

Checkland and Scholes make salient the work of Vickers (1965) and the notion of appreciative systems. We think this has added much value to the central thesis of the book. It is a meta-frame for thinking about systems, relationships, perceptions and value judgements, events and ideas, and actions. Rather than goal seeking, Vickers suggested that human perception and judgements about action are oriented toward relationships and the value associated with these. These relationships and values are filtered by an appreciation of what is happening in the world. Vickers saw the world through the metaphor of an intertwined two-stranded rope of events and ideas. Individuals appreciate the events and ideas through a frame of standards (of fact and value), and draw judgements on what to do, which in turn generate events, or possibly ideas. This on-going system continually adapts to changes in events and ideas thereby enabling shifts in perceptions, standards and value judgements of what to take action about. Reframed to the arguments thus far presented in Chapters 2 and 3, the notion of neo-liberal capitalism has been the dominant set of ideas that have evolved alongside events. The standards that shape our judgements for action have been shaped by historical expectations associated with neo-liberal capitalism. However, the current events in the world, with regard to the grand challenges and the close systemic tipping point and the radical impact to the conditions that shape humanity, may stimulate and generate new ideas—such as moral capitalism, responsible leadership and virtue ethics. In a major way we hope the appreciative system is at a point in time in which new standards of expectations, new appreciations of relationships, and appreciation of stakeholders' value is leading to new judgements on organisational action. Leadership is fundamental to changes in an appreciative system—leaders have disproportionate influence to shape sense-making of events and ideas. In Archer's (1995) terms organisational leaders (or agents in her terms) have significant influence to maintain the system (morpho-stasis)—sustain neo-liberal capitalism—or change it (morpho-genesis)—to pursue moral capitalism.

So this is our meta-systemic frame that informs on our appreciation to take action with regard to the hierarchy of the system associated with the grand challenges. We now apply Checkland's work and in particular soft systems methodology (SSM) to help construct the good dividends system.

Good Dividends—A Systemic Frame

We need to say at the outset that the system we shall offer up here is not reality. It is our appreciation of ideas and theories. Our work here draws on research and case studies that have collectively informed our conceptualisation of a system. We are seeking to inquire into how the four cornerstones we established in Chapters 2 and 3 can be addressed within an organisational context. In major part this book is less of an explanation of what to do and much more of a process of exploring what might be possible: 'bring[ing] about improvements in areas of social concern by activating people involved to reflect upon and debate perceptions of the real world structured by the systemic models' (Checkland and Scholes, 1999: 28). Working with SSM the first step is to name and then understand the problem situation. In Chapters 2 and 3 we have sought to unpack this. The second step is to establish a 'root definition' for the system. This is the system's purposeful human activity. Our root definition for the good dividends system is:

> *To generate value for stakeholders that in turn generates value for owners/shareholders, accomplished through leaders' attention to societal purpose and fiduciary duty that achieve the good dividends, but controlled by appropriate governance and measurement, in order to realise moral capitalism and address the grand challenges that face humanity.*

This book is guided by this root definition. It seeks to establish a system that is intended to lead to a transformation—echoes of one of the ambitions we outlined at the beginning of Chapter 1. To elaborate on the root definition step 3 of SSM seeks to understand relationships, power, constraints and beneficiaries of a human activity system that is based on the root definition. Checkland helpfully offers a mnemonic (that is partially memorable) of CATWOE to capture these elements. The system of the good dividends, that we will outline shortly, is at the organisational level (in terms of systems hierarchy). We have used CATWOE (1999: 35) below, assuming a for-profit business:

> Customers—the beneficiaries of the transformation: *purchasers of the service/product; suppliers engaged with the business; employees contributing to the transformation; 'one-planet' communities impacted by the business; and the shareholders/owners through receiving good dividends—greater, more sustainable and ethically derived.*
>
> Actors—Those who will implement the transformation: *Employees, suppliers and leaders. Customers and communities are also actors that enable the transformation within the notion of good dividends (more on this shortly).*
>
> Transformation—Conversion of inputs to outputs: *Human, physical, social, reputational, operational and financial capitals utilised to achieve the good dividends through the activities and responsibilities of the actors.*
>
> Weltanschauung—the world view that makes the transformation meaningful: *The necessity to address the grand challenges that face humanity and that moral capitalism is a most powerful mechanism for achieving this.*
>
> Owners—Those who can stop/enable the transformation: *Shareholders/ owners of the business; managers as fiduciaries for the owners/ shareholders.*
>
> Environmental constraints—elements outside the organisational system that are (current) givens: *legislation; attitudes of investors; availability of skilled labour; media; etc . . .*

The next step, the exciting step in terms of the book, is to turn the root definition, informed and enriched by the CATWOE, into a transformational system of purposeful human activity. 'The modelling language is based upon verbs, and the modelling process consists of assembling and structuring the minimum necessary activities to carry out the transformation process [. . .] In general we aim for 7 +/– 2 activities' (1999: 36). Peter Checkland draws on cognitive psychology that suggests this is about the maximum number that the human brain can readily work with. Importantly though this does not limit the scope and depth of the system. Returning to the notion of hierarchy in systems thinking, each activity forms a new system to which a root definition would be crafted and a transformation system of 7 +/– 2 would be created. This is the essence of the book structure. We shall examine each of the activities as sub-systems; but always keeping in mind that each system needs to be seen as part of the whole for the emergent properties of the greater system to be realised.

So, to the good dividends' system shown in Figure 4.1. It is based on the activities of the business so it will at first sight seem most familiar with regard to the first four dividends: the financial dividend, the human resources dividend, the operational dividend and the brand dividend. And two less obvious dividends: planetary dividend and the social innovation dividend—linking innovation with social need. Through enabling social purpose to be pursued these six dividends are systemically connected in order to achieve the emergent property of the system—that of realising moral capitalism. The system requires governance to control what is occurring to ensure the fiduciary duty is met. Informing governance is the necessity of performance measurement—to ensure the system achieves what it is meant to in terms of four 'E's (adapted from Checkland and Scholes, 1999: 42): efficacy—the system delivers the six dividends; efficiency—the outputs of the system (in terms of the six dividends) divided by the resources consumed; ethicality—the system enables employee practice virtues thereby generating internal goods (excellence of service, quality, etc.) along with external goods (productivity of products and services, employee remuneration, and profit); effectiveness—the system generates an emergent property, that of realising moral capitalism and therefore acting on the fiduciary duty to enrich business value contemporaneously enabling social purposes to be achieved in terms of social impact.

As mentioned previously this system is being offered to frame and stimulate inquiry and learning into the possibilities of how responsible leadership, focusing on societal purpose, can enable practice virtues and internal goods to flourish within organisations, and as a consequence engender moral capitalism to become operationalised and address the grand challenges. As the primary purpose of the system is to enable such an inquiry the suggested system of good dividends should not be judged on whether it is valid, but rather whether it is defensible—is the system logical and does it draw upon the root definition for which it is based? (Checkland and Scholes, 1999: 41). We hope though that the system continues to be rooted in 'common-sense'. In that way, it does have strength of reach and resonance to the real-world complexity. The system is then an abstract conceptualisation of how business activity may be structured. We wish now to proceed through the system explaining what has been designed.

Each of the boxes shown in Figure 4.1 is an activity; and each box is, in a sense, the root definition of a sub-system—where the detail of the action can be developed therein. The arrows suggest the notion of yield, or bring forth, or enable. The system is captured within a boundary to illustrate how the system is enabled by responsible leadership, and that the system is measured and controlled in terms of achieving the root

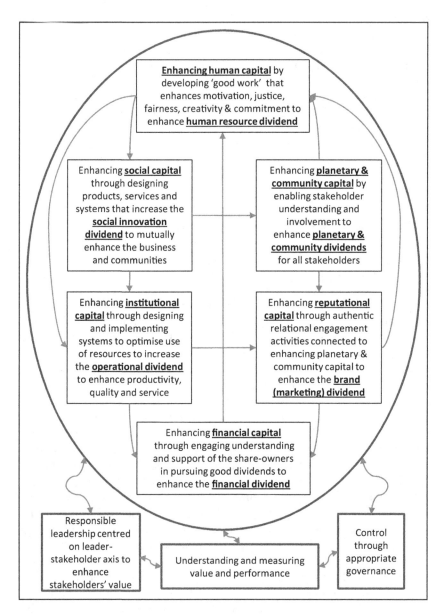

Figure 4.1 A System of Good Dividends

definition of the system. Each activity is systemically connected to others (rather than linear cause and effect process). This is why we have not numbered the activities implying some form of logical sequence. So, an examination of the system could commence at any point.

We have chosen to commence at the financial dividend. Our reasoning is the focus of leadership attention, or lack of it, with regard to the value of people, and other intangible capital assets—that are significant to the realisation of the good dividends. We start with the present and the orientation of senior leadership communication of the financial dividends to the key business stakeholder—the investors. Steve Young, Sam Rawsthorne and Luke Hildyard examine the dearth of attention from board leadership to intangible assets, and in particular with regard to human capital. It appears that investors presently do not expect human resource capital to be measured. Neither board leadership nor investors appear to see the importance of human capital maximisation—or at least reporting the same. The case thus needs to be made of the need for leadership to understand human resource capital and how it needs to be valued if good dividends are to be obtained. We return to the financial dividend within Chapter 11. Anthony Hesketh explores value and its measurement related to the six capitals, but in particular he responds to Young and colleagues' chapter and seeks to provoke a revolution in financial measurement that would unshackle CFO's from neo-liberal capitalism; but perhaps more importantly catalyse investors to expect good dividends from their investments through attention to maximising all the capitals and not just the fixed tangible assets. It is very hard to imagine how the good dividends (and aligned maximisation of the six capitals) could occur without leadership attention to the human resourcefulness (HR) dividend. It is thus the next dividend we shall address in this book.

Robyn Remke and Steve suggest the HR dividend argues for a movement. A movement away from the neo-liberal perspective of traditional HR approach with regard to structures of control and managing policies that creates such control. And a movement towards human resourcefulness—employees having a desire to invest of themselves into strong engagement with work because of what it offers to them. This resourcefulness orientation is centred on purpose, fulfilment, curiosity, achievement, satisfaction and ownership. The consequence is employees who are more resilient, adaptable, flexible and responsive because they choose to be in order to achieve what matters to them. Concomitant to this orientation to human resourcefulness is the need for aspects such as equality, well-being and remuneration to be addressed. Using the leadership lexicon of transformations and transactions (Bass and Avolio, 1990)—it is found that both are necessary, but alone are not sufficient. A case study is outlined of a HR manager seeking to realise human resourcefulness, but the realities of her context inhibit such realisation—a consequence of a neo-liberal HR director who halts progress. We suggest that by reframing HRM through a responsible leadership perspective the HR capital (the human resourceful-ness) can be realised as the HR dividend, but it does require leadership to break the historic orientation of HR and pursue resourcefulness and poli-cies that would enable resourcefulness. The emergent HR dividend is sug-gested to yield two particular dividends: social innovation and operations.

The ability to undertake social innovation draws from a sense of employee purpose and desire to contribute to organisational activity emanating out from the HR dividend. Social innovation is about exam-ining the organisation's products, services and systems to see how they can be enhanced to add value in terms of external goods (e.g. what the service does for the customer and in return the profitability and therefore remuneration to employees) but also internal goods (as contributions to society for societal or environmental enhancements). In essence, social innovation views ecological and social problems as a source of innovation and value generation (Hart, 2005). Social innovation is rarely undertaken intra-organisationally. It typically is a collaborative process of engaging stakeholders in sourcing of ideas, or used as concept development, or to test new concepts in practice (Juntunel, Halme, Korsunova and Rajala, 2016) to develop mutual sustainable interests that exist between commu-nities, suppliers, customers and the organisation (Hörisch, Freeman and Schaltegger, 2014). Steve and Minna Halme suggest social innovation is likely to be the least understood of the dividends, and perhaps the most complex in terms of maximising social capital to generate value for all relevant stakeholders. They provide three case studies to illustrate three different types of social innovation related to the experience of organ-isational leadership engaging with social innovation. The social innova-tion dividend offers up innovations aligned with planet and community interests and looks to the operations dividend to turn these into value generating products, services or systems.

The operations dividend is enabled by both the HR dividend and social innovation dividend. Operations management is the most well-developed orientation towards addressing the grand challenges with regard to pro-cesses such as lean, cradle to cradle, reverse supply chain or green logis-tics. Such processes focus on the thoughtful use of resources, for example: reduction of waste, reduction in engaged time, reduction in energy usage, reduction in materials consumed and the development of products through recycled materials. All of these have potential for reductions in cost, and indeed would seek to enhance productivity—both in terms of more effi-cient use of resources but also with respect to innovative use of resources. However, the chapter highlights the limitations thus far in pursuit of the operations dividend from a sustainability perspective. The operations dividend is most tangible and in theory most achievable. But, the ability to maximise on these cost reductions or productivity advances depends on people: employees' impassioned sense of purpose to persist in identify-ing process improvements; to be curious, enthusiastic and committed to explore what is possible, learning, testing, questioning and experimenting. Steve Eldridge, along with Steve, suggests the need for operations management to focus on value realisation, rather than cost minimisation, through attention to a combination of two emerging areas—sustainable operations and behavioural operations—that can reframe traditional operational approaches. To illustrate their argument they apply ideas from lean thinking within a case study of a most unusual context—that of police work with attention to homicide investigations. The case opens up the considerable scope for the realisation of the operational dividend across all sectors and all sizes of business. The operational dividend is directly linked to the financial dividend. It is, however, most important to our planet and our communities—enhancing or not damaging the environment or communities. And as a result of enhancing our planet and our communities the operations dividend helps to realise the brand dividend through improving the reputational capital of the organisation.

Like the operations dividend, the brand dividend is most readily understood. It is increasingly becoming part of discussions with regard to business value (see Chapter 11). The brand dividend draws on reputational capital. It is associated with the value placed on the strength of the organisation's brands in terms of product and service recognition and associated customer loyalty. In the context of the good dividends the brand dividend is enhanced through the other dividends:

- The HR dividend offers a strong sense of employee commitment to products/services and the organisation they are employed by in the interactions with customers.
- The operations dividend offers quality, timeliness and reliability to the offering; the planetary dividend offers validity of the organisation's authentic engagement with tangible outcomes manifest in the world.
- The social innovation dividend provides plentiful opportunity to involve customers in exploring potential solutions whilst at the same time enabling product/service differentiation.

The aspect of active involvement is vital. Involvement engenders a sense of loyalty, attachment and feelings of being part of a community. This generates highly desirable outcomes for an organisation in terms of brand equity and associated sustainable brand value. The Unilever Sustainable Living Plan has been doing just this. They have proactively used their investment into the operational dividend, which has begun to generate tangible planetary dividends (see Chapter 8), and as a consequence sought to engage customers in an educational awareness-raising process, with respect to specific grand challenges, and to develop a 1 billion community with the hope of generating proactive advocates of the brand (Polman, 2017). Malcolm Kirkup and Katalin Isles unpack the nature of a brand, the good dividend that branding can help deliver for businesses, how a purpose-driven brand is developed, and the challenges for leadership in building a sustainable brand. They illuminate the discussion through a case study of a leader's narrative—that of Kresse Wesling, co-founder of Elvis & Kresse. The leadership case study explores the building of a business around a brand anchored to addressing Kresse's moral outrage associated with the vast scale of waste generated by society. Her mission? To build a business that rescues and transforms waste, but that also delivers a social purpose.

And, so to the sixth dividend, the planetary dividend. This is perhaps the most demanding in terms of translation to everyday activity for most organisations. For NGOs and social enterprises this work has been done at the inception of the organisation—its societal purpose(s) established as the reason for existing. What should a for-profit organisation focus on with regard to advancing the human condition? Which grand challenge is the one to address? Why grand challenges when there are plentiful local community challenges? How can the selected challenges be digested for easy consumption in everyday organisational discourse and activity that adds value to the organisation? And how can this be done in a manner that it is not a cost but instead yields value to the other dividends including the planetary dividend? We seek to answer these difficult questions in Chapter 10—where Thomas and Nicola lay out the philosophical and moral basis for the planetary dividend and explore leadership as stewardship, through the illustration of climate change and our commitments to disadvantaged people and future generations. The planetary dividend is also explored in Chapter 13—where Luke seeks to realise the planetary dividend in his business through focusing on the Sustainable Development Goals in a manner that adds value to the business, his stakeholders, his local community and the planet. But at this point we signal the fundamental importance of this work. The planetary dividend is the core to the moral outrage we mentioned in Chapter 2—the necessity for all organisations to act now. Without moral outrage, research shows us that, however strong the economic case, organisations still don't take action. Leaders do not easily engage in conversations about societal purpose (Kempster et al., 2011). On one level there is no need to as followers do not have an expectation that this is part of everyday work, and so have little anticipation that discourses would engage in the same. On another level it is so difficult for many leaders within for-profit organisations to distil out the societal purpose that the business contributes to. And on the third level there is great difficulty in speaking about societal purpose without fear of cynicism, or not knowing how to integrate such a conversation within everyday work. Perhaps then this is the greatest challenge to current leadership practice, in terms of being so out-with learned expectations of organisational leadership, namely: to identify societal challenges, identify how these add value and understand how to engage people in exploring and addressing societal challenges as part of everyday activity. However, there is ironic good news. There are plenty of challenges to select from! If the planetary dividend is embraced it sustains the HR dividend, and the social innovation dividend, and the brand dividend. Of course, if there is no tangible evidence of these dividends being realised then aspects of employees' sense of purpose, motivation and commitment are likely to decline. The human resourcefulness that is suggested to yield the other dividends would wither and, as a consequence, the need to rely on traditional HR transactional approaches.

The leadership commitment and engagement in realising planetary dividends is so very important. Important for the planet, but also important for the sustainment of the sense of organisational purpose and thus the necessary human resourcefulness. In Chapter 3 Thomas and Nicola have put forward the argument for responsible leadership as the approach that would yield the most good dividends. However, responsible leadership needs to be complemented by structures of governance to support and sustain the leadership orientation. It is for this reason that in the final section of the book we address the need for leadership to embrace different governance models that would support value generation across the good dividends. In Chapter 12, Randall Zindler takes a leadership practitioner's perspective to governance, reflecting on his experience and that of others. He highlights a range of governance approaches most suited to responsible leadership. The penultimate chapter, Chapter 13, again takes a leadership practitioner's perspective of seeking to try out the good dividends. Luke Freeman, CEO of a small business, approaches implementation by starting with purpose connected to the planetary dividend using the sustainable development goals. With support from Steve and Stewart Barnes, he explores the leadership challenges that this generates. The book draws to a close in Chapter 14 with a call for collaborative engagement. Steve and Thomas speak of the opportunity, and need, for organisations to learn and explore together. They speak of collaboratory engagement and the hope for the development of a learning community.

The system thus drawn in Figure 4.1 illustrates activities that enable each other. Drawing on systems thinking it would be expected that an emergent property would become manifest. We anticipate this would reflect the operationalisation of moral capitalism through the good dividends. Assuming systems hierarchy the emergent property becomes an activity in a higher system. A root definition of such a higher system becomes very grand and ambitious:

A system to generate social change by societies demanding action regarding the grand challenges through the realisation of moral capitalism and alignment of stakeholders, in order to improve global well-being.

The system shaped by such a root definition is shown in Figure 4.2 with an equally ambitious title:

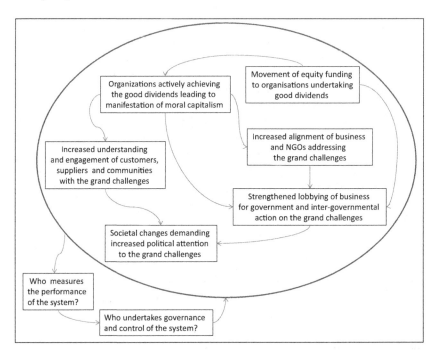

Figure 4.2 A System to Improve Global Well-Being

We shall not describe this high-level system. Its purpose is to illustrate a possible emergent property of the good dividends system. Perhaps a most intriguing aspect of the high-level system is the two questions regarding governance and measurement. Who would do these activities? And who is the owner(s) of this system who could enable it or stop it? These questions open up much bigger issues that are beyond the scope of this book. They speak to aspects that are so profoundly important. Who manages the earth system? Perhaps Lovelock (1979) was right when he offered the *Gaia* hypothesis that the conditions for life will be maintained by life for its survival—a system in which organic systems interact with the inorganic in a self-regulating manner. Let's hope we remain part of the organic system!

Part 2

5 In Search of the Financial Dividend of the Workforce

Evidence from FTSE-100 Companies' Annual Report Disclosures

Steve Young, Sam Rawsthorne and Luke Hildyard

Introduction

The financial dividend derives from deploying corporate assets productively. Financial management and financial reporting have traditionally focused on fixed assets. Increasingly however, the spotlight is falling on intangible assets including reputational capital and human capital (Lev and Gu 2016). This attention to intangible assets resonates and aligns strongly with the arguments articulated in Chapter 1 with regard to maximising dividends through the utilisation of the six capitals. Within this framework, maximising the financial good dividend is a question of how effectively corporate leaders are able deploy and manage intangible resources. Anthony Hesketh explores the link directly between intangible assets and value creation in Chapter 11. Our goal in this chapter is to examine the orientation of board leadership to intangible assets within the financial communication process, with a specific focus on human capital. In particular, we seek evidence on the following two questions: how do businesses report their utilisation of intangible assets to a key corporate stakeholder (shareholders)? And what attention do CEOs and CFOs give to the intangible capital asset of human capital? The importance of this focus is worth emphasising: all else being equal, it is hard to conceive of the good dividend argument gaining traction with CEOs and CFOs if leadership teams do not see value in communicating the importance of intangible human assets to investors. Accordingly, we believe it is necessary to understand the prevailing approach to communicating corporate performance and value creation before considering the remaining good dividends.

As intangible assets such as brand recognition and human capital continue to replace traditional fixed assets as the primary driver of business success (Lev and Gu 2016), the importance of the workforce agenda moves increasingly centre-stage. This chapter therefore explores the financial good dividend from a workforce perspective: the view that an organisation's approach to recruiting, training, retaining and motivating its employees represents a critical determinant of its ability to create and maintain value for investors seems uncontroversial (Pensions and Lifetime Savings Association, 2016). Indeed, investor representative bodies such as the National Association of Pension Funds (2015: 7) go as far as to conclude that ". . . [T]he people who constitute a company's workforce are in many cases a firm's *most* valuable asset" (emphasis added). However, while boards of directors regularly make generic claims to this effect along the lines of "people are our greatest asset", in reality the amount of detailed commentary that companies provide to external stakeholders about their workforce policies and practices is surprisingly low. This lack of foregrounding by many organisations has led some commentators to conclude that human capital represents the ultimate undervalued intangible asset, with senior management and institutional investors all too commonly viewing and reporting the workforce as a cost (National Association of Pension Funds, 2015).

Economic theory has shifted its view of spending on human capital dramatically over the last century. Until the early 1960s, the dominant view among economists was that investments in human capital represented a cost to be minimised or offset since the resulting benefits accrue primarily to the individual rather than the organisation. Thereafter, theory started to emerge highlighting the workforce (human resources) dividend associated with investments in training, engagement and other initiatives designed to enhance employee commitment and satisfaction. Given the differing theoretical perspectives on the direction and strength of the link between investments in human capital and financial returns for capital providers, a large body of research has sought to examine the relation empirically. Recent reviews of the literature such as Bernstein and Beeferman (2015) conclude that compelling evidence exists to support claims that a well engaged, stable and trained workforce, which operates within a supportive environment, is one which is likely to be more committed and productive and, in turn, be more likely to drive long-term business success.

If the "people-are-our-greatest-asset" rhetoric is justified then one would expect to see companies treating information about human capital with the same rigour and accountability as they afford to financial reporting. In particular, articulating the link between an effective and motivated workforce and the source(s) of comparative advantage that create and sustain shareholder value, and then providing details about the specific policies and practices of this comparative advantage seems like the logical outcome of a system that places human capital at the centre of corporate success.

We use the corporate disclosure policy on workforce-related features as a lens through which to draw inferences about an organisation's perspective on human capital and the perceived magnitude of any workforce dividend. Holding proprietary disclosure costs constant, we hypothesise that if companies truly believe the rhetoric that employees are critical to corporate success then boards will face powerful incentives to explain how their human capital assets drive strategy, contribute to growth and align with the creation of long-term shareholder value. Conversely, we interpret low transparency on workforce-related matters or a largely compliance-focused approach to workforce reporting as evidence inconsistent with employees representing the heart of strategy, competitive advantage and long-term value creation (despite vague public platitudes to the contrary). We use recent guidelines issued by the Financial Reporting Council (2014) and the Pensions and Lifetime Savings Association (2016) to evaluate workforce reporting practices for the largest companies listed on the London Stock Exchange.

Our analysis of annual report disclosures provided by FTSE-100 constituents as at July 2017 highlights significant diversity in practice and attitude. While some companies' workforce reporting policy follows best practice guidelines very closely, a significant fraction of companies provide very little meaningful information beyond the statutory minimum. Accordingly, while few senior management teams would contest publicly the view that a well-trained and highly motivated workforce is a critical determinant of corporate success, poor reporting on such matters suggests the rhetoric lacks substance for many companies. Conversely, a minority of sample companies explicitly recognise and actively pursue a material HR dividend.

To the extent that FTSE-100 constituents typically have access to the best resources to support workforce-related investments and also tend to apply best practice annual reporting policies, our results may serve as an upper bound on the value that boards attribute to human capital. If this is indeed the case then perhaps the UK's ongoing productivity puzzle is potentially not so puzzling after all. Drawing on Chapter 2, there is a strong argument that limited attention to the relationship of the HR dividend within public discourses on reported financial performance speaks to the taken-for-granted assumption of neo-liberal capitalistic attitudes. The final section of this chapter offers an alternative framing of financial reporting that draws on the assumption that moral capitalism is the underlying business assumption. To reach this point, we start by outlining the background to our research, focusing in particular on the costs and benefits of expenditure on human capital. Then we outline our research approach and methods, present our empirical findings, and discuss the possible consequence of reframing financial reporting that gives emphasis to human capital.

The Costs and Benefits of Expenditure on Human Resource Capital

Prior to the early 1960s the prevailing view among economists and managers was that the benefits of on-the-job training and investment in human capital more generally accrue primarily to individual employees because they are mobile and can always leave for a higher-paying position at another company. From this perspective, the gains to enhancing human capital are captured mainly by the individual and as such represent an incremental cost for the business that by implication management should seek to minimise. In the event organisations elect to invest in their employees, this perspective suggests companies should seek to offset the cost by paying lower wages. The view that spending on human capital represents a cost rather than an investment is reinforced by conservative accounting rules, which treat training and other workforce-related expenditures as a period expense because the future payoffs are uncertain and hard to quantify.

Becker (1964) altered this traditional perspective by arguing that companies also benefit directly from enhancing employees' skills and support even if the individual enjoys subsequent transferrable wage gains as a result. Under this perspective, theory holds that training enhances employee knowledge, skills and abilities, which improves outcomes such as productivity, product and service quality, and customer satisfaction. These factors in turn can lead to higher sales, profitability and ultimately company valuation. We refer to these benefits as the workforce dividend (or the human resource dividend).

Bernstein and Beeferman (2015) surveyed the literature on human capital for the Investor Responsibility Research Center Institute. They gave the example of 92 empirical studies examining the association between workforce polices and traditional corporate financial performance indicators widely used by institutional investors. These traditional financial indicators of performance include total shareholder return, return on assets, return on earnings, return on investment, return on capital employed, profitability and Tobin's Q. The majority (67) of the studies reviewed report positive correlations between training and workforce policies with investment outcomes. The diversity of industries and countries to which the evidence applies lends further weight to the findings.

While the majority of early empirical work in the area sought to assess the impact on performance of a wide spectrum of individual workforce policies, later studies proposed the view that companies realise the largest gains by adopting a portfolio of complementary workforce-related policies. These policies include training, teams, employee engagement and profit-sharing arrangements to form a "high performance work system". Beginning with Huselid (1995), a large body of research has sought to test the association between high performance work systems and financial performance. Findings suggest that a holistic approach to workforce training and support delivers more significant gains with respect to financial outcomes (e.g., Tobin's Q and return on capital employed) than a piecemeal approach focused on individual workforce practices in isolation.

Despite mounting evidence of a positive association between workforce-related investment and financial performance outcomes, concern over endogeneity bias makes causal inference difficult. For example, while many studies interpret the positive association as evidence that investment in human capital leads to superior performance, an equally plausible interpretation is that better performing firms choose to invest more in human capital because they can afford to do so. Omitted variable bias may also explain the results if workforce investment correlates with fundamental factors such as superior strategy, tone at top, or investment in other intangible assets that directly lead to better performance. Third, a broad range of observable and unobservable factors may mediate the impact of workforce investment, leading to what is often characterised as the "black box" problem. This, of course, is a central philosophical tenet in this volume and indeed the structure of the book seeks to open this black box through a systemic and inter-disciplinary approach. For example, it seems highly plausible that employee training and engagement contributes positively to job satisfaction, which in turn leads to higher productivity and superior financial performance. In this scenario, workforce investment affects performance indirectly through its impact on enhanced job satisfaction and commitment rather than via a direct channel running from specific initiatives to greater productivity.

Corporate Reporting on Workforce-Related Issues

Corporate disclosure on workforce policies and spending provides an interesting lens through which to understand the value organisations assign to the HR dividend. All else being equal, if corporations view the human resource as a core asset and a critical element of their sustained competitive advantage, which determines corporate success, then one would expect management to highlight this link in their external communications with shareholders and other stakeholders. Conversely, if companies give less weight to human capital relative to other assets, such as technology or physical infrastructure, in their communications on periodic performance and value, then one might reasonably infer that boards view their workforce less as a critical resource requiring investment and more as a factor of production.

Despite consistent research evidence demonstrating the materiality of the HR dividend, the amount of information traditionally reported by companies to their shareholders and other stakeholders on human capital policies and their effects is surprisingly low (National Association of Pension Funds, 2015). Given the costs associated with investment in developing human capital assets and the benefits such investments appear to deliver, companies' reluctance to disclose details of their activities and the performance-related benefits resulting from such investment seems counterintuitive and more consistent with a workforce-as-a-cost perspective.

A range of (non-mutually exclusive) factors may explain companies' reluctance to provide disclosures on workforce practices. One possibility is that failure to disclose may simply reflect a perception among corporate boards that workforce training and well-being is so axiomatic to corporate success that explicit discussion is unnecessary, particularly in an already over-crowed annual report. An alternative view, of course, is that the central importance of the workforce agenda is precisely why companies should be discussing the topic openly in their annual reports. At the other end of the spectrum, lack of disclosure may reflect the low status companies afford to investment in human capital and the workforce agenda despite the large body of empirical evidence to the contrary. Lack of transparency may therefore send a signal to investors to probe management more forcefully on their workforce-related policies, both in absolute terms and relative to their peers. If human capital is a source of company-specific competitive advantage then perhaps management and shareholders will prefer to avoid disclosures that could provide important insights to competitors (Verrecchia, 1983).

Accounting and legal considerations may also account for low disclosure levels. Specifically, companies may prefer to avoid any disclosures predicting the potential benefits associated with human capital given the high levels of uncertainty surrounding the payoffs to such investments and the resulting lawsuits or reputation loss that could be triggered by unfulfilled predictions. Finally, despite a growing focus by the investment community on non-financial risks and rewards characterised as environmental, social and governance (ESG) factors (explored in Chapter 12), investors have traditionally not pressed companies to report publicly on workplace-related policies as they have on other ESG topics such as the environment and corporate governance. The reason(s) for this apparent lack of interest in transparent reporting remain unclear.

Survey evidence based on companies in the UK and the 13 other countries reported by the Task Force on Human Capital Management (2003) suggests that a lack of disclosure transparency does not reflect the absence of relevant data: companies consistently indicated they were capturing significant data on workforce-related activities including training, leadership and career development, remuneration policies and whistle-blowing arrangements for internal reporting purposes. Instead, responses suggested the reluctance to disseminate information on human capital more widely was due to one or more of the following four factors:

a.   Commercial confidentiality or sensitivity of the information.
b.   The absence of clear reporting guidance or accepted practice.
c.   Lack of available time and resources to support high quality external reporting in this area; and
d.   No obvious value to the provision of such information.

These responses suggest two mutually exclusive explanations for the lack of reporting on workforce-related issues. The first is that human capital is a critical determinant of corporate success, but companies elect to provide little voluntarily information on their activities in this area. Justifications b) to d) by contrast are more consistent with boards viewing their workforce as a cost or risk to be managed (and minimised) rather than a priority factor that helps create and sustain long-term value.

In the following sections we use company disclosure policy on workforce-related issues benchmarked against best practice guidelines to distinguish between these two perspectives and provide additional insights regarding the value senior management attach to human capital as determinant of corporate success.

Disclosure Requirements and Guidelines

Bernstein and Beeferman (2015: 45) conclude that evidence supporting the gains from investment in workforce policies and practices is sufficiently compelling to motivate companies to report systematically on their training and other human capital policies with sufficient clarity and depth to enable investors to assess alignment with business strategy. Partly driven by the productivity puzzle and partly by concerns over short-termism (Kay Review, 2012), policymakers and investor representative bodies in the UK have recently moved to encourage reporting in this area (Financial Reporting Council, 2014; National Association of Pension Funds, 2015; Pensions and Lifetime Savings Association, 2016).

In recognition of the evolving importance of human capital assets and associated reporting practices, the Pensions and Lifetime Savings Association (PLSA) published guidance for its members in the form of the PLSA Workforce Toolkit (hereinafter PLSA Toolkit). The PLSA represents over 1,300 UK pension schemes with hundreds of billions of pounds of global corporate assets under management. The PLSA Toolkit aims to provide pension fund managers and other investors with a mechanism for exercising their stewardship responsibilities by identifying the type of workforce-related annual report disclosures they should look for from investee companies (PLSA, 2016). The PLSA Toolkit identifies the following four key workforce-related themes that investors should seek information about and that corporate reporting should discuss: workforce composition, workforce stability, workforce skills and capabilities, and employee engagement. The Toolkit also identifies seven metrics (gender diversity, employment type, pay ratios, staff turnover, accidents injuries and illness, investment in training and development, and employee engagement score) that should collectively help to provide insights about performance on the four themes. Finally, the PLSA Toolkit highlights additional features of high quality workforce reporting including clear links with strategy, business model and risk management.

There are clear guidelines now in place regarding the type of workforce-related information companies should be providing to furnish investors with a clear understanding of role that human capital assets play in the value creation process. Systematic failure on the part of boards to disclose such information must either be driven by extreme proprietary cost concerns or lack of clear company-level narrative about the incremental returns to superior workforce-related policies and practices.

The Question We Sought to Address

We use the emerging workforce-related disclosure requirements and best practice guidelines for large companies listed on the LSE to shed light on boards' perceptions of the role human capital plays in determining corporate success. Specifically, we use prevailing best practice reporting guidelines as a yardstick to assess how companies perceive their workforce. We interpret high and comprehensive levels of disclosure linking workforce features directly to company strategy and business model effectiveness as an indication that reporting entities view human capital as a critical asset that drives long-term value creation. Conversely, we interpret low or fragmented levels of disclosure in the face of increasing calls for greater transparency as evidence of a more compliance-oriented approach that views human capital as an unavoidable cost or risk rather than a source of sustained competitive advantage and central pillar of corporate success.

Measuring Workforce-Related Disclosures

The PLSA Toolkit provides both a guide to best practice reporting on workforce-related matters and a mechanism for evaluating the quality of current reporting practices in the area. We use the PLSA Toolkit as the basis for constructing an annual report-scoring tool, which we then apply manually to gauge workforce reporting quantity and quality in FTSE-100 companies' annual reports for fiscal year 2016. Figure 5.1 summarises the key elements and structure of the Toolkit.

The core of the Toolkit involves four workforce themes (composition, stability, skills and capabilities, and employee engagement), seven metrics that help to quantify workforce themes; the degree of alignment with strategy; and an assessment of workforce-related risks and associated risk mitigation strategies. Summary details on each of these dimensions together with our approach to scoring relevant disclosures are provided in the following sections.

Sample and Data

We evaluated workforce-related policies and practices through the lens of annual report disclosures provided by constituents of the London Stock

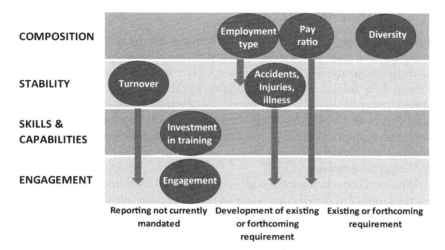

Figure 5.1 PLSA Workforce Toolkit

Exchange's FTSE-100 index as at 1st June 2017. We focused on annual report disclosures as opposed to other reporting channels such as separate corporate social responsibility reports or company websites for two reasons. First, since the annual report is the primary disclosure channel for companies to report on periodic financial performance and longer-term valuation creation, evaluating workforce-related disclosures within the context of the annual report helps to capture alignment with performance and strategy. Second, our focus on the annual report ensured consistency with the PLSA's primary focus on the treatment of workforce-related reporting practices in companies' primary mandated annual disclosure to shareholders.

The list of FTSE-100 constituents as at 1st June 2017 was obtained from the LSE website www.londonstockexchange.com/ (Prices and Markets section). Two companies were excluded: Scottish Mortgage PLC because it reports no employees due to its investment trust status and Coca-Cola Hellenic Bottling Company AG given its idiosyncratic features and its partnership arrangement with The Coca-Cola Company. Accordingly, the final analysis is based on 98 companies.

The most recent annual report available for each company at 1st July 2017 was collected from Perfect Information (www.pi-navigator.com/) or the investor relations section of the corresponding company's website. The majority of annual reports (59) relate to December 2016 year-ends. Of the remainder, 28 reports are for year-ends before December 2016 and the remaining 11 reports are for year-ends in 2017.

How Much Attention Do Companies Give to Workforce Issues in Their Annual Report?

Panel A in Table 5.1 presents summary statistics for the workforce *Themes* category. The most frequently discussed theme is employee composition, with the majority (63%) of companies providing meaningful commentary in their annual report. The decision by 35 companies to eschew this theme is surprising given the prominence of equality and diversity related issues in both the PLSA's Toolkit and the broader societal dialogue. A substantial number of companies also provide information on the importance of workforce skills and investment in training (51) and procedures for engaging employees (33).

While collectively the evidence reveals non-trivial levels of commitment by the largest UK-listed companies to the workforce agenda, the number of non-disclosers across key themes is surprisingly high given the central role that workforce-related considerations are predicted to play in delivering corporate success. Nowhere is this lack of traction more apparent than in relation to the workforce stability theme, with only 10 FTSE-100 annual reports referring to the matter directly. It is also surprising that only half the sample provide meaningful commentary on workforce skills and capabilities, particularly if organisations really do believe that a well-trained and highly skilled workforce is fundamental to long-term value creation. Since all sample companies almost certainly operate extensive training programmes, the decision not to report on such investment and associate it with value creation is perplexing.

The final row in Panel A reports aggregate results for the four themes. The typical (i.e., median) company discloses material information for two (50%) of the four PLSA themes. These findings suggest that while key workforce topics identified by the PLSA are being addressed in

Table 5.1 Disclosure Scores for Workforce-related Themes Identified in the PLSA Toolkit

	n	*Mean*	*St dev.*	*Max*	*Median*	*Min*
Panel A: Workforce themes						
Composition	98	0.643	0.482	1.000	1.000	0.000
Stability	98	0.102	0.304	1.000	0.000	0.000
Skills & capabilities	98	0.520	0.502	1.000	1.000	0.000
Engagement	98	0.337	0.475	1.000	0.000	0.000
Themes_Aggregate	98	1.602	1.013	4.000	2.000	0.000
Panel B: Workforce themes & metrics						
Composition_metrics	98	4.724	0.743	7.000	5.000	2.000
Stability_metrics	98	1.184	1.196	4.000	1.000	0.000
Skills & capabilities_metrics	98	0.745	0.737	3.000	1.000	0.000
Engagement_metrics	98	1.051	0.967	3.000	1.000	0.000
Themes & metrics_aggregate	98	7.704	2.032	13.000	8.000	3.000

companies' annual reports, the extent of the issues covered falls well below both the gold standard considered necessary for effective stewardship and also the level one might expect to see if management really believed in the value of the workforce dividend. Only three companies (Royal Mail, Whitbread and Wolseley) provide material narratives on all four themes, while more than 25 per cent of sample companies restrict their focus to one or fewer themes.

The variability in disclosure levels evident in Panel A across *Themes* and companies suggests variation in the perceived importance of both specific aspects of human capital management and the HR agenda more generally. The disparity in disclosure practices is more pronounced than one might expect to observe given the relative homogeneity of sample companies in terms of their size, geographic reach, economic importance and public profile. FTSE-100 companies routinely benchmark their reporting approach against best practice in the index and so some similarity in the treatment of critical success factors is expected. While the precise nature of what companies report and how it is presented is expected to vary with company and industry specific policies, the complete absence of commentary on multiple factors, viewed by the PLSA as fundamental dimensions of human capital, is surprising.

One explanation for low levels of reporting on key workforce themes is that boards view such matters as so fundamental to corporate success that explicit discussion is deemed unnecessary: the value of a high quality, motivated workforce is a corporate hygiene factor whose importance does not warrant explicit mention in an already over-crowded and ever-expanding annual report. Such an argument is hard to support, however, given some of the redundant content companies elect to include in their annual reports. An alternative and more troubling conclusion is that the lack of coverage by many companies reflects the relative low status of workforce matters in the list of corporate priorities.

Panel B of Table 5.1 presents descriptive statistics for aggregate disclosure scores for *Themes* inclusive of information concerning *Metrics* relating to a particular theme. The maximum score for the composition, stability, skills and capabilities, and employee engagement theme is nine, seven, four and three, respectively.

In addition to being the most frequently disclosed workforce theme, composition is also associated with the highest number of disclosed metrics: the median company reports information on four metrics alongside a discussion of the composition theme itself (median score = 5.0). Disclosure levels for the remaining three themes are much more limited, with the median company *either* commenting on the theme *or* providing information on one related metric (but not both).

The disparity between workforce composition and the other three themes is driven to a large degree by mandatory reporting requirements in this area rather than consensus among companies that workforce composition is the critical dimension of human capital. For example, CEO pay relative to the next highest paid corporate employee (typically the next-most senior board member) is a required disclosure under the Directors' Remuneration Reporting Regulations (revised 2013) and gender pay ratios are a mandated disclosure from April 2018 for UK companies with at least 250 employees (The Equalities Act, 2010 (Gender Pay Gap Information) Regulations 2017). Accordingly, a significant fraction of the disclosure activity documented for the sample appears to reflect externally imposed reporting requirements rather than a voluntary disclosure decision. As soon as spotlight shifts to metrics and themes where no disclosure mandate exists (e.g., aspects of diversity such as age, ethnicity and sexual orientation; use of zero hours contracts; mental well-being; etc.) then transparency levels tail off dramatically.

Figure 5.2 plots aggregate workforce disclosure score by company, presented in rank order from the company with the highest score to the organisation with the lowest score. The aggregate disclosure score for each company is the sum of its aggregate theme-level scores from Panel B in Table 5.1. The maximum score is 23 (i.e., four *Themes* plus 19 metric-related elements) and the minimum is zero. The median company has an aggregate disclosure score of eight and as such falls well below the PLSA's gold standard level of transparency. Even the most committed discloser only reports half the information (score = 12) recommended by the PLSA, while the least enthusiastic company discloses only three elements in the Toolkit.

Collectively, results reported in Table 5.1 and Figure 5.2 reveal relatively low disclosure levels for the typical FTSE-100 company and substantial cross-sectional variation in the prominence boards give to the workforce agenda. The universal corporate rhetoric about employees being the most important asset appears not to be reflected in many companies reporting approach. In sum, a surprisingly small fraction of UK-listed blue chip stocks provide significant information on their workforce policies and practices.

Is the Focus on Value Creation or Compliance?

If human capital forms a central pillar of strategy and business model then one should expect companies to discuss the role of their workforce when articulating how they create and maintain shareholder value. The PLSA's Toolkit proposes two dimensions to this narrative: explicit commentary on the links between strategy and workforce matters, and detailed exposition of precisely *how* workforce-related policies translate into sustained comparative advantage (as opposed to boilerplate platitudes).

The first two rows of Table 5.2 provide details of disclosures linking workforce to strategy. The good news is that the majority of companies (70%) provide some explanation of the channels through which a high-quality workforce contributes to corporate success (e.g., by driving

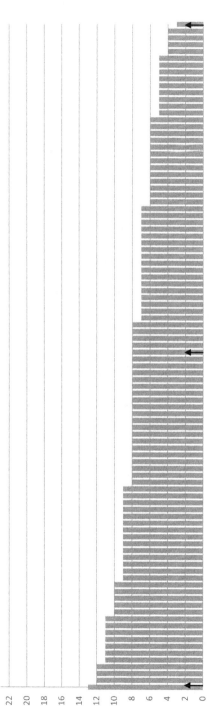

Figure 5.2 Distribution of Aggregate *Themes* plus *Metrics* Disclosure Score Ranked from Highest Scoring Company to Lowest Scoring Company

Notes:
The 98 FTSE-100 companies in the sample are rank-ordered based on their aggregate disclosure score for the four PLSA themes plus the 19 performance measures associated with the seven PLSA metrics. The maximum possible value for this score is 23 (information disclosed for all themes and performance measures) and the minimum possible value is 0 (no information disclosed on any theme or performance measure).

Table 5.2 Disclosure Scores Relating to Strategy and Risk Management

	n	*Mean*	*St dev.*	*Max*	*Median*	*Min*
Links to strategy	98	0.429	0.497	1.000	0.000	0.000
How strategy is supported	98	0.704				
Risk management	98	0.908	0.290	1.000	1.000	0.000

innovation [Convatec] or winning new business [Compass Group]). Most companies therefore acknowledge the HR dividend explicitly in their annual report. However, less than half of sample companies (43%) are able to articulate a clear association between their workforce, business model and sustained comparative advantage. More worrying still is the evidence that only a third of companies (32) disclose both a clear articulation of the linkage *and* a well-defined explanation regarding the specific role of the workforce in relation to strategy execution. All else being equal, this minority of companies that acknowledge and communicate their workforce dividend publicly are those most likely to be realising the tangible benefits of human capital identified in extant research. In contrast, there is a risk that the remaining two-thirds of the sample that provide either a negligible or incomplete public narrative about the contribution their employees make to sustainable comparative advantage are failing to maximise the returns on their human capital assets.

The almost universal treatment of human capital from a risk viewpoint contrasts with results for strategy. Precisely why companies appear more inclined to link workforce disclosures explicitly with risk rather than value creation is not immediately clear. One possibility is boiler-plating: many reports include in their risk assessment section a statement along the lines of "The loss of management or other key personnel or the inability to identify, attract and retain qualified personnel could make it difficult to manage the business and could adversely affect operations and financial results" (e.g., Unilever: 39). A more pronounced link between workforce issues and risk may also indicate that boards (a) find articulating workforce-related risks easier because the outcomes are more tangible or (b) possess a poor grasp of their corporate strategy and the role that human capital plays in driving business success. A third possibility is that boards are more concerned about the risks associated with employment laws and equal opportunities (suggesting a compliance or public relations approach to disclosure) than the benefits of a highly motivated and engaged workforce. This compliance-focused explanation is consistent with evidence presented in the previous section that a material element of workforce disclosures is driven by externally imposed reporting requirements. Collectively, these results suggest that (some) management teams may be prioritising the downside risks of their employees over the upside potential of a highly trained, motivated and committed labour force. Realising the full economic returns to investment in human capital may therefore require a substantial change in mindset on the part of some boards.

Does Disclosure Policy Provide a Consistent Picture?

Companies with a clear strategic vision of the role that human capital plays in delivering corporate success and an effective plan for implementing that vision are expected to adopt a coherent and consistent policy toward workforce-related disclosures. In particular, companies that understand the upside value of human capital and therefore take a more strategy-focused approach to workforce disclosures are also expected to provide more information on *Themes* and *Metrics*. Table 5.3 correlates disclosure scores for workforce themes and metrics with companies' propensity to articulate clearly the contribution that human capital makes to value creation.

Consistent with expectations, all Spearman correlations illustrate positive relations and only the stability and engagement themes are insignificant at conventional levels. Companies that highlight the strategic value of their workforce also back this up with more information of the type recommended by the PLSA, while companies that provide little strategy-related workforce narrative tend to be less forthcoming about themes and metrics in the PLSA Toolkit. The evidence suggests significant differences in the way companies view human capital and that despite robust evidence of a material HR dividend, a substantial fraction of companies seem unwilling or unable to capture this dividend.

The findings suggest that most companies in the sample stress the downside risks associated with human capital whereas only a subset of entities explicitly recognise and actively pursue a workforce dividend.

Table 5.3 Spearman Correlations for Toolkit Themes with Strategy Risk Management (Two-tailed probability values reporting in parentheses.)

Workforce theme	Strategy score	Risk score
Composition	0.301	−0.090
	(0.003)	(0.381)
Stability	0.049	−0.010
	(0.634)	(0.926)
Skills & capabilities	0.501	−0.022
	(0.001)	(0.827)
Engagement	0.125	0.002
	(0.221)	(0.982)
Themes_aggregate	0.211	0.073
	(0.037)	(0.477)
Themes & metrics_aggregate	0.331	0.128
	(0.001)	(0.208)

Summary and Conclusions

Our objective in this chapter is to use corporate reporting on HR-related matters as a lens through which to assess the value that senior management attach to their workforce as a source of sustained competitive advantage. Theory and evidence suggest that a highly trained and well-motivated workforce contributes positively to corporate performance and shareholder value creation in the medium to long term. The question we seek to answer in this chapter is whether corporate narratives regarding competitive advantage and sustained shareholder value creation reflect the central role that an effective and motivated workforce is predicted to play in delivering corporate success.

We use best practice guidance from the Financial Reporting Council (2014) and the PLSA (2016) as a framework for assessing annual reporting policies on workforce-related matters and perceived value of the HR dividend. Findings for constituents of the FTSE-100 index of the largest companies by market capitalisation listed on the London Stock Exchange present a mixed picture. While beacons of best practice exist where senior management place workforce practices at the heart of their strategy for delivering corporate success, the median FTSE-100 company appears to adopt a compliance-driven approach to reporting in this area. Rather than providing detailed information on workforce practices and HR policies designed to enhance skills and productivity, the typical company makes generic statements concerning the importance of its workforce to sustained corporate success without providing substantive narrative commentary or data to support such claims. Even though most senior corporate executive teams are quick to proclaim human resources as a key business asset at a general level, few are able (or willing) to articulate a clear link between specific workforce practices and long-term value creation in their annual reports to shareholders. Based on this evidence, we conclude that many companies may be failing to capitalise on the full value of the HR dividend.

Collectively, our results suggest many companies continue to view labour as a commodity factor of production rather than a specialist input that requires investment and careful nurturing to ensure maximum returns. Evidence that some companies appear to overlook the value of their human assets may also suggest broader structural problems with respect to the standard of cultural and ethical values both within organisations and in relation to their interactions with external stakeholders. Consistent with the view that the HR dividend represents a latent source of value in many companies, institutional investors, shareholder advisory bodies such as the PLSA and ShareAction, and stakeholder lobby groups such as The High Pay Centre are focusing greater attention on workforce policies and practices. Whether sustained external pressure is sufficient to unlock latent HR value is unclear, as are the reasons why (at least some) companies fail to embrace the value of an appropriately trained and motivated workforce despite consistent evidence concerning the tangible economic benefits of such an approach.

In conclusion, we speculate on an alternative framing of financial communication where the intangible asset of human capital receives greater attention. In particular, reporting could attach more prominence to dimensions such as recruitment, attrition levels and employee engagement, including quantitative information on well-being, diversity and the strength of employees' positive identification with the organisation. Reporting would speak of:

1. Measuring the level of understanding and the degree of engagement with the business's societal purpose at various levels of the organisational hierarchy (e.g., board, management and front-line employees).
2. A focus on measures of employee skill development, along with leadership and team development investment and the measurement of the outcomes of such training.
3. Measurement would go beyond the internal to embrace investor understanding of the value of engaging in the pursuit of societal purpose (see the UPM case study in Chapter 7).
4. A balanced approach to performance measurement combining short-term and medium-term financial planning that embraces maximising all capitals—drawing on the suggested measures of the other dividends.
5. Governance reporting that approaches shareholder value maximisation through a broader stakeholder perspective.

Collectively, these measures would indicate the strength of how the business seeks to maximise human capital and capture the emergent human resource dividend utilised in maximising the remaining dividends.

Through a better understanding of the intangible asset of human capital, its dividend to the business, and its presentation within the financial reporting process, we speculate on the reaction of external stakeholders—shareholders and potential investors. We suggest they would become increasingly knowledgeable of human resource capital and anticipate useful development of the same. Shareholders, and prospective investors, would expect to see such commentaries. In a sense, the fiduciary duty to shareholders would be underserved if such intangible assets' value were not being examined, measured and proactively maximised. It seems highly plausible that investors would seek to optimise their investment portfolio towards organisations that seek intangible asset maximisation and demonstrate robustly how this was being achieved. We shall develop these arguments in subsequent chapters, most notably the next chapter and Chapter 11.

6 From Human Resources to Human Resourcefulness to Realise the Human Good Dividend

Robyn Remke and Steve Kempster

In Search of Resourcefulness

Human resourcefulness is the heart of all organising and is at the heart of the human resource dividend. Connecting with Chapter 5 and to give value to this dividend, Gallup (2018) suggest that when employee engagement is high the dividend (in the form of earnings per share) is approximately 150 per cent above the industry norm. The intangible human dividend from resourcefulness is thus most tangible.

But let us start with an apology—the use of the term human resources. We know. It is a terrible term. From the start, we are reducing human workers to a *mere* resource. It is an unfortunate expression, routed in a history that hasn't always been kind to workers. In truth, we would welcome a change. And in fact, many organisations have changed what they call their HR departments, although we are not sure the names Talent Management, People Operations or Employee Success are much better. But, as Human Resources is how it is most well known, perhaps we can start by using it (and its spawn, Human Resource Management—HRM).

With that apology out of the way we now offer another. We write about HR and HRM with very broad strokes and generalities. This isn't entirely fair, but it is done to make a greater point; this chapter isn't meant to provide a comprehensive overview of HR/HRM history, theory and practice. We will briefly provide some historical and theoretical context, but we hope to get quickly to the point of the chapter, which is to highlight how we can think about HR and HRM as a way of contributing to achieving the good dividends.

We should also warn you that we are both rather critical of much HRM. Not because we think it is unimportant; just the opposite. We think people are the most important part of organising, but we too often dedicate too few resources, too little time and energy, and not enough concern towards our organisational members. HR/HRM is an essential but far-too-often overlooked function of all organisations. In fact, organisational scholars Wilcox and Lowry (2000) go so far as to suggest

HRM is comprised of the implicit and explicit choices that are made about the way people are managed at work—whether these choices are carried out by line managers, are the result of a formal HRM function, or are integral to the institutions is inconsequential. All organisations can be seen to practice HRM in one form or another.

(2000: 30)

Therefore, if all organisational practice is HRM, it seems obvious that smart leaders don't just take HRM seriously; they make it their priority. No other aspect of organising can happen without people. There can be no good dividends without people. It is axiomatic but worth stating: it starts and ends with people.

HR is uniquely poised to produce good dividends because HR speaks to a form of moral capitalism rooted in the human aspect of organising. It is for this very reason that Wilcox and Lowry (2000: 29) argue 'ethical considerations emerge in most if not all areas of HRM practice.' If we think of ethics beyond merely right vs. wrong, we can see how all HRM engagement has the potential to enable ethical virtues or align purposes for employees and stakeholders alike. HRM is both the outcome and the process by which work becomes meaningful for employees. The key to actualising good dividends is to move away from thinking about HRM as a form of static organisational function. Instead, we can think about HRM as a framework by which all organising is made meaningful. Resourcefulness is the outcome of shifting our understanding of organisations to organising—leadership to leading—management to managing. Resourcefulness is the state of being ready to resource—to think, reflect, act and pursue in ways that are not only aligned with the organisational purpose, but manifest and communicate that purpose for others. We shall assert that Responsible leadership (as outlined in Chapters 1, 2 and 3) is the catalyst by which the process of resourcefulness is made manifest.

The structure of the chapter is as follows. First, the current HR assumptions and outcomes of control are elaborated—the rhetoric and reality of HRM. Second, we explore the outcome of this control as the inability to create and sustain resourcefulness through HR policy and practice and highlight what is being lost through such HR control—limited creativity, no sense of purpose to the work, severe questions around quality, productivity, and customer service. Third, we apply the key principles of responsible leadership to HRM and outline the notion of responsible HRM as the catalyst that generates human resourcefulness. Fourth, we explore a leadership case study. It is a narrative of Pernille as seen from her team speaking about her approach at seeking to realise responsible HRM. Fifth, and finally, we outline the nature of resourcefulness as the process by which the HR dividend is realised by looking back at the case study.

What is HR?

Human resource management (HRM) is a rather elusive or even ambiguous phrase that is used to describe a variety of concepts, managerial approaches and practices. But, at its most basic, HRM is simply about work (Grugulis, 2017). HRM is concerned with what happens to people and with people while at work and while engaged with work. Boxall and Purcell (2011: 1) state simply, 'HRM refers to all those activities associated with the management of work and people in organisations'. HRM is about management, organisation and organising. Or, more specifically, how one manages and organises workers. But these definitions lead one to wonder, *what isn't HRM?* Or, *how is HRM different from general management?*

While *management* developed as an organisational concept during the industrial revolution, HRM is a relatively young idea. Originally described as personnel management, HRM was borrowed and then adopted by British managers from their peers (and competitors) in the United States. HRM was the management fashion du jour in the 1980s and 1990s. With attention being paid to the needs of increasingly busy workers, and the development of technologies such as the fax machine, laptop and high-speed internet that enhanced the ways we work, programmes such as family leave, flexitime, workplace development and worker well-being became just as central a concern for HRM departments as the more traditional tasks associated with payroll, recruitment and hiring, and pension management. But, despite efforts to be more humane, often reflected in changes to the names of HR departments mentioned earlier, HRM remained a managerial prerogative. Building on growing enthusiasm for a neo-liberal, market-driven business orientation, and benefiting from the decline of trade union membership and collective organising, HRM functioned as a form of managerial control disguised as a progressive employee-centred organisational strategy.

There are numerous ways to organise HRM models and theories, and this chapter will not serve as a comprehensive review. Indeed we seek to resist a temptation to meander through various cul-de-sacs of theoretical discussion, and thus minimise theoretical discourse (and excessive referencing). However, it is helpful, and necessary, to recognise the variety of approaches to HRM. Inherent in the debates about the definition and place for HRM are differing frames of reference for understanding HRM and organising in general: unitarism, pluralism and radicalism (Grugulis, 2017). Unitarism describes the perspective that there is a uniting, unitary viewpoint within an organisation, and this viewpoint is that of management. The dominant perspective in the majority of HRM textbooks and public press books on management, unitarism assumes that all organisational members support the overarching organisational goals and plans, regardless of whether they individually benefit, or whether the goal or directive is sound or not. It is assumed that not only does management speak for all organisational members, but that all organisational members support management's plans. Management is viewed as benevolent—what is good for management, is good for the organisation, and good for all organisational members. The unitarist HRM function then is to create, perpetrate and maintain the unifying vision for all organisational members to serve the organisational need, which thus serves the members.

It does not take a die-hard Marxist to find this perspective unrealistic. On further inspection, this perspective is not only unachievable, but it is undesirable. A forced unitarist approach will necessarily mask over and erase desperately needed diversity, contradiction and even conflict. Difference and dissent are a natural part of working life and contribute to organisational growth, innovation and creativity. Pluralism not only accepts this reality of working life, it celebrates these aspects of organisations and situates HRM practices right in the heart of these intersecting trajectories. The radicalist perspective assumes that the division between management and workers, employers and employees, is unresolvable, unbreachable and enduring. To that end, HRM is a control mechanism by which workers are manipulated into satisfying the goals of the organisational elite.

Given these three perspectives, arriving at a definitive definition for HRM can be challenging. The classic and oft-cited definition for contemporary HRM suggests:

> human resource management is a distinctive approach to employment management which seeks to achieve competitive advantage through the strategic deployment of a highly committed and capable workforce, using an integrated array of cultural, structural and personnel techniques.
>
> (Storey, 1995: 5)

We suggest this definition captures much of what HRM addresses in most organisations and is therefore a useful point of reference.

Bratton and Gold (2015) use the metaphor of waves to describe the evolution of HRM. The first wave is focused on the notion of hard and soft HRM. Hard HRM views workers as resources in the production process, thus necessitating control (Legge, 2006). Soft HRM, in contrast, encourages an investment in employees as human capital to facilitate increased motivation, job satisfaction, and ultimately, commitment for superior performance (Legge, 2006). What emerged was a bundled approach of HRM including both elements of hard and soft models. The second evolutionary wave of HRM took a more strategic approach with supporters arguing that HRM must be an integral function of all organisational planning and management. This approach segued into the third wave, an orientation away from strategy to performance: how do HRM policies and practice enhance organisational performance?

These three perspectives, or evolutionary waves, oversimplify actual HRM theorising and HRM practice. However, they help to highlight the complexity associated with the concept of HRM. So, how do practitioners actually navigate this tension and *do* HRM?

Most HRM practitioners and managers operate with feet in all three camps: address the hard and the soft, pursue a strategic role of HRM and seek to link HRM to organisational performance. HRM practitioners also recognise the unitary vision whilst at the same time recognise the inevitable tension that occurs through pluralism, and indeed suggest that at times it must feel like that radicalist opposition of workers with employers is a given of organisational life. Emergent from this bundle of practice issues is the reality of a major tension: HRM seeks to serve the individual worker and the organisation simultaneously. The next section explores this tension and the implications of HRM in practice.

What is HRM in Practice?

To better understand how HRM practices happen in the workplace, we need to briefly explore some fundamental beliefs about work that guide our own practices. Many of our workplace policies are rooted in an overly simplistic understanding of organisations. We create false dichotomies between employer/employee, manager/worker, productivity/worker well-being, but in truth, work is highly symbolic and meaning-full. We are often simultaneously managers and workers, productive and well. These concepts are not fully oppositional, but they can create conflicting or contradicting tensions for individual workers.

Further, work always happens in a physical, socio/political and historical context. Boxall and Purcell (2011) remind us that 'work is a negotiated order . . . their job is worked out (negotiated) over time' (2011: 9). Organisations are not neutral places of association, '[t]hese negotiations, implicit and explicit, formal and informal, are not conducted on a level playing field, since the power relations at work are [typically] unequal' (2011: 9).

We also cannot characterise employees as one homogeneous group. Individual workers are infinitely complex—they are not 'mindless believers nor cultural dupes' (Grugulis, 2017: 12). Employees may genuinely appreciate and engage with some HRM initiatives while resisting, rejecting or ignoring others. Indeed, they may exhibit a healthy dose of scepticism or even cynicism about the motives of the HRM initiatives while participating in and benefiting from these practices. Employee attitudes about their work may have more to do with the larger organisational context, or sense of organisational purpose than a specific HRM initiative.

With all these variables at play, it is not surprising to discover that our attempts at doing HRM and our ability to understand HRM have no clear prescriptions for success. We are left with the outcome that HRM is often confused and at tension with itself, regularly ignored and undervalued. And, if we are completely honest, much of what we deal with at, and with, work is from time to time 'simple cock-up. . . . Poorly thought out plans, duplicated work, inconsistent orders, and contradictory messages are part of the realities of work' and no HRM strategy can fully erase or mask this reality (Grugulis, 2017: 11).

Regardless of whether you subscribe to hard or soft HRM, consider HRM a strategic imperative or a performance enhancer; the outcome of all HRM is a tension to serve two masters (employers and employees). As a result, HRM policies tend to reflect the discourses associated with soft, people-oriented HRM, while the practices orient around hard HRM strategies of efficiency and capitalisation. In calling her textbook *Human Resource Management, Rhetorics and Realities*, Legge (1995) wrote about the struggle to fulfil the promises of HRM, and in fact, organises her text on 'personnel management' around the paradoxes and contradictions of HRM. The rhetoric of HRM is often a fictional aspiration when compared to the reality of HRM organisational practices.

With the tension between hard and soft, and rhetoric and reality, HRM has sought to add value. Always with an eye towards competitive advantage, HRM saw an opportunity to position itself as a supportive method by which senior managers could enhance productivity, performance, and ultimately, profitability (or so they hoped). Taking a 'soft' view towards their employees led to a resource-based view of business where their employees provided key competencies—creativity, innovation, technical knowledge—that were essential to business success (Legge, 2006). These attitudes towards workers led to the creation of surface-level HR practices such as family leave programmes, leadership development certifications and diversity training initiatives that were often heavy-handedly applied to all employees, regardless of context, need or appropriateness. In addition, much rhetoric was dedicated towards improving a range of themes: organisational cultural development; work reorganisation (the introduction of flexitime, telecommuting, workplace flexibility); worker development and learning; enhanced performance appraisal; elaborate reward schemes; more thoughtful and intentional recruitment, especially in light of changing diversity expectations; mandatory anti-harassment and anti-bullying programmes to promote workplace safety and security; and intensive internal and external communicative strategies towards employee branding and organisational reputation alignment. Indeed, management was captivated by the promise of improved performance with an employee-centred workplace that included the efficiency and predictability that universally applied 'best practices' would insure. In principle, HRM sought to create highly committed workers who were inspired to contribute to the needs of the organisation—in major part the restatement of the unitarist doctrine.

However, research shows that the climate in organisations is one of insecurity. For example, many men and an increasing number of women are either refusing family leave altogether or returning to work prior to the completion of their leave (Hewlett, 2007; Moe and Shandy, 2010). In part the rhetoric and weak implementation of HRM policies suggest HRM practices still fail to capitalise on the attributes of their workers because they treat these practices as 'fixes' for workplace problems. Continuing on the example of maternity leave, the policy fixes the problem that women need time off from work to deliver and then care for an infant. The value of the leave exists only as much as it allows the woman and/or man time away from work with the safeguard that she/he is able to return to work on an established date. 'Smart' managers, however, recognise that maternity leave is merely the label associated with a fundamental change in how this worker engages with the world and her work. Her resourcefulness has changed and she is not the same employee returning from an extended vacation. While many women attempt to downplay this change for fear of experiencing discrimination, there is plenty of evidence to suggest that it happens.

In essence there is little evidence that these HRM practices and policies are grounded in a larger sense of purpose or organisational virtue. Because they tend to be reactive in their design, the practices act like stop-gap measures to help workers work more. Increased cynicism about workplace loyalty and commitment understandably has left many workers to wonder about the usefulness of many HRM practices. Despite its best efforts, HRM has never achieved priority status within businesses (very few invitations to the C-suite, I'm afraid) and has been routinely under-resourced and arguably overlooked in strategic decision-making processes. In addition, whether cynicism or just poor implementation of uninspiring initiatives is to blame (or perhaps both?), HRM has failed to take hold in the larger managerial mindset and HRM has maintained a second-class position. This is in part because there were no significant changes to either organisational performance or employee experience. Some of the HRM failures are a result of poorly designed plans, ineffectual implementation and/or under-resourcing of initiatives.

By the Great Recession in 2008, most organisations failed to appreciate the reasons for HRM and declined to support HRM initiatives, especially when they struggled to merely keep on the factory lights. The credit crunch, the recession that followed and the pursuit of austerity has set an organisational climate that has brought the rhetoric and reality tension into sharp focus. The 'hard' side of HRM—policies and control—has been to the fore. The rise of the 'gig-economy', and the corollary of portfolio careers where individuals expect little from the organisations have occurred at a time when HRM within organisations have had many functions outsourced—particularly the softer aspects. The consequence has been to leave HR teams light on the ground to do anything other than move from crisis to crisis. To a great extent the unitarist dream is broken in the wake of the re-energised neo-liberal agenda as a strategy for survival of both the organisation and the employees.

As a consequence, we are now at a crossroads. To continue down the road of a neo-liberal orientation to HRM captured within the rhetoric of the veneer-thin soft orientation and the ever-increasing reality of the controlling hand in the pursuit of hard HRM, resulting in a parsimonious radicalism of employee engagement with the organisation. This will lead to ever-greater control and distancing between employer and employee. Along this road we find it hard to imagine where the employee commitment, creativity, desire for quality and customer care will emerge from. Or at this prescient the crossroads to pursue a different course—take the fork in the road towards realising the HR dividend through resourcefulness of people. In Chapter 5, Steve Young and colleagues described the lack of attention to the intangible value of the human resource. In Chapter 11 Anthony Hesketh will suggest how this intangible HR value can be measured. We are on the cusp of change. Our role in this chapter is to offer a glimpse of what might be realised by taking the fork in the road—to follow the direction sign toward responsible HRM and the realisation of human resourcefulness.

The Fork in the Road: Towards Responsible Leadership as a Catalyst for Realising Human Resourcefulness

The human resource dividend is not easily achieved and even most traditional transactional HRM is plagued with very meagre results. The crux of the HRM problem is the need to simultaneously support employees' interest and organisational interest, which we often believe are oppositional. HR practitioners, mired in this tension, often find themselves stuck in an impossible, no win situation. But, borrowing from the concept of responsible leadership, we can reject the oppositional tension and reframe HRM as an opportunity to accomplish good dividends. The focus of responsible leadership, simply, is to understand and deliver value to stakeholders. Imbued in moral capitalistic orientations rather than neo-liberal assumptions, responsible leadership does not box itself in about the details of the binary employer—employee conflict. It is always rooted in stakeholder theory, which means stakeholders—all stakeholders—come first. HRM, recast through the tenets of responsible leadership, does not act in the singular interest of the organisation or as an agent serving the corporation's needs. Rather, it seeks to address a configuration of needs—the corporate body, the employees, the customers and suppliers, as well as our one-planet community. In this way, HRM, through the lens of responsible leadership, becomes a stakeholder mechanism, which seeks the mutually beneficial development of all.

Conscious not to contribute more rhetoric in conflict with reality, as described earlier in the chapter, we suggest responsible HRM (RHRM) is substantially different from previous approaches to HRM. First, as just described, RHRM assumes a stakeholder philosophical approach, which includes not just employees and the organisation, but, with equal consideration, all stakeholder voices. The traditional dichotomy of employee/ employer is dissolved. Second, is in the operational dynamic of responsible HRM, which we unpack below. Chapters 2 and 3 detailed the intricacies of responsible leadership, so we will move directly to the application of those attributes and principles to HRM. It is from this application that we show (in a normative manner) how human resourcefulness becomes manifest.

Responsible leadership is centred on understanding and aligning the purposes of the stakeholders. Such purposes are oriented towards societal needs, but in balance with organisational, employee, customer and community needs. Alignment of stakeholder activity towards realising these purposes is key. Interpreted into HRM speak, policies for HR control become reframed as policies for enabling and realising purpose alignment between the employee and the organisation. For example, appraisals/ annual reviews would seek to make prominent the need to sustain alignment of the employee's sense of purpose with that of the organisation. The old currency of KPIs, targets and objective setting may still exist, but would be reframed to fit to the language and spirit of aligned purposes purpose.

Responsible leadership seeks to overtly pursue an ethical policy within the enactment of management practice. In this way, purpose and ethics are intertwined. Similarly, the pursuit of ethics in everyday organisational policies and practices becomes manifest in the HRM arena as a salient value-based system. For example, HR practices such as remuneration, promotion, recruitment and employee well-being are transparent and ethically managed in the interests of both the organisation and employees. It would, therefore be irresponsible, and unethical, to have remuneration levels for senior management beyond an agreed proportion of the lowest paid (see Chapter 12 and discussions by Randall with regard to structures and mechanisms that explicitly take on board a responsible approach to governance). To give focus to this point in 2016, the average pay ratio between FTSE 100 CEOs and the average pay package of their employees was 129:1 (Shand, Kalinina and Patel, 2017). In contrast, compare this to the highly successful Mondragon cooperative in Spain's Basque country where the ratio is limited to a maximum of 10:1! (Roche, Freundlich, Shipper and Manz, 2018).

Responsible leadership assumes decisions are taken with regard to the short-, medium-and long-term needs of stakeholders. Placed within the frame of HRM this speaks to aligning the needs of employees with the organisation. Rather than the neo-liberal sense of human resources to be used and then discarded, there is a valuable recognition of the partnership alignment. The needs of both are being met in a mutually reinforcing manner. As such, communication on organisational strategy and performance would be transparent, timely and made available at a variety of regular touch points throughout the year, including appraisals.

Linked to the medium- and long-term goals is the responsible development of employees, which considers the skills required for the organisation placed alongside the needs of individuals as they progress in their careers. For example, honest and safe-guarded conversations about maternity/paternity arrangements, part-time work, job-shares and portfolio work allow employees to plan career development in intentional and positive ways. At the same time, these strategic conversations enable the employer to proactively facilitate and capitalise on opportunities that benefit the organisation. Through responsible conversations that have been part of the various HRM practices mentioned above, organisational restructuring (organisational development) would be approached as a partnership. RHRM is, therefore, a process of collaboration that seeks to meet aligned needs and purposes. In addition, transparency, the hallmark of responsible HRM, emerges throughout all the HR engagements we have outlined and minimises resistance to change from all stakeholders. Resistance is reduced because stakeholders see (and believe) they are the instruments *and* beneficiaries of the change. So, while the old axiom *people are not resistant to change, but rather are resistant to being changed* often rings true (and problematic!) in traditional HRM, RHRM reframes organisational change into an inclusive engagement of all stakeholder parties.

Finally, we envisage the scope for HRM to move beyond the controlling (sometimes policing) function and fully embrace a strategic leadership role. A responsible leadership role for HRM seeks to engage with employees and with the C-Suite. In the C-Suite responsible HRM enables the board to be clear on organisational purpose and pursue this in alignment with employees, within the products and services as a purpose-driven brand (see Chapter 9), with suppliers and with respective community stakeholders, and with the rapidly growing investor community interested in purpose-driven responsible investments (see Chapters 10 and 12). In this way the leadership role is to articulate and pursue responsible HR as the core that runs throughout the organisation's approach with stakeholders. In essence we envisage a much greater senior leadership role for HR if the good dividends are desired . . . and why wouldn't they be?

RHRM offers a very different sense of orientation and feel with regard to the field and the profession. The usual role of having to defend and protect the organisation by controlling the employees (with employees as unintended casualties) has been replaced with a HR role that catalyses engagement and partnership. As a result, the dividend of resourcefulness is achieved. To better understand some of the ways RHRM plays out in practice, we spoke with one of the leading HR professionals who helped lead the change to RHRM in her organisation, ScanDan Bank (please note that all names have been changed to protect the privacy of the HR professional and the organisation).

RHRM in Practice: A Leadership Case Study

The clanking of champagne glasses finally silenced the packed atrium of the beautiful ScanDan Bank building. Overfilled to capacity, not only was all of HR there, but members of other departments, and fans of Pernille had come to wish her well and to say goodbye. As the atrium finally fell silent, in good proper Scandinavian tradition, Christian began the toasts—one of many—that would acknowledge and honour all that Pernille did for ScanDan Bank and wish her well as she moved on to begin her own HR consulting firm. But, because Christian had only known Pernille for a few months having only recently taken on the HR director position, his toast was kind, but short. He noted that Pernille was known and loved by everyone, was a maverick in her approach to HR and was always pushing the envelope—an only slightly veiled indication as to why he and Pernille did not always agree on how to *do* HR.

After 13 years in HR and Talent Development, Pernille was leaving ScanDan Bank, one of Scandinavia's largest banking institutions. Within her work in HR, Pernille had special responsibilities for talent development, which included leadership development, and diversity and inclusion. Pernille was widely regarded for her revolutionary and even 'radical' approaches to HRM. Christian brought years of HR experience to ScanDan Bank when he was hired to replace the outgoing director. Instead of promoting someone from within Nordic Bank, the board thought it was wise to bring in Christian, someone well connected to the Nordic banking industry and well known to most of the board members and senior managers. ScanDan Bank's strong reputation for appealing HR strategies and practices, employee satisfaction and retention, and community engagement made the offer of director impossible for Christian to resist.

Christian took a very methodical and intentional approach when he began at ScanDan Bank. He knew that the HR functions were already very good and he took pleasure in reassuring the employees that he had no plans to 'fix what isn't broken'. This was music to Pernille's ears because she had spent the past 13 years cultivating a unique and highly effective way to *doing* HR. But, that was never her intention. She was just trying to do a good job.

In her early years as a HR practitioner, she was frustrated that many of the well-intentioned efforts of the senior management and HR business partners were not helping to make employees happy, nor more productive and the organisation was not achieving its goals either. Through trial and error, reading, observing, asking questions (and even a MSc along the way!), Pernille began to change the way she fulfilled her HR responsibilities. Faced with moderate success, she pushed further and began to question the basic principles of what HR is and how it operates within ScanDan Bank. Over time, she shifted her thinking away from the more traditional approaches to HRM that she learned in university and in her early working career and developed a more relational and responsible approach to her engagement.

By the time Christian arrived on the scene, Pernille was one of the top HR business partners in ScanDan Bank and was widely acknowledged for her skill, especially in her HR areas of leadership development, people management, and diversity and inclusion.

After nine months working with Christian, Pernille decided to leave ScanDan Bank. Despite a supportive CEO, it was clear to Pernille that she and Christian did not share the same vision for responsible HR. Christian made it clear that he found Pernille's approach unusual, unsettling, and most importantly, difficult to measure using traditional HRM metrics. In that context, Pernille felt unable to continue her work at ScanDan Bank and left to pursue other options.

Returning to Pernille's leaving party, what Christian's toast lacked in depth and detail, Pernille's colleagues were quick to contribute in spades. Eric, the CEO, toasted Pernille's creativity and bravery—always willing to try something new, even if there wasn't a clear indication that it would work. It was clear he was sad to see her leave and was, perhaps for the first time, realising the size of the Pernille's contribution to ScanDan Bank's success. Other colleagues toasted to her strong work ethic, consideration of other workers, and HR innovations such as her infamous Human Ground Rules, her check-in and check-out exercises, and her nagging persistence that everyone has potential. As the toasts and tributes concluded, it was clear that Pernille not only shaped how ScanDan Bank did HR, but how ScanDan Bank worked. Everyone was impacted by her efforts and many of her colleagues were feeling rather annoyed that Christian was unwilling to make an effort to keep Pernille at ScanDan Bank. He seemed so stuck in practices and metrics from the past that some of the HR team members wondered when was the last time Christian actually *did* HRM. Perhaps he was so far into management that he was no longer knowledgeable on what good HR is and does for an organisation.

After the final toasts, Pernille and the senior managers left to attend a private goodbye dinner. The crowds thinned as others returned to work or headed home. The melancholy members of her immediate work group pulled close the chairs that were strewn around the atrium, and tracked down the remains of several half-consumed bottles of champagne. Declaring that it was a shame for everything to go to waste, Eric placed the remaining platters of hors d'oeuvres on the tables next to the gathered chairs. Relaxing a bit, the work group sat in silence as they each considered their own futures at ScanDan Bank. Dorte announced, to no one in particular, that regardless of who they promote to replace Pernille, she was sure they would not have to work as hard as they did for Pernille. But the work would not be as rewarding. It wasn't that Pernille was overly demanding. It's just that she saw the job, her job, their jobs—the world—differently. Pernille did not just *do* plain old HRM—she wanted her work to matter and to matter for others. And, she expected it to matter to the members of her team too. Pernille saw the big picture. HR wasn't about getting the employees to complete the right training sessions, fill out the appropriate paperwork, and fill out the necessary government reports each year. HR was about the people—all people. All stakeholders. Everyone is important. Pernille always saw ScanDan Bank as more than a bank. It is a community of people, situated in a specific location (along the banks of a beautiful canal!) that affected its physical environment, and contributed to larger social and political debates. This perspective—this stakeholder perspective—permeated everything Pernille did.

As the remaining champagne was consumed, Pernille's team began to reminisce on what it was like to work for Pernille. Annette noted with a laugh,

> you could not work with Pernille and not know about her rules. Her Human Ground Rules. These rules were what set her apart. They were different from what we learned in uni and where I worked before. But, there is no denying it: Pernille is all about her rules.

The rules were clear and unequivocal. Everyone was expected to follow the rules.

The rules were the enactment of a very clear and well-developed ethical position. But these weren't just Pernille's ethics—these ethical perspectives were rooted in the purposes and values of ScanDan Bank. Pernille tried to take a light-hearted approach towards the rules as a way of insisting that her team members also follow the rules. This was, for Pernille at least, a way of ensuring that the purposes and the ethics of the organisation were aligned for all stakeholders.

No one was ever entirely sure how many rules compiled the Human Ground Rules, but there were a few that emerged as constants. First and foremost, everyone is a human. Each and every person has thoughts, feelings, ideas and struggles that are equally real and legitimate. The ground rule insists, therefore, that all voices be acknowledged, an enactment of Pernille's stakeholder perspective. Pernille was often heard reminding her group that ScanDan Bank is people and those people are connected to people. ScanDan Bank is part of a community, and as such, is responsible to and for those fellow community members. Implicit in this first rule is the realisation that because everyone is a human, everyone is also more than just a worker or employee of ScanDan Bank. Everyone has lives that extend beyond the ScanDan doors, and those workers, family members of employees and community members have goals, desires and objectives that relate to ScanDan Bank. Making sure those goals, desires and objects were met was a daunting task and required the efforts of the entire senior management. Programmes such as their leadership and skill development courses, as well as their volunteer support programmes, helped the individual stakeholders, including customers, have a better sense of collaborative purpose.

Rochelle led the group to raising a glass to those dreaded check-in and check-out exercises,

> Ugh. I hated that we had to start with the check-in/check-out. I wanted to just get started with the meeting. But, I have to admit, I usually enjoyed hearing from you all. And, you will not believe it, but when I ran the Group 5 meeting last week, I started with the check-in/check-out. I couldn't help it. It just felt natural!

Pernille insisted everyone 'check in and check out' before each meeting. These exercises go back to the rules. As a consequence of the first rule, everyone has the right to be heard. Pernille was really good at developing innovative practices that helped employees develop a voice in their day-to-day interactions. The 'check in and check out' exercise was used at the beginning of every meeting. Regardless of the objective of the meeting, agenda item number one was always a quick exchange when Pernille asked the meeting participants how they were doing and how they felt about their work. Specifically, she asked if there was anything preventing them from achieving their objectives and goals or was making their work more difficult. She didn't offer solutions—in fact, she intentionally just listened. But she took notes and then, when she was able or it was appropriate, she addressed whatever challenges emerged from the sharing. Despite the exercise taking about seven to ten minutes at the start of the meeting, Pernille was convinced that it was worth the time and effort. She learned specifics about how her colleagues were doing and what challenges they were facing. The 'check in/check out' exercise helped her stay connected to her colleagues and fostered camaraderie between employees.

It was easy to poke fun at the exercise, but in a moment of champagne-induced honesty, the work group admitted that it was useful to them too. They got to know each other and even form partnerships and alliances, share information and knowledge, and provide support in ways that more formal networks do not usually allow. The exercise humanised everyone and helped develop a relational rapport between Pernille and her colleagues and between the colleagues themselves. This relational approach proved essential as ScanDan Bank faced various changes, which seemed like a regular occurrence. Pernille provided consistency through the changes, even when the changes were unpredicted or unexpected. In those times of uncertainty, Pernille's work group and others that she worked with drew on the strength of their relationships to create security and inspiration. They trusted each other and that allowed for increased flexibility, agility and even nurturing, if needed.

David, with his glass raised high, recalled how annoyed he would get when Pernille would just assume that everyone was trying to do their best—another of Pernille's Human Ground Rules. Regardless of how bad the situation, or difficult the individual, Pernille always treated everyone as if they were doing the best they could. It drove David crazy, but deep down, he admired Pernille's ability to operate from this assumption and saw how beneficial it was for her and the organisational members. For Pernille, this ethical practice was the embodiment of the values of ScanDan Bank. Giving 'their best' was indicative of not only what was expected of them as an employee, but revealed the ways in which their purpose for their work aligned with the larger organisational purposes. Everyone has 'off days' and may not always be able to give 100%, but Pernille insisted that if your interactions were guided by the assumption that your colleagues or other stakeholders were giving their best, you were in a better mindset to make sure that the outcomes were achieved for everyone. When David pushed back and challenged this rather basic and simple assumption, she insisted that her years in HR confirmed her belief. How could David argue with that?

In the lull of the conversation, Lise, toasted Pernille's leadership:

> She never talked about herself as a leader except when she talked about conscious leadership, but she seemed to understand her responsibilities as a leader. I would not have thought of myself as a leader, but when she encouraged me to complete the LeadAct program, I actually surprised myself. I actually like leading and I am pretty good at it. Who knows, maybe I will apply for Pernille's job!

Lise's comment led to a round of cheers and drinks as each team member considered how Pernille's leadership had affected their own work experience. Along with the idea that everyone usually tries their best is the rule that all stakeholders have potential. Even when facing strong resistance or cynicism, Pernille assumed every stakeholder had potential, which meant every interaction included the opportunity (and obligation) for acting responsibly. Stakeholder potential required listening, thinking differently and possibly even taking a risk on an employee. But, it also meant benefiting from enhanced creativity and innovation. This rule influenced Pernille's shift away from traditional leadership development programmes to establish a variety of practices that helped create what

Pernille called her 'leadership pipeline'. These programmes include the LeadAct programme that Lise completed. Pernille understood that not all employees want to follow the same career path or progress at full speed. And, they may approach or 'do' leadership differently. Therefore, it is important to offer a variety of methods by which individual employees can develop their leadership skills. In doing so, more employees are encouraged to engage, and it provides greater predictability and flexibility to senior managers as they promote and recruited top performers. Pernille called this approach 'conscious leadership'—something that she often referenced with her team members, but also with her senior managers and other team leaders. This shift in developmental education had also enabled Pernille to include areas of learning that are often excluded or marginally included in traditional programmes. Issues such as unconscious bias and inclusion awareness are now central concerns for all employees because they were integrated into all the educational interactions.

Later that evening as Pernille rode home on her bicycle, she felt good about leaving—finally. Nine months ago, Pernille had no intention of leaving ScanDan Bank. Nevertheless, she finally felt comfortable that this was indeed the right decision. As her mind drifted to her team members, she thought about all the 'lessons' on HR that she had tried to implement and hoped her team would continue with their good work. She often stressed that the full machinery of the HR process goes on in every aspect of work, even when it is hidden. All practices, all interactions and all managers are responsible for contributing to the alignment of values that constitute a responsible approach to HRM. Nothing is exempt. She felt rather sad that she wouldn't be able to see her team continue with their good work.

And, it was good work. Pernille often worried that the busyness and mundaneness of day-to-day work would cause much of their HR work to go unnoticed. However, she was pleasantly surprised by how complementary her colleagues outside of HR were in their toasts and how much they did in fact notice. Pernille credited this awareness to the strategic communication that she used to signal and affirm the values and purposes of their work. She was methodical in her intentional communication about the ways in which the specific HR practices—including small practices such as how you conduct a meeting, to more formal practices such as annual evaluations and promotion—affirmed the values that unified all the stakeholders. Pernille wasn't sure if anyone had noticed, but so many of her colleagues talked about the positive organisational culture and the ways she had contributed to this positivity, it seemed that her colleagues had noticed—or at least they did now! Now she just hoped Christian would not interfere too much and allow her team to continue doing what they do best.

Resourcefulness as the HRM Dividend

Pernille's departure speaks volumes as to the importance of responsible leadership, especially from senior managers, within organisations. Pernille was, in many ways, the embodiment of responsible leadership for her colleagues and team. In comparison, however, Christian failed to provide the leadership necessary for Pernille to continue in her work. Pernille's case also highlights one of the difficulties of pursuing RHRM, namely, securing full buy-in from senior management and colleagues. Most challenging if neo-liberal HR assumptions predominate. Notwithstanding ScanDan Bank's strong reputation (and many awards) for outstanding employee relations and support Christian was unable to shake off his deeply ingrained and rather neo-liberal approach to workplace relations. He was unable to envision a more responsible workplace and the benefits from employees taking responsibility and emergent human resourcefulness. Many of the practices that Pernille used, which we highlighted above, are radically simple. But, they created significant impact and facilitated dividends that transcended the traditional limits of HRM. Through these simple approaches the tension that hangs over traditional HRM regarding serving employees and serving the employer was removed. The simple leadership approach sought to be responsible to all stakeholders through aligning and realising interests around the business purposes and objectives.

At this point, we hope to have established the need for a reframing of the 'human resource' from traditional HRM to RHRM. In short, traditional HR, in essence is about control—exacting out the transaction between the employee and the organisation in pursuit of the organisational objectives. It focuses on contingent reward and corrective action to follow and fit with contractual and legal requirements. Its emphasis is on control. But importantly it does give consideration to considers employee fairness and equity of remuneration important and clearly valued aspects of RHRM.

RHRM reminds us that the transactional HRM approach is far from sufficient. RHRM is transformational and provides a sense of support, encouragement and development, aligned with valued purpose of work and opportunity for workers and stakeholders alike. RHRM facilitates intellectual curiosity and creativity, which will enable organisational members to give of their best. Importantly, workers are willing and able to give their best because the work matters to them. It provides some sort of fulfilment and achievement. To be clear, RHRM isn't just another management fad, addressing the same old HRM in a new sparkly frock. RHRM is a radical shift away from thinking of employee stakeholders as resources and defining them as human *resourcefulness*.

So, what is resourcefulness? Well, human resourcefulness is the reconceptualisation of HRM as an ontological process. The idea of resourcefulness isn't entirely new: some consultants and scholars talk about resourcefulness as a strategy for increasing employee potential (Kanungo and Misra, 1992; Varghese, 2018). But, MacKinnon and Derickson (2012) take a different view when they suggest community resourcefulness is 'better understood as a process, rather than as a clearly identifiable condition amenable to empirical measurement or quantification' (2012: 264). If we extend their concept of community resourcefulness and situate it within a managerial organisational context, we can see resourcefulness as a 'relational concept. . . . It is the act of fostering resourcefulness, not measuring it or achieving [it]' (MacKinnon and Derickson, 2012: 264). From this perspective, resourcefulness is the way in which you *do* RHRM. It captures the move away from transactional, end-oriented control-dominated HRM practices and moves towards organising interactions that facilitate the HR good dividend.

At the heart of it, resourcefulness is a localisation of agency and authority to individual organisational members and all stakeholders. They each become integral components to the larger process of organising. Organisational purpose alignment transcends stakeholder group boundaries, which enables each stakeholder to advocate for his or her own interests without fear of those interests impeding the interests of others. They freely advocate for their own purpose because all perspectives and vantage points are valued. This enables individual managers to participate in a dynamic engagement with each of the stakeholders (or stakeholder groups) and develop a relational approach to their management. Resourcefulness encourages stakeholders to be adaptive, agile and critical. They become resilient and persistent in their achievements and they develop and share knowledge and skill in collaborative ways. Managers benefit from increased confidence and assurance because resourcefulness expects that the organisational members are prepared for eventualities through the development of capacity alongside capability.

Resourcefulness offers out the potential for dividends because the work—whatever it is—matters to employees and stakeholders alike. It matters to the employees that high standards of service are offered to customers because the success of the product or service matters to them because of the purpose associated with it–the purpose enhances the one-planet community in some way. Of course, it matters to the organisation for purpose and human resourcefulness to be palpable; for example employee commitment, enthusiasm and creativity with resulting reductions in sick-days, employee attrition, enhanced quality, productivity and financial benefits. And finally, it matters to employees gaining the benefits of resourcefulness as a sense of worthy activity and fulfilment along with fair and equitable remuneration. This is the thesis of the good dividends and gives weight to the significant nature of HR resourcefulness.

A Fork in the Road

We assert that there is a necessity for HRM to become core to organisational strategy and to leadership. HRM is more than a function in an organisation. There is a need for policies and control but only to the extent that they help support and serve an organisation's ability to realise human resourcefulness. Human resourcefulness is the fulcrum to leverage the organisation's good dividends. We suggest RHRM is the mindset by which resourcefulness is achieved, and resourcefulness is the process by which the HR dividend is achieved. In Chapter 1 and Chapter 4 Steve, Thomas and Ken explained the pivotal role of the HR dividend to the realisation of social innovation dividend and the operational dividend.

We spoke earlier of a fork in the road with regard to HRM. It is of course the same fork in the road with regard to neo-liberal vs. moral capitalism. Organisational leadership does have a choice and it is a stark choice. Continue with more of the same—the neo-liberal approach to HRM—and you will not be alone. Many will continue down that well-trodden road as after all 'no one was ever sacked who ordered an IMB computer!' Alternatively, you can embrace RHRM and pursue something of the 'rules' that Pernille practiced. In choosing this path, you seek to realise resourcefulness—a very different journey for leaders, for employees, for families, for communities and for our planet. The consequences of HRM as business-as-normal, is clear. But, if the alternative journey where the intangible human capital is of great value, where people are helped to realise their purposes, and where good work should be the expectation, then the ideas and hopes contained in the subsequent chapters will be of great interest.

7 Social Innovation Dividend

Leading Stakeholders in Value Creation for All Our Futures

Steve Kempster and Minna Halme

Introduction

Social innovation (SI) is defined as 'the commercial introduction of a new (or improved) product (service), product-service-system, or business model which leads to environmental and/or social benefits (Hansen and Grosse-Dunker, 2013: 2407–2408) that enhances business value. It is centred on the fundamental need to balance economic, social and ecological needs and generate value for stakeholders, notably shareholder/owners. In this way SI speaks directly to notions of moral capitalism as described in Chapter 2 for an overt and deliberate attention to developing products, services, business models and systems of the organisation to generate economic value through attention to societal and ecological needs. We suggest that the SI dividend is a critical mechanism for: enabling product and service differentiation—enhancing the brand dividend; for linking organisational purpose and individual purpose in a stream of activity; for feeding into the operational dividend; for relational engagement of stakeholders—as a mechanism for employees, suppliers, customers, communities and NGO's / charities to understand and participate in realising the dividend for our planet and our communities.

Relative to the other dividends academic attention has been limited and is significantly less developed, particularly with regard to pursuing SI. Of the little research that has been undertaken (which we shall briefly review here) it is focused at a strategic and business model level. A good example of this is Hart's important text 'Capitalism at the Crossroads.' Hart (2010) advocates for disruptive innovation with attention to the Base of the Pyramid (BoP), through which the social and environmental grand challenges can be embraced and alleviated through capitalism—not viewing the BoP simply as a market place for exploiting, but rather as partners adding collective value (2010: 228). Although Hart speaks about the considerable potential for SI, attention is at the strategic level. The work does not explore the complexity of enabling SI and gives only limited attention to how SI may be enacted. In essence, there is a dearth of attention and guidance towards implementing SI and the role of leadership in such enactment.

As a consequence, we suggest that SI is the least understood of the dividends being explored in this book and perhaps the most complex. Complex in four key elements: first, leading engagement of employees to embrace the concept and value of SI whilst developing a powerful and supportive guiding coalition; second, identifying SI value generating opportunities for a range of stakeholders; third, engaging and leading a range of stakeholders at different stages; fourth, leading processes to exploit the value from SI. Robyn Remke, with Steve, in Chapter 6 have offered helpful insight into the first key element. So, our assumption here is that employees embrace the need for SI. Thus the HR Dividend helps enable the realisation of the SI Dividend if the remaining elements are in play.

Prior to addressing these three elements, we first briefly critique the emergence of SI. We explore the nature of SI, and why SI is increasing in attention (in no small way with the link to financial performance). Subsequently we look at the link of SI with stakeholders and the complexity of managing this dynamic to deliver mutual value. We consider the notion of a maturing engagement in SI and map such maturity with three different forms of SI. Using the preceding discussion, we examine three case contexts in which SI has occurred—seeking to understand how SI has been undertaken from a leadership of purpose perspective.

The Case for Social Innovation

We offer that SI could be considered as both a blessing and curse. We shall address both of these aspects. First as a blessing, SI is seen as a significant source of sustained growth (Hall and Wagner, 2012), and, in the language of dynamic capabilities, extend organisational capabilities that may be hard to replicate, and create the potential for competitive advantage (Eisenhardt and Martin, 2000). Additionally, SI opens up significant opportunities to pursue new markets (such as 'base of the pyramid' markets, Hart, 2010; Halme, Lindeman and Linna, 2012); but also provides processes to enrich customer relationships through dialogue with customers to develop products and services—extending the reputational dividend (Taghian, D'Souza and Polonsky, 2015). Further, SI offers a platform for knowledge and learning, and stimulating avenues for advancing the operational dividend in terms of process improvements (Majumdar and Marcus, 2001; Yin and Schmeidler, 2009). Finally, and a corollary to the previous 'blessings' of SI, research has shown a positive relationships between: SI and firm performance (Seelos and Mair, 2007; Hall and Wagner, 2012; Mikolajek-Gocejna, 2016), SI within corporate responsibility and financial performance (Margolis and Walsh, 2003; Orlitzky, Schmidt and Rynes, 2003), and SI enhancing corporate reputation and increased product sales (Taghian et al., 2015).

It should be noted, however, that the relationship between CSR and financial performance is weak when CSR is treated as a 'bolt on activity.' In Chapter 2 the issue of sustainability integration as central to organisational strategy and activity was highlighted drawing on Minna's work (Halme and Laurila, 2009). Steve addresses this notion of integration within the field of leadership development (Barnes, Kempster and Smith, 2015) using Peter Checkland's notion of 'marbles and birds' nests.' The 'marbles' represent the individuality of activities that stand alone. They can look most attractive and indeed be polished up to become objects of beauty, and perhaps be admired; but they cannot integrate. Drawing on systems thinking outlined in Chapter 4, it is not likely that emergent properties can be obtained—where the whole is greater than the parts—through the marble's approach. Yet there is an understandable tendency of management to pay attention to neat, discrete (shiny and attractive) activities that can be measured. In contrast are the 'twigs' of the bird's nest; alone these twigs may seem unattractive, and difficult to measure their contribution, but drawn together they form an effective and elegant system. The value of each 'twig,' the value of SI activity, is in the connectivity and embeddedness to the whole business system. SI then, needs to be seen as an integral part of the business model rather than an occasional initiative.

It is in search of this integration and connectivity that the 'curse' forms: '[T]here are two generic reasons why SI has still to live up to its fledgling expectations: First it is difficult process fraught with uncertainty and risk; second, innovation does not occur in a vacuum, being shaped by a wide range of stakeholders' (Hall and Wagner, 2012: 186). We need to emphasise that the first reason is common to all innovative processes (Schumpeter, 1934; Hall and Wagner, 2012: 186). Rather, it is the second element that is difficult because of the need to obtain value for a range of stakeholders, and value realised through a process of engagement with a range of stakeholders.

The systemic reach across the organisation coupled with the complexity of multiple stakeholder engagements suggests the necessity of considerable senior leadership motivation and commitment to SI. We shall address leadership motivation and commitment within the case studies in the second half of the chapter. At this point we assume such leadership commitment is present and we examine the engagement of stakeholders.

SI and the Engagement of Stakeholders

The recent movement away from closed innovation—protecting ideas and knowledge for use in products or services—and towards open innovation—a deliberate flow of knowledge inwards and outwards through the organisation closely coupled with others outside the organisation (Chesbrough, 2012)—necessitates a very different approach to working with stakeholders. For SI to occur requires open innovation and stakeholder engagement to be closely coupled together (Gould, 2012). A mechanism is required for this to occur—that of leadership.

Too often stakeholder management is viewed as managing stakeholders in order to minimise impact on the organisation. From an SI perspective, stakeholders become an opportunity rather than a threat. Prominent to SI are the employee-stakeholders who have been identified as a central hub and dynamo for user innovation (Gambardella, Raasch and von-Hippel, 2016). For example, and going back more than two centuries, Adam Smith (1776/1937: 17) highlighted that 'a great part of the machines made use of in those manufactures in which labo[u]r is most subdivided, were originally the inventions of common workmen, who, being each of them employed in some very simple operation, naturally turned their thoughts towards finding out easier and readier methods of performing it.' We wish to make salient the role of users as stakeholders in the SI process. This includes employees, but also customers as often being heavily engaged in the co-creation process. 'Lego, for example, invited consumers to create designs of toy robots and construction models, write applications for the robots, and offer them to other consumers on its website' (Ramaswamy and Gouillart, 2010: 2). User co-creation of innovative value can also occur with suppliers within the value chain (Hall and Wagner, 2012).

Moving beyond user innovation from the primary stakeholders, secondary stakeholders—such as communities, NGOs, social enterprises and charities, and indeed universities—have much potential to add value towards open and co-creative innovation (Kazadi, Lievens, & Mahr, 2016). Indeed Goodman, Korsunova and Halme (2017) argue that in SI secondary stakeholders may create greater value than primary through the variety of roles and radically different value insights that can occur during SI.

The inclusion of such a breadth of stakeholders returns us back to the blessing and curse analogy. Kazadi et al. develop the 'blessing' of open innovations using combinations of primary and secondary stakeholders as a source of resources which may create valuable knowledge and, if well managed, create advantages over the competition (2016: 526). This perspective is an extension of stakeholder theory (Freeman, 2000). In many respects stakeholder theory was an early and well considered nudge to the business world towards considering the purposes of an organisation beyond profit and to a 'sociological question of how organisations affect society' (Laplume, Sonpar and Litz, 2008: 1153). Value to the organisation becomes manifest through the orchestration of a network of stakeholders (Goodman et al., 2017). Kazadi et al. (2016), suggesting that such a network offers up ideas at early stages of SI and as a testing ground for the emergent and developed ideas. Goodman et al. (2017) have identified that stakeholders can occupy a variety of roles and at different stages of the SI process, as well as roles that help to bridge across the stages.

The two aspects of, first, engaging a range of stakeholders in different roles, and second, generating co-knowledge (and co-value) for the organisation and the participating stakeholders, returns us to the 'curse' of the complexity of engaging with stakeholders in SI. Prior to addressing the 'curse,' the opportunities that networking and relationship engagement create must not be rushed past. In the case studies examined by Kazadi et al. (2016) they identified significant motivational impact on employees. There was a clear sense of purpose and novelty to the engagements, as well as curiosity and intellectual stimulation by being exposed to very different ideas, different people with different perspectives, and often different and challenging contexts.

Back to the complexity curse of SI. Kazadi et al. (2016) underscored the difficulties of involving stakeholders in innovation, highlighting, for example, the need to address the following: find the right stakeholders to work with; understand the competencies of stakeholders to engage with, compounded by the variety of stakeholder organisational structures and cultures; address the varying interests, conflicts and powers of different stakeholders; motivate stakeholders to participate and sustain such participation through understanding the different aspects of value for respective stakeholders; whilst at the same time managing the flow of knowledge and insight that has value to the organisation and to stakeholders. For those balancing all this it must at times feel like a curse.

Little attention has been given thus far to the micro activities of organising the SI process. Both the Goodman and Kazadi studies focused on the importance of a maturing relational engagement associated with mutual value identification and value generation—typically these studies highlighted time periods of one to four years. As way of example of maturing relationships in SI, Steve was working on a joint event with Eric Guthey of the Copenhagen Business School. Various for-profit organisations had been engaged with the Danish Red Cross (DRC) to help address refugee assimilation into Danish society and had been working with the DRC for at least year. It became strikingly clear that DRC did not have an in-depth understanding of how value was being created for the businesses. There was an assumption that the businesses were taking on refugees as a philanthropic act. Discussions revealed much greater value generation—value was around business reputation, employee morale, staff retention, and, for one business, reductions in workwear (Kempster, Guthey and Uhl-Bien, 2017).

Engaging multiple stakeholders—primary and secondary—in processes of SI is complex but there is much potential for value generation. But there is an overt need for leadership to align value opportunity with organisational experience, organisational strategy and leadership ambition. It is to this we turn next.

SI Enabled by Shifts in Organisational Orientation and Maturity

To obtain the potentially transformative effect of engaging in SI requires careful balancing of action to the organisational context. That is balance the organisations experience and maturity of SI to the range of complexity. The recent work of Adams, Jeanrenaud, Bessant, Denyer and Overy (2015) is most useful for such maturity balancing in framing a contextual pathway for leadership engagement with SI. Their research highlights a typology of three SI contexts that reflects a movement from limited primary stakeholder involvement to multi-stakeholder engagement and we shall go through each in turn:

SI as operational optimisation: an 'internally oriented perspective [-] doing the same things but better approach' (2015: 9). In part it can be a reactive response to comply with legislation. Or it can be a proactive approach to pursue processes oriented to productivity, efficiencies, service engagement and ethical requirements within the organisation. There might be reach to supply chains through imposing systems of control to minimise reputational risk to the business. Employee and supply chain user innovation dominates 'the doing the same thing but better' SI approach. These approaches to SI are not core to the business model, rather are focused on operational improvement. Our Case Study 1 with SOK explores SI as operational optimisation.

SI as organisational transformation: A shift in emphasis externally in orientation with regard to going beyond doing no harm and overtly seeking to realise benefits for society. The focus is centred on connecting the value chain through primary stakeholders—embracing a more fluid permeable boundary around the organisation. There is a greater attention to social aspects alongside environmental (2015: 11). Features of organisational transformation would reflect process systems (highlighted in Chapter 8 to follow this) such as circular economy, sustainable supply chains, or frugal innovations to serve BoP markets (Halme et al., 2012; Levänen et al., 2016). Financial measures are transformed to embed SI as a core strategic activity and become central within the business model. Case Study 2 looks at UPM as organisational transformation and winning new market opportunities.

SI as systems building embracing societal change: Aligned with the systems argument outlined in Chapter 4, the essence of the third orientation is the consideration of social innovation beyond the organisation—'doing good by doing new things with others' (Adams et al., 2015: 13). The accent here is on collaboration and networks that enable 'a set of actions that shift a system—a city, a sector, an economy—onto a more sustainable path' (Draper, 2013: 11). Adams et al. advise that there have been few studies that examine this space (the work of Selsky and Parker, 2005, is a notable exception that explores cross-sector social oriented partnerships). Rather it is very much industry led. Examples offered include: Nike—and the project called LAUNCH, an open innovation to make transparent the materiality impacts on their supply chain 'through working with material scientists, governments and investors and consumer groups' (2016: 17); Unilever and the 'Sustainable Living Plan' focused on global health, food and energy with the supply chains, customers, NGOs and governments; and Sony through the 'Forum for the Future' looked at 'how technologies might redefine lifestyles in 2025' (2016: 15) working with writers, designers, technical and sustainability experts. Case Study 3 with St1 explores an organisation seeking to undertake SI as systems building toward societal change.

At first sight, SI as systemic social change appears most ambitious, risky and potentially a distraction from the purposes of the organisation and the associated fiduciary duty to serve share/owners. Although Chapters 1 and 2 have outlined the business case for organisations becoming involved in social change, caution must be sounded. Of the few cited cases of being involved in this space the repeated message is one of organisations needing to simultaneously engage in SI as systemic social change whilst maintaining current business practices and allowing the knowledge and insights to migrate across. The challenges of undertaking multi-stakeholder activity in SI have been highlighted earlier and systemic social change compounds the complexities further.

For the most part the progression through the three types of SI reflects the maturity and experience of organisations engaging in this space. We suggest that leadership is a critical intervening mechanism for such alignment—calibrating the scope of SI, assessing the maturity of experience in the organisation and guiding the level of engagement.

Leadership of SI

What is striking from reading the literature and research regarding SI is the limited attention to how SI occurs and to what stimulates decisions and actions to engage in SI. It is the purpose of this chapter to address this question and, in particular, to understand the role of leadership in engendering attention to SI and guiding action to realise value from SI. Our supposition is that senior leadership is instrumental in this process in terms of the following: power to make change occur; sense-making to convey purposes of involvement; governance to shape buy-in to the scope of change; performance measurement to control what is being pursued; and symbolic role modelling through engagement in activities to demonstrate the value of involvement. Drawing from Adam Smith (1759) we assume leadership is the '(in)visible guiding hand' that is absent from overt attention in research to date.

Questions that form around leadership of SI as the guiding hand that has thus far been overlooked reflect the following: Why take a lead?

How did leadership develop and embrace others? What leadership issues were overcome and how? Who had to be convinced and how? What organisational structures emerged, how and why? How did the leadership structure of an organisation support or hinder progress? What were the governance aspects that had to be addressed? What is the relationship of risk and leadership appetite? How does leadership grasp and develop opportunities? Here are some of the questions that lie unexplored, yet so critical for SI to take root. Reflecting the review we have summarised thus far in this chapter 'the [SI] process tends to be socially very complex' (Perl-Vorbach, Rauter and Baumgartner, 2014: 176). The influence of leadership is fundamental to steer a course of order and direction through this complexity.

It is our intention in the case study research that follows that we seek to nudge towards some of the above questions and at the same time integrate the extant knowledge and emerging principles of SI we have reviewed.

The Three Case Studies

Case Study 1: SI as Operational Optimisation as 'Doing Same Things Better'

> **Lea Rankinen, VP Sustainability, SOK Finland**—*a senior manager reporting to the CEO and the board, and seeking to realise SI through business unit directors. SOK is owned by approximately 40 per cent of Finland's population as a cooperative and it is the third largest company in the country.*

The leadership narrative of the case highlights the important of social capital and strong internal reputation, structural positioning, role clarity and being in tune with the cultural practices of an organisation. Lea has been with SOK for over 15 years, has undertaken many roles in a variety of business units, resulting in significant network basis and trusted reputation.

SOK is Finland's largest retailing company, a cooperative owned by its customers. It operates in Finland, the Baltic countries and Russia. Its biggest business area is supermarket trade, followed by fuel sales and service station stores, hospitality business, hardware trade and banking.

SOK is a co-op. It is owned by 2.3 million customers. As such it sets up a different agenda and stakeholder relationships than as a shareholder company or private firm, or family business. Lea explained the purpose of SOK to maximise benefits for the customer-owners. To do this they seek to be 'as efficient as possible to give value to customer-owners.' The size of ownership and profile of SOK means that 'we are so large in Finland that everyone has an opinion about us and many millions as owners.

What people think about us really matters.' Stakeholder engagement with customers is thus in the DNA. A core activity is the continuous tracking of purchasing data and customer opinions to understand and refine benefits for the customer-owners.

The organisational context needs to be considered through the lens of Finnish culture—an orientation to action, process and measuring implementation. It is from such action that arguments and narratives emerge. Lea comments: 'We get things done . . . we learn from one area and then spread out.'

So what was the context for leading SI at SOK? Lea explains that various executives had explored the sustainability agenda. On the one hand, it was seen as being too far behind rivals to make significant changes, and a concern persisted whether SI would be commensurate with the purpose of the business to maximise benefits to customer-owners. For example, this key stakeholder was not pressing for such changes.

It was in this context that Lea became Sustainability Manager in 2011, located within the communications department. Her first action was to understand the scope for change. She commented on engaging others 'in an old-fashioned way. Setting up an advisory group . . . we did a SWOT analysis and scoped out ways going forward.' Of significance for Lea was 'how this built up networks and levels of trust as discussions on SI slowly began to take root.'

Whilst this was occurring Lea was most visible to key internal stakeholders—prominent senior leaders at board level and head of the business units—extending and strengthening her network and gathering stronger credibility in the business scope for sustainability. In 2014 there was an important restructuring. Sustainability was taken out of communications to become a new unit that reported directly to the COO (who is the deputy CEO). Lea became VP for Sustainability with a brief to 'challenge the board and be a watchdog . . . generating the case and momentum for sustainability.' This brief, title and restructure is significant to leadership influence. It gave power and access to influence and connect—reinforcing the social capital that had become established. 'My role is to make sure the board understand the issues. I had [name withheld] come up and say "what is all this about human rights?" So I had to explain in detail, the impacts, and now he is fully on board.'

Returning to the ongoing action, the Advisory Board, through the external members, had challenged SOK to go beyond responding to customer-owners, but to be ambitious and shape the debate on important issues. The outcome of this work (over 18 months) was the establishment of a social innovation strategy on issues that matter to grow stronger and be aligned with the organisation's sense of its purpose to generate benefits for the customer-owners. It was based on four key areas, 100 sustainability actions and 10 performance indicators that were to be reported to the board. The four areas were: for the good of society; climate change and the circular economy; ethical operating culture and human rights; and well-being and health.

The aspects of sustainability were illustrated and highlighted by Lea through the case for human rights. This became a prominent area for SOK to help drive SI. For example, human rights have significant potential if mishandled to damage reputation, particularly within the context of procurement/supply chains. Lea had a strong insight into the potential costs and benefits associated with pursuing human rights:

> Costs: the cost aspect links to a clash with the core business strategy for efficiency and value for money (an expectation of customer-owners) if approaches to human rights imposed on suppliers increase costs;
>
> Benefits: the benefits of pursuing human rights through imposing criteria on suppliers may stimulate SI through developing closer relationships and also encouraging the support of process innovation. For example, support and guidance is made available to reduce waste, lower energy costs, stimulate employee engagement (through enhanced employment practices) that connects with process changes for enhanced quality and efficiency. Much of the foregoing can offset supplier increased salary costs of advancing employee human rights. And all this would stimulate a growing interest and awakening desire for sustainability for SOK at board level.

This was the business case Lea argued for human rights. It also offers a detailed insight to the leadership work of Lea where she challenged the Board to embrace—'a very significant change in mind-set.' This is the essence of Lea's narrative to enable SI through influencing the board and senior managers of business units of this argument.

At the same time that this narrative and argument were being developed was the 'Adrian House—name changed' incident—a whistle blower from a SOK supplier. Lea and the VP Procurement visited a supplier in [name of country withheld] to understand the issues that had emerged of human rights allegations from one of SOK's suppliers. They spoke with the Unions, employees and Adrian House, who had completed a report for Finnwatch (Finnish civil society organisation focusing on CSR) regarding the working conditions of a juice factory supplying to SOK. SOK advised the supplier to apply human rights to the employees' working conditions. In return they would support the supplier to progress with approaches to SI. The supplier refused, and the relationship was terminated. Over the next two years SOK supported and eventually acted as defence witness for Adrian House who was being pursued by the supplier company. There was a gradual and careful ramp up of Board support for supporting this legal action' after.

The Adrian House case was a watershed for SOK and Lea's leadership in terms of SOK embracing sustainability. By supporting the case the Board signalled and affirmed the necessity of the four sustainability themes. The media engagement highlighted SOK's position and enhanced SOK's repositioning and overt commitment. Lea comments: 'when the Adrian House case occurred we were ready to be open . . . there had been a two-year journey of action inside SOK on this.' The approach in the group and now with suppliers was 'to take care of people and the environment . . . we were now promoting human rights and encouraging action in a variety of ways.' The sense of a maturing organisation in terms of engaging with SI is captured with the current comment from Lea: 'At this moment I am developing the policy for radical transparency where we go beyond auditing . . . we expect to share all data openly within the next 6 months.' Commenting on the engagement of human rights across the Board, Lea gives the example of the VC Procurement: 'he is now fully on board with human rights, we have a very close working relationship stimulating change throughout the supply-chain.'

Summarising the situation Lea comments, 'our position now is we want to do good—and for SOK this makes good business sense. For example, and linked to the four key areas, all business units are pursuing circular economy [. . .]. We are going way beyond communications and for reputational gain; but to understand and develop key leverage areas that all parts of the group can build upon. This is about the big issues.'

In a sense, Lea, the Board and the Business Unit Directors have travelled a journey of growing in confidence to undertake SI. It started in a safe, conservative and traditional way. Through action, through organisational restructuring, and through Lea's social capital, distributed leadership has spread across the group and there is new confidence to now begin to reframe the benefits to customer-owners. The influence of distributed leadership now frames societal expectations of SOK to take the lead and responsibly seek to shape all stakeholder attention towards key issues. The approach that occurs in a structured way throughout all the business units is a focus on the 'circular economy'—all business units develop action plans and Lea meets with them all each month to go through the progress on these, linked to the four action areas. In essence 'what we learn somewhere we spread across other areas. We take a holistic view—including the supply-chain. Processes have led to our approach to SI becoming part of the DNA [. . .]. The mind-set change has occurred . . . but it builds on our approach. It builds on Finnish culture "we get things done!" We have not done this through big pronouncements of transformation . . . we pursue action to get ownership and have targets to measure how we are doing. Action and implementation builds in the commitment.'

Looking back, Lea comments on her leadership that she has been enabled and supported 'to be brave, and to be disruptive to my own group but working within the way we do things.'

Case Study 2: SI as Organisational Transformation and Winning New Market Opportunities

Jussi Pesonen, CEO and member of the board UPM—Finland's fourth largest business. A strategic change orientation with responsibility for strategy and allocation of resources to SI. Attention to addressing shareholder needs.

The Trend of global paper sales was one of decline from the late 1990s into the 2000s. In 2006, the decision was taken that paper production could not be the central focus of the business. 'Fifty per cent of the people said the paper demand would come back. We have seen this before and it always comes back. Paper will always be needed.' UPM was (and is) an asset rich business based on forest and integrated production processes associated with mills. The business had been going since the 1890s with many people being employed for many generations in the business. Indeed, Jussi is such an example 'being with UPM now for over 35 years. Before that my father was a paper mill director.'

In this context the decisions that had to be taken were more than just business in the interest of the shareholders. The decisions were highly personal, anchored to a way of life, a set of values and relationship with a biomass of deep intrinsic value. Associated with these values were the core business values of efficiency and minimisation of waste. These aspects had made UPM most successful. Jussi comments: 'This was, and is, the DNA of the business. We were not speaking then about sustainability but it was core to us, a responsible approach to resources which made good business sense then, and now.'

Jussi comments on how change occurred: 'Our Board believed we could do it ourselves. No matter what happens we need to change, do things differently. Very skilful organisation, integrated organisation, strong back bone. The choices were either to acquire new related businesses away from paper, or stick to core business and innovate. We believed in ourselves, our technical capability, our commitment to biomass.' This was around 2006. A decision was made to close Voikkaa paper mill [near Helsinki]—'toughest decision of my life. About half the views were against this decision. We had to make 600 people redundant and they did not understand why this mill had to close. The decision split the company.'

The approach they went for was sustainable innovation around their core capabilities and processes. But first the business model had to change. It needed to move away from an integrated approach to producing paper. Jussi emphasised that 'where in 2005, 80% of the revenue were in paper. Now, in 2017, paper is only 25%. We always wanted to reduce our waste, reduce water consumption, reduce energy, better use of raw materials, but we were just one product' more of an efficiency mindset—but good for sustainability. We didn't have a clue how to turn this mindset into a new business. Now paper is just one of six products.' Three of these were in existence, plywood, packaging and paper. But three new areas were to be developed: biofuels, bio-composites and bio-chemicals. None of this was known. This was completely new for the industry.'

The purpose of UPM became known as 'Biofore—recyclable and renewable biomass, combined with innovation, efficiency and responsibility. Responsible business can be efficient and profitable.' This is critical to the UPM story. Walking into the HQ for the interview the name of the building is 'Biofore House.' Biofore was not a mission statement or strategy; it was and remains their core purpose. It connects the soul of the business, its history and employee sense of belonging to the way forward. It speaks to a responsible orientation that engenders ownership and pride. At the time of the restructure it became disseminated internally. It provided the communication to employees of how the restructure hung together—the core roots of biomass. But it spoke to the values of the business with regard to 'stewardship of the resource, and with regard to efficiency and responsibility.'

The biofore approach first focused on excellence with regard to performance in terms of quality and environmental performance. These early steps gave assurance to shareholders. 'The shareholders didn't understand Biofore. "Why are you doing this?" We had to show performance. Now we have over 25% of fund managers actively seeking to support the sustainability agenda. Normally this would be about 10%. It shows the shift that has occurred and how we are seen by shareholders.'

Once the performance changes had been delivered Jussi realigned the R&D investment: 'Using the 80:20 rule we moved from 80% being paper and this became 20%. The 80% moved to bio-fuels, bio-composites and bio-chemicals. This of course was a significant move. We didn't have the competences for the development of these areas. So people were recruited. What we did know in our DNA, as engineers, was addressing efficiencies and waste. The waste from pulping provided the opportunity to develop high value-added products.'

'We quietly undertook experiments. Lots of piloting—growing the scale of experiments until we knew we could do this. Myself and my senior management team spent considerable time networking and enabling the piloting to move forward. We were humble enough to make things happen before we announced things.'

We probed Jussi on how the social innovation occurred. 'It was from our core approach to employee engagement. This was central to Biofore.' He advised us of the strategy of employing learning and development, training, safety and remuneration. He was most proud, rightly so, of UPM being in the top 1 per cent of global companies for these elements— cited prominently in the annual reports. But this was not separate or additional to Biofore. The central purpose encapsulated in Biofore was enabled through employees. In this way the purpose of work was readily understood.

'Innovations came from the efficiency driven period (2006–2012). In 2008 innovation attention was also focused on safety. For example, we have had a period of six years without an accident—good from a social perspective but also good for performance.' Jussi comments that 'our forest management is top of the index for sustainable management, we have been for many years and we are remain so now.' The essence of Jussi's comments was to suggest that to be a 'biofore' company they must live the elements every day—more than an initiative, but a clear sense of purpose that permeates throughout. The company has received various awards and recognitions. 'But I must tell you we did not go out and say our strategy is "biofore." We did the hard work internally getting things moving. Once it was well in place, when we had the firm steps and the results were coming in from the innovations, we started to tell people outside. They didn't understand this biofore but they did see what we were achieving.'

Jussi offered examples of the social innovations occurring. In 2012 'we invested in a major biofuels plant—the only one still in the world based on wood biomass.' The bio-chemical innovations are undertaken in partnership with a range of stakeholders. 'These innovations occur as a consequence of teams of people pursuing a clear purpose.'

'Bio-composites—all started from recycling—a waste pulp that was burnt—we decided to do something with this waste. What can we do with this? Create a composite? Environmentally friendly by using a waste that was bad for us and customers and turn [it] into a valuable product. Establishing a circular economy. Waste has been in this industry for years. Now we use waste in a range of valuable products—this is our circular economy. We take wood from the forest and now we make new high value products. Crodex—£100 per a gram—used for cell cultivation—from the waste of paper production. Make heart cultivation using these products!'

Further evidence of the standing of UMP as an employer of choice was the high attraction for new recruits, 'people want to work here.' Equally, the business has very low attrition, absenteeism and sickness days. The business has acquired various and many awards, such as the sector leader award of Dow Jones Sustainability Index, ranked as industry leader with a gold-class distinction in Robeco-SAM's annual Sustainability Year-book (2016); and a global leadership position of CDP's Forest Program (2016). This reinforces their external reputation, but also the employee sense of positive identity associated with the business. The recognition of the company in the standing and contribution to the Finnish economy is well understood, but also the company provides a clear beacon for illustrating 'how responsible business can be efficient and profitable. The shareholder reaction and education to the business model speaks to this.'

Our sense making of the leadership is one of clarity of purpose anchored in the history and culture. This is a long-term view and in no small way does the association with biomass and the cultivation of the renewable resource speak to a broader sense of stewardship. At the same time, the approach to SI is rooted in efficiency and minimisation of waste—they had the resource, and the mindset to minimise waste, and had the clarity of purpose in terms of clear business units to find high value-add products from this waste to align with the business model.

In terms of SI development in the business, they have moved out from type 1—an internal focus and now are readily engaged in type 2—working with stakeholders to generate product offerings. The clarity of the strategic focus has minimised the complexity of stakeholder engagements. UPM have become most sophisticated in working with selected stakeholders.

Case Study 3: SI as Systems Building Toward Societal Change

Mika Anttonen—Chairman of St1—entrepreneurial founding leader and a self-made billionaire. Does not have shareholders to manage. Orientation towards achieving personal purpose. Highly prominent entrepreneur and societal influencer in Finland, in particular in the area of sustainable development and economy.

St1 undertakes second generation biofuels, wind-power and geo-thermal energy. Mika acquired a portfolio of petrol stations from Exon in 2006 and a further portfolio from Shell in 2010. The business model is based on income from petrol stations, corporate accounts and energy sales. The biofuel utilises biowaste collected from bakeries, foodstores, breweries, food processors and other outlets, such as restaurants. St1 have plants generating biofuel, which is made available in the 1,400 petrol stations in the Nordics. St1 also invests in wind-power plants and geo-thermal heat.

Speaking about the business and the employees' understanding of its purpose Mika comments that 'everybody understands the business is in fossil fuels and understands this allows us to invest into new solutions.' There is a palpable entrepreneurial feel to the business approach linked with an excitement and sense of purpose in seeking to tackle the big sustainability questions by showing what can be achieved.

The interview with Mika is dominated by his personal sense of societal purpose. The business is a means to an end. 'I wish not to make money, I have enough, I seek to change the world. It's our responsibility to find solutions. The Nordic society is the best model in the world but it requires us to take our responsibilities very seriously. It's about duty in society as much as it's about rights, and this is not prominent. The purpose of the business is not to convince customers they should use biofuels—rather these are made available.'

Instead, as Mika puts it, 'the business seeks to utilise its profits by investing into R&D to change the world. It's our responsibility to find solutions. Start with the big figures, population growth. Half the world population barely surviving—they are not thinking about carbon. So we have to change our lifestyles first. We need a whole system view—need the system to stimulate innovation through necessity. Need innovative solutions that will solve the problem.'

His major concern relates to the lack of systemic connectivity of what he sees happening in the world. 'The push for electric cars will not solve the big issues.' He speaks of rebound effects. 'How will we generate the electricity? There are not enough windmills or rivers to dam. Will we move to nuclear power stations [and see] proliferation all over the world? This seems highly unlikely, and strategically most dangerous in terms of geo-political issues. Further, the oil industry will move away from gasoline but persist in the production of heavy crude oil products. The key is to understand systemically at a global level the picture and find local solutions aligned to this. But who is doing this work? Our response here is to offer ways forward.'

Mika speaks of the carbon foresting in the Sahara Project. Mika describes with passion a project he is currently investing in, 'carbon farming.' He describes how they are preparing a plan for solar panels to desalinate the seawater and use this for growing a forest in Saharan Morocco. He outlines how the forest will capture the carbon. 'Biomass production would become established. Pulp production and associated biomass products offered (for possible scope see the UMP case study above). Local economies transformed. Communities enriched. Ecology transformed from desert to forest. As this spreads across the Sahara so climate forecasts show how this can lead to the rains returning. The potential of a virtuous cycle, all drawn from SI. (More on how this occurs in St1 shortly). "Our estimates show that the cost should be much less than generating biofuel." So we shall start as we always do with a pilot to prove the model, and then we shall lobby the EU for CO2 sinks to be accepted away from the EU.'

St1 is investing in scientists' work on a plan for 'Making Sahara green again.' This is about demonstrating the potential of what might be and subsequently pursuing partnerships for making it happen. 'We shall make the knowledge freely available'—a form of knowledge philanthropy.

So how does SI operate in St1? Mika's answer stems from the overt sense of purpose in the business. 'We are a CO2 aware energy company. We sell fossil fuels and invest the profits in R&D renewables. We have a culture here of asking questions. The biggest is why do we come to work? Everyone is engaged in questions. And everyone knows that the business must balance making profits to invest in SI as well as protect the sustainability of the business. This purpose is motivational. Of course remuneration is important but for this generation purpose is significant.'

Responding to the question how do you get buy in he answers: 'by leading from example, words tied to actions. On our website we have 101 assertions (ideas and arguments)—from the employees, not me.' We asked how do these ideas translate across into SI. 'There is a straight connection to our business activity. Ideas and actions—this is my leadership principle. But the ideas also come from various stakeholders we engage with.' He is speaking about users, supply chains, but mostly from 'scientists . . . we have had hundreds of ideas but only 2 have been developed so far.' Mika offers the example of the City of Espoo and the geo-thermal project that came this way. 'Drilling a hole for getting "deep heat" from 4.5 kilometres. Very exciting.' Mika explains the technical details and then comments: 'It will be a game changer. It has the potential to deliver 10% of the city's energy needs. If it works it will become a scalable model for other cities and we will make this knowledge available.' He commented on the contract negotiation with the energy supplier: 'When we started this project and I did the deal with [name of contractor withheld] we had to agree on the cheapest energy unit price, that they currently have. He said to me we couldn't do a project like this because we have to get a suitable return on equity. Stock listed companies are never going to address the big societal questions.' Again, Mika is questioning the ability of organisations and indeed politicians to see the greater systemic picture.

'Last year we made 260 million Euros profit, then the taxes. After that we had 200 million free cashflow that we put to SI projects. I'm not putting the jobs at risk. I don't have a bonus. People here see the investment. This guy is not bullshitting—this purpose is more important for [the] young generation. I don't need any more money—I want to deliver solutions. But not empty promises.'

Returning to the 'assertion' ideas Mika comments: 'From our employees we get ideas. In mid-2017 we collected these 101 "assertions" from our employees of what we should do, how and why in order to make the world a better place. We have these on our website.' We asked if these have come to fruition. 'A few, not many yet. But there's one about to be announced. Very exciting to do with refinery. I cannot say more at this stage.'

We asked how can Mika leverage the ideas they are generating to change the world: 'First, I have to prove it works in real life, get it "rock solid" get it to the market and then get the ball rolling globally. Get the big guys involved. [If the] carbon farming example works, then we get Al Gore or Barack Obama involved. If in 5 years' time it is working in real life—then I will contact the most powerful people on the planet to get it going. You can see what we have done, we want to share the knowledge, not holding back the IP. These things don't happen if we all don't participate. We are working with [name withheld] of a satellite measuring system to measure the carbon capture. It will tell us how much it costs to take the carbon—the costs look less than biofuels right now. Instead of only biofuel we should build carbon sink in [the] Sahara. Don't need tax-payers' money. Just need it measured and accepted. The business logic has to be there. The numbers we have done add up. The answer is that we need more biomass. There will be a natural tipping point. When there are enough Sahara carbon forests the climate will change. The rain will come back. That's what the Institute of Meteorology are saying.'

We asked him what key lessons would he pass on to others seeking to undertake SI. 'To analyse your own business segment of the global situation. Do it in an honest way. Draw conclusions on what your business can do to support the most sustainable solutions. You need to understand the global system. Harmony between the global and the local. We need to be more educated on the global system to generate aligned local actions. We should ask ourselves: how would an African young man see the same stuff and then try and find harmony.'

Our interpretations of leadership of St1 in this entrepreneurial context suggest the most salient notion of purpose infused into all activities. Employees are an integral part of SI activity balanced alongside the necessity to be profitable. In many respects this means accepting some contradictions of a business model that draws profits from fossil fuels and invests these into SI.

An approach to leadership is one of role modelling. Mika commented that he does not need money. The accounts show the employees how profit is invested into SI, and that SI is being made available for others to learn from. Thereby reinforcing the narrative of the purpose and aligned action in pursuance of the purpose.

Open innovation was striking in this case study. It rather suggests that the type 3 typology of systems change SI is captured by Mika's leadership approach. That is the notion of pursuing SI by generating a business model that pursues knowledge generation and making that openly available for others to engage with this activity is rooted in a global systems perspective. We did not speak of this approach as type three SI in the interview, but it does give insight into how leadership may approach a system's change orientation. However, Mika's situation may be very unique—not needing to serve shareholder for immediate return on investment. Jussi's leadership approach to SI at UPM does speak to the growing shareholder interest in responsible business through engaging in operational type 1 SI first (demonstrating the performance capability) and then progressing to type 2 SI. It might be that if Mika's Saharan project succeeds UPM may become a partner and thus move into systems change on a scale that has significant reach and impact for humanity and realise a major planetary dividend.

For all the cases there is a grounding of action in the reality of needing to demonstrate success. Mika's approach, which reflects type 3 SI as systems change, seeks to show the world the opportunities that exist to gain greater systemic impact. UPM as transformational SI seeks to convince shareholders and partners. While SOK as type 1 operational optimisation—the 'same things but better'—seeks to catalyse an interest and ownership of sustainability challenges with the main board, divisional directors, customer-owners and their suppliers. In this way leadership within SOK has established the ground and business case, from which greater scope and reach of SI could follow as they progress into type 2 S1.

We wish to emphasise though that the SI typology (Adams et al., 2015) is not necessarily a progression. The case studies seek to illustrate the sensitivity of leadership by recognising the context, aspirations and sense of purpose. All three cases speak to the notion of responsible leadership by focusing on leader-stakeholder interaction as the primary concern—seeking to generate value for the organisation and stakeholders over the medium term.

Concluding Thoughts

SI is perhaps a difficult concept to embrace within the business model. It is the least understood and offers substantial challenges in terms of openness to and with stakeholders, engaging with an understanding of where value is generated for stakeholders and managing such stakeholder value realisation. However, we suggest SI offers distinctive competitive advantage to a business because it offers a platform for the deepening of the business engagement with key stakeholders in the realisation of all the six good dividends. In the introduction of the chapter we suggested there were four elements associated with SI: leading engagement of employees to embrace the concept and value of SI whilst developing a powerful and supportive guiding coalition; second, identifying SI value-generating opportunities for a range of stakeholders; third, engaging and leading a range of stakeholders at different stages; fourth, leading processes to exploit the value from SI. We have outlined elements two and three and embraced aspects of one that had previously been explored in the preceding chapter. The first three elements create a platform from which the fourth can occur. It is to the operation dividend we next turn in order to understand how SI can be exploited and value realised through operational processes.

8 Operational Dividend
Realising Stakeholder Value

*Steve Eldridge, Steve Kempster
and Andy Webster*

Introduction

Operations management is fundamentally about identifying value and delivering this. In the context of the good dividends value—both identification and delivery—is associated with the customer (to help realise the brand dividend), and of course with the financial dividend; but importantly value is but also associated with the dividend for our planet and our communities. To this end the chapter seeks to show how these dividends can be realised through applying lean thinking to a service organisation—a police constabulary in the UK focusing on homicide investigations.

There is much complexity though with discerning how value is understood and identified with customers and other stakeholders, and with the processes of delivering such value. For example, value for communities might be a reduction in waste, pollution, energy, or noise. Value is also in the creation of employment directly and through supply chains. Value might be found in the support of technical training in community colleges required for the organisational operations. Value for employees might reflect engagement in developing processes, taking initiative, questioning assumptions; in this way, value for employees might reflect ownership and control of operations, rather than a mechanistic assumption of labour to implement others' decisions. Understanding value then is not straightforward, but it is critical. However, a preoccupation with identifying and realising value across stakeholders is not the dominant discourse in operations management—with managers or academics. In major part this reflects the dominance of the neo-liberal discourse, highlighted in Chapter 2, that has shaped leadership of organisations in the pursuance of cost reduction and the exploitation of resources. The essence of the argument of this chapter is the need to shift operations management from being captured by neo-liberal capitalist thinking to become the hand maiden to enable the moral capitalist agenda explored in Chapter 2: a shift from exploiting resources to the responsible pursuit of value through engagement with resources—material and people.

For this shift in operations to become manifest there needs to be a similar shift in leadership commitment and orientation. A shift in operational leadership orientation towards seeking to realise the resourcefulness of people (described in Chapter 6) along with enabling the social innovative stakeholder approach (described in Chapter 7). In this chapter we shall describe these two shifts as behavioural operations and sustainable operations. Drawing on traditional operations methods, such as lean thinking, and with an attention to organisational purpose and sense of responsibility for the impact of resources on our planet and our communities, leadership of operations would seek to realise value for customers and other stakeholders. For example, responsible operations would pay much attention to the use of energy, waste reduction in all forms, and designing products capable of being recycled. It would be the intent that the outputs of the operational dividend are thus realised for all of the business's stakeholders. Thus, operational dividend (the operational outputs) is the realisation of value. For the purpose of this book that is the realisation of the good dividends.

In this chapter the orientation toward value realisation will be taken through the lens of an operations manager. We wish to critique ideas on operations management and the realisation of value applicable to the role of an operations manager. Perhaps too often operations management is dominated by product-based businesses, and too little attention is given to realisation of value in service offerings. We hope to create a balance here. There are some sections that do speak (too much) on the ideas related to products. However, we seek to address the balance by making the case study a focus on a service context. We hope that the chapter can be read as applicable to operations managers from both contexts. We further hope that the chapter will stimulate ideas and reflections, but also be challenging to assumptions in both service and product organisations.

To give context to the argument for realignment in operations management from delivering cost minimisation to delivering value maximisation we shall first explore (albeit briefly) the history of operations management (OM) and the development of what we describe as "traditional" OM. From establishing the convention of operations management as inputs-process-outputs we overlay the different concepts that have emerged, such as time and motion, craft, batch and line, TQM and Lean. The development of these concepts and ideas rooted in the input-process-output axiom is towards value realisation oriented to the customer. We explore what value might be and for whom and illustrate the complexity when situated amongst the array of stakeholders. The growth of debates and ideas associated with sustainable operations management can be seen to grow out of an appreciation of stakeholder value. We outline the key ideas, notably cradle-to-cradle and reverse supply chains, captured in the notion of sustainable operations management (SOM) and speak of the significant potential of SOM, as an operational dividend, to contribute to the brand and reputation dividend and of course the planetary dividend. However, we advise caution with regard to progress in the area to date by highlighting the relatively limited practice-based engagement with these concepts. One of the causes for limited take-up is associated with the strikingly restricted examination of people in the discussions of operations management. How might people (employees, suppliers, customers) engage in the inputs-process outputs relationship to realise this value? In the lexicon of operations management, a new concept of behavioural operations management (BOM) has begun to emerge. We suggest that through drawing together SOM and BOM (excuse the abbreviations) leadership of operations can realise the brand and planetary dividends. We utilise the concept of lean within a case study to illustrate our argument and apply such thinking to an unconventional context for lean thinking—police work, and in particular, homicide investigations. The case study pursues the challenge of value identification and delivery across the case study stakeholders. In this way we hope to illuminate the scope and reach of reframing police work and the identification and realisation of stakeholders' value that would allow the ideas to be applicable to all contexts, manufacturing, services, health, local government and so forth.

Conventions and Definitions of "Traditional" Operations Management

Operations management developed as an academic discipline in the latter half of the last century with a foundation of empirical work in the manufacturing sector that has accumulated almost ever since the beginning of the industrial revolution. The relevance of this initial work to the service sector was recognised and, hence, old-fashioned manufacturing management was renamed as "operations management" to encompass this inclusivity and the diversity of applications. We define it simply as: "the activity of managing the resources which are devoted to the production and delivery of products and services" (Slack, Brandon-Jones and Johnston, 2011: 4). Underpinning this definition is the notion that an organisation can be represented as a process. A typical representation is shown in Figure 8.1.:

Operations managers seek to achieve the appropriate balance between efficiency (for example, a high yield from the transformed resources, and a high utilisation of the transforming resources) and effectiveness (for example, products and services that add value for customers supplied in a timely manner).

Control of this process and the achievement of efficiency and effectiveness can be measured using the five performance objectives: quality, cost, speed, dependability and flexibility. Using the resource-based view of the firm (RBV), achievement of these objectives can be linked to the development of "competitive capabilities" such as quality, cost, delivery and flexibility. The RBV perspective has been extensively researched in the

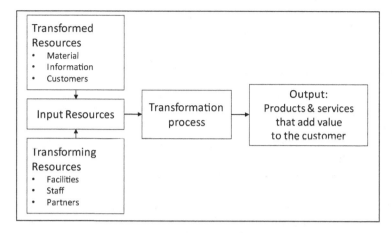

Figure 8.1 Operations as Input, Transformation and Outputs
(adapted from Slack et al., 2011: 10)

manufacturing sector (see, for example, Hayes and Wheelwright, 1984; Schoenherr, Power, Narasimhan and Samson, 2012).

The basic process model can be applied within the service setting although the role of the customer in the process and perceptions of value need to be reconsidered (the customer can be an input resource (co-production) to the process; the customer's experience of the process will add/subtract value). Nevertheless, this model is sufficiently robust for most operations within an organisation. Extending its scope to encompass all stakeholders in the sequence of operations from the source to the market leads to a definition of supply network management:

> "Supply network management is the management of the interconnection of organisations that relate to each other through upstream and downstream linkages between the processes that produce value [dividends] to the ultimate consumer in the form of products and services" (adapted from Slack et al., 2011); but also value/dividends to other stakeholders, owners, employees, suppliers, and our communities and our planet.

This definition takes us further than the simple "factory physics" of operations management and has led OM researchers to extend their understanding of organisational behaviour and inter-organisational relationships. Similarly, the extension of supply networks to encompass a "cradle to grave" approach to sustainability has given rise to topics such as reverse logistics and sustainable product/service design. However, the underlying principles of efficiency and effectiveness in operations still remain, though neither term is meaningful without a definition of "value" [dividends] in operations. The following section explores the conventional notions of value and how they have developed in operations management.

Advances in Traditional Operations Management

Taylor's Scientific Management represents the first serious attempt to offer an analytical perspective on managing an operation's resources. Wren suggests that "it is important to see Taylor in the context of his era, an era of needed reform" (Wren, 2011: 19) and this finds support with Grachev and Rakitsy adding that Taylor's work was "particularly conflicting with post-industrial society" (Grachev and Rakitsky, 2013: 513). Whilst it is important to recognise the historic and socio-economic landscape in which it was positioned—an age dominated by traditional industry—there remains a view that many of his insights are still valid today (Locke, 1982). Indeed, the application of time and motion study to all, but especially human resources, to improve an operation's efficiency and effectiveness still pervades organisations in the twenty-first century whether the operation is a car assembly line, a management consultancy, a university, a pharmacy or a call centre. His view of humans as machines, whose work could be redesigned and optimised, attracted criticism. In effect, reducing the cost of a product/service and improving its availability to the market, but was being achieved by exploiting vulnerable or unsustainable resources. This neo-liberal orientation persists and is relevant, as well as prevalent, today.

Interestingly, post-war initiatives emerged that began to address these concerns. The focus on the achievement of product/service quality became particularly fashionable during the 1970s and 1980s. Total Quality Management (TQM) was seen as the way to improve efficiency and effectiveness in a way that was more optimistic and inspirational for an organisation's employees and its customers. TQM embodied notions that quality capability is a source of competitive advantage and should be achieved by, among many methods, establishing team working as the norm for empowered staff and making sure that customers and suppliers were involved in a process of continuous improvement. Interest in TQM faded away in the 1990s. Perhaps it was too difficult to sustain within Western organisations owing to its key requirement for sustained senior management commitment to long-term culture change. Or, on the other hand, managements commitment to a neo-liberal orientation, which dominated in the 1980s and was enabled by flexible labour laws, undermined the ability to gain the TQM dividend. Robyn and Steve's discussion in Chapter 6 speaks to this with regard to realising the necessary human resourcefulness for TQM to bear fruition.

An interesting departure in TQM research is the work of Genichi Taguchi (1986). His initial focus was on the practical use of statistical techniques to improve quality, but he produced a model of the 'quality loss function'. He proposed that if a product deviates away from its target specification then the *loss to society* varies parabolically with the size of the deviation. The point being that time, material and human contribution is wasted from generating a valuable output for society; wasteful of the potential human resourcefulness in a virtue practice orientation (MacIntyre, 1985), in which excellence has not been achieved.

The notion of lean production and, more generally, lean thinking, arose as the next significant operations improvement approach. Its roots can be traced back to Taylor's scientific management and, also, to the elements packaged in the West as TQM though embodied for years in what has been described as the "Toyota way" (Morgan and Liker, 2006). The original conception of lean was not overtly preoccupied with sustainability— it was not the prevalent discourse of the time. It was focused on customer value and improving this through better use of resources. However, lean speaks to many aspects on which sustainability is centred—and we shall develop this further when we explore sustainability operations.

Although Ohno at Toyota is recognised as pioneering Lean Production, it is W. Edward Deming's seminal *Out of the Crisis* that has challenged thinking and practice (Deming, 1982). He posited an alternative route to operational efficiency, focused on flow and not the measurement of individual activity functioning within it (Deming, 1982). Furthermore, together with Ohno (1988) and Womack and Jones (1990, 1996) he was explicit that production must focus on what is adding value (dividends to customers in order to maximise financial dividends to owners). Therefore, any activity that consumes resources, but does not add value, seen through the eyes of the customer is waste and waste must be eliminated. He identified seven types of waste: transportation, inventory, motion, waiting, over production, over processing and defects. Subsequently, researchers have proposed additional wastes, notably the failure to exploit employee creativity (Liker, 2004), or more broadly the notion of resourcefulness. A fundamental part of Ohno's approach was to ensure work was visible and solve problems as and when they occurred. To do this it required worker empowerment, allowing production to be stopped so a solution could be found to prevent further errors. Womack and Jones (1996) observed this within Toyota in all areas of the organisation; not just the production lines. This enabled Womack and Jones to propose a framework for lean thinking, which embodies five simple steps: specify value; identify the value stream; create flow; operate a pull system; strive and for perfection. Value is what the consumer values and the process that creates this is the work stream. Flow is the movement through the organisation and emphasis is placed on removing barriers between organisational, suppliers and customers with the key focus on creating value. Pull recognises that customers want to choose the value (goods) they require as opposed to the push of goods to a market that has no need for them.

Perfection seeks to eliminate waste by eradicating defects. The notion of striving for perfection assumes the employee wishes to strive. We shall address this shortly under behavioural operations management, but suffice to say that this is not as straightforward as elegantly described in the lean manual. Further, and most importantly, step number one (specify value) is the most difficult. Little attention has been given to understanding and realising this value. In Chapter 7 Steve and Minna unpacked in some depth the necessity of realising value across stakeholders for social innovation to become manifest. The work undertaken there is thus complementary to this chapter and we shall draw on that work within the case study further on in the chapter.

As a footnote to this discussion we highlight the ambiguity and paradox of value and the implications of such ambiguity in realising value and thus realising good dividends. As described earlier, the conventional process of operations management delivers products and services that add value for the customer. In simple terms, if customers have the capability and resources to do the transformation themselves then they would if the cost of doing so is less than the price of the product or service if they purchased it. The added value of the operation is simply the price paid by customers for those activities that they cannot do or do not wish to do. Consequently, operations managers focus on reducing non-value-adding activities (aka the "waste") within their operations. Some interesting paradoxes emerge from this focus on waste reduction. For example, the adoption of plastic packaging in grocery supply chains has greatly reduced the amount of food spoilage (though some would argue that it is still too high), but, inevitably, much of this packaging is effectively single use and its environmental effects are well known. Do consumers value aesthetics and ease of use over permanently disfiguring the planet in a locality often many miles from their home? In this context, circular supply chains add no value in the eyes of the customer unless they are a part of the operation's brand values. Similarly, no customers would like themselves to be treated inhumanely at work but they are quite happy to drive technologically advanced cars that are available at an affordable price. These have been produced using process designs in which humans are incorporated as cost-effective machines. These are simple, perhaps simplistic, interpretations of how the notion of adding value for one group of stakeholders actually subtracts value for other stakeholders. This might be seen as an inevitable outcome of the simple, reduced process model used in operations management. The next section considers the steps being taken to develop a more holistic, sustainable and systems-based approach.

Towards an Integrated Approach to Realising Value: Embracing Sustainable and Behavioural Operations Management

We start this section recalling a helpful definition of operations management as the: "design and management of the transformation processes in manufacturing and service organizations that create value for society" (Chopra, Lovejoy and Yano, 2004: 1). The definition captures the essence of the role of operations enabling the good dividends—"creating value for society". But we respectfully add "profitably" in order for the processes to be sustainable in all three elements of sustainability: economic, environmental and social. Within the operations management field the emphasis on sustainable OM is mostly toward the balance of economic and environmental. For example, *lean* methodology was driven out from an economic orientation linked to customer value—a transition from "lean operations, to lean enterprises and finally to lean consumption" (Kleindorfer, Singhal and Van Wassenhowe, 2005: 483). The environmental gain is the reduction of waste. Lean thinking is connected with supply chain thinking and the development of closed loop supply chains with businesses taking full responsibility for the entire lives of the products; and more recently reverse supply chains where the customer returns the product and the chain is concluded when the business is able to extract/recycle remaining value from the product—recycling materials or generating energy through incineration. There is much excitable discourse in the sustainable OM field around these themes. The idea of "decoupling economic growth from increasing resource use as well as promoting waste reduction or minimization" (Gregson, Crang, Fuller and Holmes, 2015: 219) are most laudable ideals. The opportunities for the planet with regard to moving from a use of natural resources as cradle to grave— "take-make-dispose"—to cradle to cradle—where ideas of "disassembly, adaption and re-use are considered from the outset" (2015: 220) deeply connect to notions of OM generating "value for society". The natural extension is embracing customers in this process through reverse supply chains where products are returned to the manufacturer for successive value to be extracted. The necessity for supply chains (including the customer) to be ever more closely integrated is an inevitable corollary to processes enabling the constituent elements of the product to be capable of re-use. For both the development of lean thinking and, with regard to maximising product recyclability, close relationships with stakeholders are thus necessary. However, we need to go further than the environmental-economic axis. There is the need for OM to give attention to the social aspects of sustainable operations.

Sustainable operations management has not given much attention to the social aspects impacted by the transformational process, other than placed on the business by regulatory requirements. And to be a little blunt, we would assert that much of the environmental sustainability aspects we have touched on are more the consequence of accident and emergence than deliberate leadership intent, and "actual enactment is limited and fragile" (Gregson et al., 2015: 218). There are a number of notable exceptions. In Chapter 7 Steve and Minna highlighted how various corporates are pursing social innovation—becoming close to both customers and suppliers to meet social needs. The case study with SOK gave insight to the impact on reputational capital of the activities of suppliers. The case illustrated social aspects in terms of employment conditions, welfare and human rights. A further high-profile corporate example is that of Unilever and the Sustainable Living Plan (Unilever, 2017). Through the commitment of the CEO and the C-suite they have sought to commit the business to a range of social and environmental sustainability outcomes as a result of attention to their operational processes. For example: a reported reduction of waste by consumers by 27 per cent and by 2020 a reduction of 98 per cent from Unilever operations going to landfill; reduction in water usage target by 2020 by 39 per cent; a target of 100 per cent sustainably sourced agricultural raw materials by 2020 (currently reported 57%). On social measures there are targets for human rights in supply chains and in the business, opportunities for women and a focus on inclusive business—for example smallholder businesses and small retail outlets. In broad strokes the marketing agenda seeks to impact 1 billion customers with regard to generating healthy lifestyles, reducing environmental impact by 50 per cent and enhancing the livelihoods of millions connected with Unilever.

We highlight Unilever as an example of the reach of operations management. But we also seek to make salient the coupling of operations with brands and organisational reputation. Unilever are seeking to leverage the changes in operations to enhance the brand equity and the reputational capital. The engagement of customers closely aligned with the operational targets is a most overt example of realising good dividends. Not just brands and reputation, but protecting natural capital and realising the planetary dividend. The Unilever plan, like many other businesses, has the opportunity to generate operational dividends that will enrich our planet and our communities. Through connecting with customers and suppliers the systemic challenges outlined in Chapter 4 have significant chance to be addressed. Indeed, the Unilever plan overtly connects with the UN Sustainable Development Goals (SDGs). But it's not just the large corporates where the operational dividend can be realised and aligned with the SDGs (See Chapter 13 for an in-depth case study of a small business). Finally, the operational dividend, impacting on reputations and brands along with the planetary dividend, has a close relationship with human resource dividend—we shall address this very shortly.

In essence, sustainability operations management has a leadership responsibility. Without the operational dividend, through attention to sustainability, the good dividends remain theoretical. And here caution must be applied. Research shows that sustainability operations management is not so easily grasped (Gregson et al., 2015). Examining the issues from a practice-based perspective of the operations manager we suggest the limited pursuit of the operational dividend of environmental and societal contributions is the result of five elements: first, the complexity that is placed on an operation manager to juggle all these requirements.

For example, a manufacturing manager operating with limited resources (time, budget and support) is expected to deliver quality and consistency (minimal defects) that is cost efficient, embrace close supplier relationships in the delivery of value, whilst being responsive to changing customer needs and being compliant to government regulations; and all of that compounded by an ever-growing discourse for recycling where the discarded product can be turned into valuable alternative products. Second, is the myth of the circular economy (and notions of cradle to cradle) in the reality of business activity (Gregson et al., 2015). Third, the limited leadership desire to pursue the operational dividend that would "deliver value for society" profitably (Chopra et al., 2004)—the persistent dominance of neo-liberal operations management assumptions around reduction of cost rather than maximisation of value. Fourth, the complexity of understanding and realising value, rather than the clarity of cost reduction. And fifth, the limited attention in operational management to people in the transformational process. It is to the last of these elements that we turn to next.

Behavioural operations management (BOM) is the new kid on the block for operations management. For Steve (K) this was a striking revelation. For him it was hard to understand how the operational designs, the procurement processes, relationships with suppliers, understanding of customer value and transmitting that through the transformational process could occur without a deep appreciation of the human factor.

OM approaches have been based on the economist relational argument that humans will respond to monetary incentives—if they do not or they vary from the rational expectations then there must be communication misalignments (Gino and Pisano, 2008). Suggested definition of behavioural OM is understandably the impact of human behaviour on operational systems and processes (Gino and Pisano, 2008: 679). The seemingly very obvious issue of the impact of human behaviour on operational systems was ironically in the earliest studies of operational research (the work of Mayo, Roethlisberger and Dickson in the 1920s and 1930s cited in Ross and Nisbett, 1991: 210–212). Further validation of this axiom was the Hawthorne experiments (see John Adair's, 1984, review of these famous experiments of the 1920s) where worker behaviour was modified, not by monetary incentives, but by the simple act of being viewed in their everyday acts. In both these pieces of research the key finding was that productivity increased because the workers were pleased to receive attention. The attention, care, encouragement and sense of purpose all given to the work, of course, resonate with the central thesis of this book. The argument of the resourcefulness of people (the human resource dividend), that generate excellence of customer care, creativity and innovation, attentiveness to quality and standards, are the qualities that are so needed to implement the operating systems and procedures. So it was a great surprise for Steve (K) to realise that 2006 was the first paper on this area in the field of operations management (Bendoly, Donohue and Schulz, 2006).

OM assumes optimal systems—the most efficient and effective way (Gino and Pisano, 2008). We assert that this is rarely (if ever) achieved and certainly not without the hand of leadership being most evident. Gino and Pisano (2008: 681) beautifully capture the point thus:

> Real operating systems like factories, supply chains, and product development organizations are complex social systems where human behavior is a central driver; thus the usefulness of tools, methods, and frameworks that ignore the realities and limitations of human behavior is limited.

There is the necessity for the human resource dividend to be ever present if the operational dividend is to be realised. This point is not present in the literature of operational management. Attention is to managers, their cognition and behaviour. Little mention is made and little weight placed on employee engagement—on realising and sustaining the human resourcefulness. The fledgling research attention is focused on the problems of human behaviour (see for example Bendoly et al., 2006; Bendoly, Croson, Goncalves and Schultz, 2010). It follows the notion of transactional leadership and exception reporting (Bass, 1999), and understanding the defects in the systems and correcting them. The defects are the human behaviour that needs fixing. The operation management research is a long way from embracing leadership and the relationship this has with human resourcefulness. Yet there is a strong recognition that leadership is so important to aspects like quality, customer care and productivity (Masi and Cooke, 2000).

The link between SOM and BOM is significant to this chapter. It is about leadership and purpose. The OM scope for engagement and delivery of sustainability is considerable. After all it is in the engine room of organisational operations that the purposes of the organisation, the value generation for society, become manifest. It is through the excellence of the operations that value for stakeholders is maximised and wasteful impact on stakeholders is minimised. But it relies on the human resourcefulness engaged with the operations for this to occur. The complexity of addressing closed and reversed supply chains to design products that can be recycled, or for the service offerings to be socially innovated to help embrace community challenges in a profitable way, depends on those in leadership roles seeking to engender a strong sense of business purpose to the everyday operational activities. In Peter Senge's (1990) bestseller *The Fifth Discipline*, he speaks of the apocryphal tale of two employees working in a quarry being interviewed. Each is paid the same. Each has worked the same period of time—25 plus years. Each has the same working conditions save for having a different manager. Moving to speak to the first employee who stands close to a pile of smashed rocks and is leaning nonchalantly on his sledgehammer he asked "what are you doing?" The employee answers "smashing rocks". The researcher moves to a man standing a few metres away. Around him are neatly cut rocks, carefully stacked up. The same question is asked "what are you doing?" He answers in a proud way: "Building a cathedral!" A simple and trite tale of two different operational outcomes. Traditional OM would look at the control and regulation aspects of the smashed rocks to limit this occurring. The responsible leadership as OM (i.e. the BOM and SOM approaches) would seek to generate meaning and engagement of work to the purposes of the business. We wish to highlight though that all approaches to OM are necessary—the traditional, the SOM and the BOM. There is the need for all—all are necessary but on their own insufficient. The objective of the operations manager is to achieve a combined transformational process. We capture this in Figure 8.2.

Although this is a very simple offering, we hope it captures the essence of what is required for organisations to realise the good dividends. Value realisation is at the heart of the OM activities. We are suggesting a balanced approach in the realisation of value and sustaining such value. Society, and the challenges identified in Chapter 2, warrants the necessity for responsible leadership to become prevalent in the world of operations management.

We take up this challenge for the development of responsible leadership in an operations role. We explore and apply the ideas of traditional operations management—using lean thinking—with SOM and BOM being a focus on the realisation of value for stakeholders within the case study.

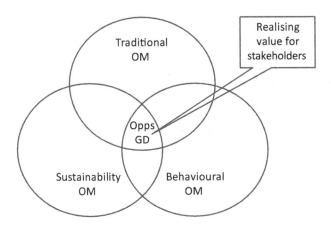

Figure 8.2 Finding the "Sweet-spot" of Operations Management to Realise the Good Dividends

Murdering Waste

As we stated in the opening paragraph of the chapter, value realisation framed by the good dividends is oriented in three ways: the customer (brand dividend), the organisation (financial dividend), and our planet and our communities (planetary dividend). The case draws on recent research in a public sector service organisation. It offers the opportunity to see the application of some of the ideas we have explored in a setting that may be untraditional to operations management. We do this in order to illustrate the scope of possibility and applicability to organisations in many contexts. We explore the potential operational dividend of homicide investigations.

Homicide is part of daily human life and its occurrence is surprisingly common. In the UK, it is the police service that has a duty to investigate it. High profile failings in the last century in the UK, such as the mismanaged Yorkshire Ripper enquiry and the failed investigation into the racist murder of Stephen Lawrence have led to significant transformation of practice (Byford, 1981; MacPherson, 1999) encapsulated by the Major Incident Room Standard Administrative Procedures (MIRSAP) (Association of Chief Police Officers, 2005). The output of this process is valuable for a variety of stakeholders. Failing to investigate properly can have far-reaching consequences for society in that it may leave a killer at large and may erode public confidence in the state's ability to maintain law and order.

However, MIRSAP is highly resource intensive, especially when compared to non-fatal investigations. Imagine a victim being assaulted by punch, knife, hammer, strangulation, gunshot or poisoning. If the victim survives, it remains an assault. An assault case is usually allocated to a detective constable to work under the supervision of a sergeant. If the victim dies as a result of the assault, it will result in the establishment of a major incident room with a senior investigating officer managing a team of between 10 and 30 staff who follow the Major Incident Room Standard Administrative Procedures process. The assault is the same in both cases though the value of the investigation is judged very differently by the police on our behalf.

A further complication to the value argument arises from when recent UK government austerity measures have forced policing to reconsider its core business and notions of value for money. This problem is not dissimilar to the one that faced the manufacturing sector in the post-war era in its pursuit of competitive advantage. Lean approaches that focus on achieving more output for less input have been successful. At the same time, the challenge of delivering policing in the complexity of the twenty-first century is different to the one that confronted Byford and MacPherson when they made recommendations for procedures. Lean presents an opportunity to make homicide investigation speedier ("justice delayed is justice denied" for the victim's family), more effective ("fit for purpose" as the politicians often declare) and more efficient ("reduce government spending" for the tax payer).

This case study, conducted by Andy (Detective Chief Superintendent, and Head of Serious Crime and Specialist Capability) adopted a lean operations approach to challenge the way homicides are investigated. The difficult first step of "defining value" was and is very difficult, so it was side-stepped in the hope that a definition would emerge during the study. So, the first step became an examination of the workflow in the major incident room of two high profile murder investigations using Value Stream Mapping (VSM). VSM is a commonly used lean technique to determine not only what adds value and what is waste (effectiveness), but also the number of steps taken to achieve this (efficiency), and the time taken at each stage (effectiveness). A combination of questionnaire surveys, interviews and focus groups were used to elicit the underlying factors behind the VSM analysis from the perspective of experienced police officers.

Andy's first conclusion was that value in the Major Incident Room Standard Administrative Procedures process was ill-defined. To Andy this came as no surprise, but it is worthwhile examining some key findings that emerged. There was a general agreement that "prosecution evidence" is a value-added output, but broader reflections on value-added activities in the process include all of these comments: "a search for the truth"; "following all reasonable lines of enquiry"; "hypothesis testing"; "what leads to evidence and gets served as evidence"; "evidence of what has happened"; "the where, the when, the how and the who is responsible"; "value is what is used at court"; "right outcome at the end of the day"; and "whatever impacts on public confidence."

This means that it is most challenging for a senior investigating officer to make a robust judgement as to the effectiveness and efficiency of a homicide investigation in terms of identifying, agreeing and delivering value. For example, if "pursuing evidence gathering opportunities" was used as the criterion then an average of 32 of the 40 actions studied in the VSM were value adding. However, if the criterion was one of "obtaining evidence used in prosecution" then an average of only 12 actions added value. Irrespective of the definition of value, there are clear opportunities to reduce waste within a major incident room. However, a comparison of these numbers at the individual case level indicated large differences between the two cases, which reflected the degree to which the senior investigating officer's (that is the leader's) strategy is influencing investigative activity in comparison to other factors such as local working practices. In other words, one process used on two different cases at two different locations with two different senior investigating officers yielded two different levels of value-adding activity but, ultimately, both yielded a successful outcome. We suggest this speaks to the influence of behavioural operations distorting value identification and realisation.

Andy's second conclusion follows on from the VSM data described above, namely: the Major Incident Room (MIR) process is inherently inefficient. This surprised him, especially as he had gone on record only 12 months earlier stating that the MIR was "fit for purpose, a good check and balance . . . a low risk option"—drawing on data from a qualitative survey of investigating officers' perceptions. The VSM data contradicted these perceptions and facilitated Andy's new perspective on the process. The MIR Standard Administrative Process (MIRSAP) was introduced with the intention of encapsulating best practice (and he hoped best value) in homicide investigations. But he had serious misgivings that the enforced standardisation/rigidity—that is treating police officers like machines—can cause inefficiencies. For example, filing a crime report (that is the recording of an incident as a crime) for an assault is a simple or, even automatic activity, which, arguably, does not add value to the investigation. In homicide investigations, seven additional non-value-adding steps are required. In the sample used for the VSM, there were four actions required as part of the standard policing process (each involving seven steps), which contributed 10 per cent of the total activity, none of which added value to the investigation. Indeed, the management information system (known as "HOLMES") designed to support investigations was perceived to create more work and more unused evidence rather than less.

Andy's study revealed that the MIRSAP process is wasteful from the lean perspective. For example, only 30 per cent of the activities studied resulted in evidence that could be used in the prosecution case. In lean terms, this is "over production". Furthermore, MIRSAP is good at harvesting material but this stock piling of information, almost never to be used, is akin to excess "inventory" and can obscure the investigation's view of what is valuable evidence. There appears to be unnecessary repetition and duplication of work in the MIR and the majority of investigating officers considered murder investigations to be over resourced, which suggests "over processing." Interestingly, a younger investigating officer observed the issue was not the quantity of staff on enquiries but the quality. From a behavioural operations perspective a lack of experienced investigators meant that often work had to be redone, incurring a different waste—"defects."

Remaining on the behavioural orientation, the most significant waste related to unused employee creativity (Liker, 2004), or resourcefulness. The findings suggested that officers felt that they could improve the way they work but are constrained from doing so. Andy concluded that policing culture is a barrier to lean implementation. He found that the investigating officers were very loyal to the HOLMES system and MIRSAP process and that this culture of "doing things by the book" could present a barrier to change. Officers had a straightforward, mechanistic approach to task completion (the officers would only carry out the exact instruction written on the action, no more no less). It is clear that this approach eliminates risk. Indeed, the MIRSAP approach has resulted in very few mismanaged investigations or high-profile miscarriages of justice. This is a good thing from the investigating officer's perspective, given the professional and personal consequence of failure. So a major finding for Andy was that any change to a leaner method of investigation would require intensive culture reorientation to ensure acceptance by the investigating officers and overcome this institutional risk aversion.

Finally, Andy concluded that this complex process was in need of a systems thinking approach. For example, the investigating officer's role permits a holistic view of the investigation but, instead, they too see the process in terms of lines of enquiry (such as house to house calls, CCTV, forensic examinations, searches, telephony and many more . . .) and clearly defined MIR roles (such as Enquiry Officers, Indexers and Exhibits Officers). The downstream "customer" of the MIRSAP process is the Crown Prosecution Service (CPS) and it was clear that there was a disconnect in terms of thinking and in terms of flow between the investigation team and the CPS. Indeed, officers complained vehemently about the lack of integration with the CPS at a systems level or collaboration at a personal level. The absence of a systems view serves to create bottlenecks and waste. All of which impacts on the effectiveness, efficiency and expediency with which justice can be delivered.

Andy's research has illustrated that twenty-first-century policing has conceptually and methodologically much to learn from the shop floor of Toyota. By further exploring these processes it offers the real prospect of delivering a service that is fit for those who tragically fall victim to the most heinous of all crimes. This research raises several points with more general relevance to good dividends in operations.

The first point is the realisation that the MIRSAP processes have run their course. They will undoubtedly continue to offer a risk-averse, seemingly fail-safe approach to homicide investigation but at a cost that is no longer viable in twenty-first-century policing. The work of homicide is greatly impacted by the increasing threats for societies around the world (highlighted in Chapter 2 as grand challenges) of terrorism, human trafficking, modern day slavery and cybercrime. Our operational approach in the UK fails to deliver an acceptable return on the investment for UK society. Reform is required for societal value to be gained.

This leads to the second point, which is defining and understanding value. A dive deeper dive into the relationship between value and evidence is essential. If the police service fails to do this, its processes will continue to be undisciplined, unwieldy and inefficient. Value in homicide investigation, must be translated into the pursuit of reasonable lines of enquiry to secure evidence and must be performed in a victim focused way. Thus, defining value is pivotal. We have identified the need to orientate the system around value for the victim. This is justice, but for the victim(s) justice may additionally relate to speed by which justice occurs. But of course value is also associated with other stakeholders: the investigating officer's purpose is related to protecting society and pursuing justice as part of that process; and more broadly, citizens wishing to be assured that justice is achieved and through a system that uses public money wisely (probably efficiently, but not necessarily if the outcome can be trusted).

This leads to the third point that realising value lies not just beyond MIRSAP and HOLMES processes but beyond policing. It requires an engagement with strategic stakeholders. With regard to homicide this includes the Criminal Prosecution Service, Forensic Services, Health (Pathology), Courts and Legal Services (Solicitors officers and Chambers). There is at present a silo approach that exists, not just within the MIR, but within the separate entities and that make up Criminal Justice System. The disconnect between them is palpable: rich in waste; not in justice.

We are deeply hesitant about prescribing a solution that embodies lean principles as, inevitably, this would be a simplistic or reduced model of what is a complex problem. So with that said, we offer an interpretation in order to guide understanding for transference of the issues to other contexts. We highlight the five steps of lean thinking that will frame our suggestions in Figure 8.3.

Value is what the consumer and other stakeholders value—in this instance, justice, in a timely and reliable manner, which uses public funding wisely. The process that creates this is the "value stream." The key from a leadership perspective is the necessity to develop the value stream in conjunction with the partners—the criminal justice system—engaged in the value stream built on a consensus of value. It requires drawing on the talents of all involved. In this way the "flow"—as the movement through the process and, which focuses on removing barriers between groups in the criminal justice system to ensure this value is not dissipated—can be advanced. The waste that is generated by the current system in

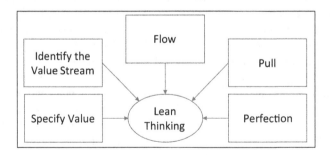

Figure 8.3 Five Principles of Lean Thinking
(adapted from Womack and Jones, 1990, 1996; Liker, 2004)

the flow has been highlighted. Perhaps the challenge in applying lean to a homicide investigation is addressing the "pull". The pull recognises that customers want to choose the value (products/services) they require rather than simply accept the products/services that are pushed onto the market by mass processes. Reframed to the value desired of the victim as justice, the value stream and the integrated flow may be capable of engaging the victim within the process where value for them is prioritised. However, the needs of the legal system for the generation of justice may limit such engagement. The final element of perfection speaks loudly to the argument in this book of generating good dividends through three aspects: first, utilising human resourcefulness—the driving sense of purpose, commitment, energy and curiosity; second, drawing on social innovation—seeking to innovate to add value (and minimise waste) through close engagement with partners; and third, operational optimisation by continuously improving operations by eliminating waste. Through such an application of lean the reputation of the criminal justice system—through value maximisation of delivering justice in a timely fashion through efficient and effective use of public funding—would be enhanced thus providing positive feedback to the partners in the process. The dividend to society and to the victim is evident throughout.

What was so striking to Andy is the encouragement that the lean thinking methodology can be embraced by homicide investigations to create not only efficient and effective processes at reduced operational costs, but, in particular, deliver value for a range of stakeholders: justice for the victim, that is delivered in a timely manner; value to police staff and engaged stakeholder services reinforcing the sense of purpose being realised through aligned and productive activity, increasing morale through effectively (and efficiently) protecting the community, and improving the quality of service to the victims' families; value to society of an effective service that delivers justice in a manner that is efficient and reliable in terms of quality of process, and that is able to give the public confidence.

Conclusion

The case study has been used to illuminate what might be possible in terms of applying operational methods to realise value. We assert that value needs to be considered to be more than just value to the customer—although most important. Framed within the good dividends argument is the need to align customer value to a broader set of stakeholder needs, notably our planet and our communities. The argument in Chapter 1 and Chapter 4 is that the operational dividend draws on human resourcefulness, and social innovation, to stimulate activity. In this way the case we have outlined provides an illustration of connecting SOM and BOM together to help realise value to society, to his colleagues and connected partner stakeholders, and of course, to victims.

In this chapter, and in particular with the case study, we seek to show what is possible in a context far removed from the usual suspects (excuse the pun) of manufacturing businesses. The case seeks to focus on a manager and his thinking about the transformational processes he is responsible for. A realisation of what might be possible using operation management techniques in order to realise purpose—protecting the community and helping to realise justice in an efficient and effective manner.

9 Achieving Good Dividends Through Brand Leadership

Malcolm Kirkup and Katalin Illes

Introduction

It is 15 years since we both awoke to realise we were part of the problem and not the solution. As an MBA Director at a prestigious business school, Malcolm was educating business leaders. He was well aware of the growing number of corporate scandals, the shameful environmental degradation, human rights abuses in supply chains and, in 2008, the financial crisis, and these were issues his MBA students' analysed in great depth. But was he changing mindsets and behaviours, and producing more 'responsible' business leaders? He wasn't convinced. His determined subsequent journey to take more direct action led him ultimately in 2010 to join Jean-Paul Jeanrenaud from the WWF and Jonathan Gosling at the University of Exeter to create a very different kind of MBA—the One Planet MBA. This was a unique, uncompromising MBA: a focus on the stewardship of natural and social capital as a central responsibility of business, with students who were keen to fight for change. Over the same 15 years, Katalin was engaged with a number of academic institutions across Europe and Asia. She observed how the limitations of Western business education models were being magnified abroad and often causing more harm than good. Business courses were being delivered wholesale without any regard for cultural differences or in-depth understanding of the specific historic, social, economic or ecological conditions. Katalin became frustrated with the limitations. She sees the need to educate the whole person and to equip students not only with technical skills, but also how to find individual purpose and become a force for good in the world. We have now joined forces at Westminster Business School in London, bringing our respective interests in marketing and leadership together. Hence our excitement when Steve invited us to present our thoughts on brand leadership.

Along our respective journeys towards understanding brand leadership, we became aware of a successful and inspirational business that walks the talk: a brand that lives and breathes the essence of 'doing good.' The case of Elvis & Kresse now features regularly as an exemplar in our teaching. The business launched in 2005, directly in response to the founders' own 'moral outrage': discovering the vast scale of waste generated by our society and, more specifically, the quantity that ends its life buried in landfill or incinerated. The founders' mission? To build a business that rescues and transforms waste, that is financially sustainable and that also delivers a social purpose. The business began by recovering decommissioned fire hose from the London Fire Brigade, transforming the hose into affordable luxury fashion accessories, and donating 50 per cent of its profits from the hose lines to the Fire Fighter's Charity. The business has grown steadily to become a powerful purpose-driven brand that generates exceptional good dividends. We were so inspired by the business that we approached Kresse Wesling, co-founder, to share her journey and experiences with us, and we are delighted that she has contributed her thoughts to support this book.

In this chapter, we seek to unpack the nature of a brand and to explore how a 'purpose-driven' brand offers the prospect of enhanced dividends. We highlight how a successful purpose-driven brand generates shared value, brand preference, enhanced reputation, lower costs and a compelling source of innovation, whilst also educating and leading behaviour change among consumers and among businesses that seek to emulate good practice. We then explore the leadership challenges facing Chief Marketing Officers (CMOs) in building purpose-driven brands: the need for clarity, consistency, authenticity and transparency, and also the challenges of maintaining the conversation with consumers through all activities, including partnerships. We conclude with our reflections on the importance of personal leadership in building good dividends. Throughout the discussion, we introduce observations from Kresse Wesling who, in our view, is a brand leader who lives and breathes the essence of 'doing good.'

Building Brands and Reputational Capital

Let's begin with the nature of a brand. A brand can be a product, a service, a person, a business or even a place that is identifiable and made distinctive by specific and unique attributes or value. In an increasingly busy, noisy and competitive marketplace, with so many choices available to consumers, it is important to be noticed and to stand out, and so ease of identification and distinctiveness are important. As Leslie de Chernatony argues, a successful brand is one that can sustain this distinctiveness and its special value over time and in the face of competing alternatives (de Chernatony, 2010). The more distinctive the better, especially if competitors cannot replicate the advantage, although the nature of the distinctiveness must be relevant, important and of value to the consumer or user. Distinctiveness is not static and it can change over time, either in response to competition, changes in consumer needs or a desire to communicate a clearer proposition.

A successful brand motivates consumers to want to reciprocate and exchange value. A brand has a set of 'assets'—the sources of influence of the brand—which can be both functional and emotional. Functional assets might include the physique of a product, its performance, its cost or consistency. Emotional assets are less tangible but, through experience or reputation, bring 'meaning' to the brand—for example, perceived reliability, responsiveness, competence, courtesy, credibility, security, empathy or trust. A strong brand will develop and nurture a set of compelling, consistent and deep meanings or associations for the brand, which are valued by consumers. This combination of assets, in turn, produces a range of benefits—some in the form of financial brand equity outcomes (and the prospect of healthy returns in the future), but others relate to the effects and influences on consumers and other stakeholders. Strong brands can generate psychological or behavioural impacts—reassurance, continuity, consistency, safety, loyalty, trust and advocacy. A brand is not just a projection to the external world, consumers and competitors. A strong brand also plays an important role in connecting an organisation emotionally to its employees, suppliers and other stakeholders. It offers a positive association to customers. The choices that we make, the brands that we buy, or avoid, reveal many of our values, personal preferences and how we are in the world and relate to the world.

So How Does a Purpose-Driven Brand Offer the Prospect of Enhanced Dividends?

Sustainably focused businesses seek to deliver 'shared value' for a range of stakeholders and not just shareholders. Porter and Kramer (2006) argue that businesses depend on the communities in which they exist and therefore need to focus on this connection in order to ensure long-term competitive success. Shared value can help secure long-term financial sustainability, but also an increase in the overall value created by improving the economic and social conditions of the communities in which they operate. In the case of brands with an environmental and social mission, a clear dividend arises from being part of the solution. For Kresse, the motivation and goal for her business is focused emphatically on this contribution. Yes, the business needs to be financially sustainable, but she argues that the finance is primarily to provide the *facility* to deliver the *higher purpose*. Her enterprise metrics focus on the extent to which she is solving the problem she set out to address—initially, the 10-ton-a-year problem associated with fire hose waste—alongside the contribution she is able to pass on to the Fire Fighters Charity. Having largely accomplished the hose waste goal by 2010, the focus is now the 800,000-ton-a-year problem, redirecting leather-offcuts from landfill or incineration. Kresse noted that the growth metric, or their concept of ambition, is aligned with waste rather than profit. "*I'm also motivated by whether or*

*not we and our employees are happy, challenged and fulfilled. Whether
we can sleep at night. On that, we do."*

From a financial perspective, a good brand that is deeply meaningful
offers the potential to win consumer preference against competing alternatives. In 2015, the Nielsen Global Corporate Sustainability Report indicated
that 66 per cent of consumers, and 73 per cent of millennials, were willing
to pay more for products sold by purpose-driven brands (Nielsen Company,
2015). For some consumers, strong brands create symbolic connections
between goods and identities, and the purchase of a congruent brand may
reinforce their self-identity and the coherency of their sense of self. This can
be particularly the case with purpose-driven brands. Furthermore, consumers with similar identities form groups and communities. Brand consumption can provide symbolic and conspicuous information about which groups
and communities we associate with, and can therefore enhance a sense of
belonging. Consumers do not just 'buy' value in a transaction: they 'create'
value from, and for, a product/service while using it. Kresse noted the particular emotional connection that attracts consumers to the E&K brand.

> *"Many of our customers save up to buy our bag because it reflects
> their values and they want to wear their heart on their sleeves. When
> people talk about statement handbags . . . well, our bags make a dif-
> ferent statement. Some buy for gifts . . . and that's because you are
> giving more than a thing. You're giving recycling and you're giving
> 'giving.'"*

The strong narrative behind the brand—both the environmental and social
narrative—encourages repeat purchases, an acceptance of the premium
price position and, importantly, active support from customers and an ongoing 'conversation,' both literally (via the web live chat and visits to the
company's workshop) and metaphorically. But it is the brand advocacy that
brings particular saliency dividends. Elvis & Kresse customers are keen to
demonstrate their support through telling the story behind the product
and the enterprise. A good brand can be a powerful educator. It can make
customers think beyond short term, personal gratification and consider the
long-term impact of their choices. By spending money on products that
do not only serve a utilitarian purpose one moves beyond the 'disposable'
mentality of consumption, contributes to the reduction of waste and makes
vital steps towards a more responsible way of living. Customer satisfaction
is multiplied by the emotional and psychological rewards of the act. By
spending money wisely, one moves from being a passive consumer to being
an active participant of the change that is so badly needed in the world.

Doing good can also provide dividends through the improvement of
an enterprise's reputation among external stakeholders. It can enhance
credit-worthiness among investors and banks. A company's environmental and social performance can be a strong indicator of corporate
adaptability, the durability of the company's competitive advantage and

the quality of its leadership. Reputation is built on trust. It is a powerful yet fragile construct that needs continuous nurturing, reinforcement and protection. Leaders have a great responsibility to act as stewards, to protect the core values of the brand and actively seek opportunities to authentically enhance product qualities, communicate the advantages of the brand and work in close partnership with the business environment and society to maximise the positive impact of the brand. A good brand always represents more than the achievements of individual leaders. It is important to serve, first, the long-term interests of the brand rather than the short-term interest of key position holders in the organisation. Brand reputation is a collective achievement and when a brand's reputation is tarnished the responsibilities also stay in the community.

A purpose-driven brand can also save costs through reducing business risks: a more responsible approach and enhanced compliance can reduce the risk of litigation, the cost of accidents and reputational damage. Strong community relations can help preserve a company's social licence to operate: ensuring uninterrupted operations, consistent access to raw materials and less resistance when entering new markets. On this latter point, a strong, *trusted* brand allows for brand extensions—allowing the organisation to gain faster acceptance when launching new products or services and reducing the communication costs, if well known.

Kresse identified a further, significantly positive, dividend arising from her brand proposition: the opportunity to use the brand's credibility to educate and encourage changes in consumer behaviour. Consumers 'learn' from brands—through classical conditioning (conditioned product/service associations with the brand), instrumental learning (positive or negative reinforcement associated with good or bad deeds) and cognitive learning (through observation). Regular customers, and those with an emotional connection to the brand, can be highly effective advocates of the mission too. The interest that Kresse has successfully cultivated through her marketing and her presence in the media has also provided the opportunity to educate scores of young people. Not to build awareness of the 'product,' but to build understanding of the environmental challenges of waste and landfill and to awaken a new generation of warriors. In the early years of the business, Kresse was invited by the Cabinet Office to be a Social Enterprise Ambassador in the UK: to visit schools and colleges, meet journalists and to present at countless functions. She made the most of the platform to educate a considerable audience. In her view, if you don't reach people you can't communicate:

> "*I feel an obligation to show people there is a different way. And I'm proud of what we have achieved. . . . So I do feel like it allows me to be bold and to make statements and ask questions and to prod and push things a little bit further down the road in the direction of something better. I can only do that because running Elvis & Kresse gives me that permission.*"

While Kresse modestly claims she is 'not yet a leader,' her influence in the sustainable fashion and repurposing sector has been significant. Since 2005 her business model for affordable but luxury sustainable fashion has been emulated by numerous start-ups and also by some corporates: "*The industry is coming to meet us, where we are, and conscious consumption is well on the rise.*" Rewarded in 2013 with an MBE, Kresse has inspired a movement that collectively produces significant good dividends.

Good dividends also arise through an enhanced connection with employees and other stakeholders. Companies with a purpose-driven agenda are better able to attract the best and brightest recruits. A strong brand—with a positive organisational culture and values—will motivate employees and build trust and faith in the organisation. Knowing what the brand stands for can provide clarity for employees and help them embody and authentically deliver a consistent experience to customers. With the right motivation and incentives, employees can also be a valuable source of innovation with a vested interest in success. As with the external projection of a brand, internal dividends can therefore also arise from a strong brand: employee commitment, responsiveness, enthusiasm, higher productivity, loyalty and reduced staff turnover (Interbrand, 2018).

Any enterprise wishing to preserve long-term survival in any market needs to be active with innovation. If the business mission is authentically motivated to solving environmental and social problems, then these problems of themselves will drive creative innovation and the results will be a perpetuation of good dividends. Kresse argues that, for purpose-driven brands, innovation is easy:

> "*We are not doing innovation in a crazy wide-open scenario. We're literally looking at a problem and it's a great way to focus the mind. We are looking at waste materials and thinking—what is it? What is it good for? What is its future? How can we extend its life and its value for good.*"

John Bessant, a colleague at Exeter on the One Planet MBA, identified four dimensions of innovation which should come naturally to a purpose-driven brand. *Process* innovation comes from a change in the way products and services are delivered. Production processes can be changed to reduce the use of chemicals, increase the durability of a product, or reduce energy, water and raw materials. Levi's concept of 'water-less' jeans demonstrates a high-profile attempt to significantly reduce water-use in the manufacturing process. *Product* innovation comes when an enterprise changes the type of products and services offered. New products can be introduced to extend the life of a product or to facilitate their recycling. Global brands such as H&M, Levi, Marks & Spencer and Zara have introduced ranges that incorporate environment-friendly raw materials such as organic cotton, Tencel and recycled polyester. *Position* innovation arises when there are changes to the context in which products are framed and communicated. Over the last decade many global brands have sought to instill sustainability within their brand proposition. *Paradigm* innovation involves changes in the underlying mental models that shape what an organisation does. Elvis & Kresse is a good example of a business repurposing waste, and another new business model is emerging for traditional manufacturers. Paradigm innovation is also possible in the service sector. 'Forma Futura,' for example, is an independent Swiss asset management company. They invest responsibly in listed companies. Client funds are invested in a manner that ensures they increase the sustainable quality of life, and at the same time, achieve a fair market return. Linked with Chapter 8 in this volume, Desso, a Dutch manufacturer of carpet tiles, is introducing 'cradle-to-cradle' systems. The business model innovation is the ambition to move from an existing take-back and recycling system to a 'product-service system.' Rather than assuming customers will continue to buy, own and dispose of carpets, products could be reconceived as services that customers lease for a given period. This saves costs on materials, keeps harmful products out of the waste stream and builds relationships between supplier and customer.

Drawing the discussion from this section together on how a purpose-driven brand generates a range of dividends, brand leadership can be seen to be closely associated with responsible leadership—certainly in the case of E&K: the long-term orientation, value enhancement to a range of stakeholders, the collaborative approach to brand development and the sustainable and arguably moral approach to connect the brand to aspects of worthy purpose.

So What Are the Leadership Challenges for Building a Strong Purpose-Driven Brand?

A brand that seeks to be distinctive and valued requires a clarity of purpose and a compelling narrative. Kresse has a strikingly simple and clear mantra, which represents the company's DNA and its brand values: reclaim, transform and donate: *"We've had 13 years to nail it down . . . it's a compelling driving force and it informs everything we do."* The products are all made from reclaimed materials—parachute silk, auction banners, sail cloth, office furniture textiles, canvass printing blankets, leather off-cuts, jute and hessian coffee bags, tea sacks and shoe boxes.

> *"If we started to make our products, with brand new materials, it would be over. And I've seen other companies do this. They start with an environmental story, then want to grow quickly and they lose it. That would be a red line for us. If pure growth was dictating those kinds of actions, we just wouldn't pursue it."*

There is also clarity in design. Whereas product design in a traditional company would start with an idea, for Elvis & Kresse, design begins with a problem. It is the material and the scale of the problem which dictate what they will make and how they will make it: "*In the case of the hose, we scrubbed away the soot and grease that builds up after 25 years of active duty and discovered a truly remarkable textile. We wanted to honour this tough, life-saving material.*" The brand values demand that design is classic and timeless and that products should be made to last as long as the materials they reclaim. There is no ostentation and no desire to make pieces that only last one season. Products are unique, hand-made and based on quality craftsmanship. The transformation process emulates Kintsugi, the Japanese art of repairing broken pottery with lacquer mixed with gold, silver or platinum, where breakage and repair becomes part of the history of an object. The refurbished pieces are worth significantly more than their new, undamaged counterparts. In Kresse's words: "*It would never be enough to give an old fire hose a somewhat useful life: we must transform it, make it desirable or useful in and of itself.*" The clarity of purpose for the enterprise is also reinforced through certification as a BCorp, guiding and reminding the organisation of the essential values for a good dividend business (see Chapter 12 for a discussion on Bcorps as a governance structure that can enable the realisation of good dividends). In an indirect way Elvis & Kresse challenges the disposable mentality of consumerism underpinned by short-term orientation. If everything is continuously replaced then nothing is really valued.

A challenge for any brand is to ensure that its values are *consistent* and reflected in every aspect of its operation. For sustainable brands this is particularly important. Seeking to contribute to an environmental cause in one part of the business, whilst burning up energy in another, will soon challenge the brand's authenticity. Kresse is emphatic about this, not least because of the scrutiny that ethical brands are subjected to. The same brand values 'reclaim and transform' inform the packaging and communication materials. The labels, the stickers, the mail pouches and the foam padding are all reclaimed wastes. Until recently, the company had not used leaflets as they were unsure how to produce them in a way consistent with their values. Kresse now rescues tea sacks, cuts them to size and prints in an ecologically friendly way: "*I prefer to wait until we can do something right. I don't wish to compromise.*"

For a purpose-driven brand, strong values must also be consistent in the way employees are recruited, managed and nurtured. Kresse is particularly proud of the contribution the enterprise is making socially through employment. In 2007 they embarked on a collaboration with Remploy, a disability specialist that supports sustainable employment for the disadvantaged. They also support apprenticeships to bring young and local people into the business: "*It is consistent with our values in so many ways. With an apprenticeship you can rescue a human being by offering that work opportunity. We can transform young people's lives with a worthwhile role and with kindness and respect.*" The company hires skilled talent too, but only if they share, or can learn and adopt, the company's values. This is important to Kresse: "*At one time our Employee Handbook was just one sentence—'If you litter, you're fired.' It set the tone because we all take this business and our example very seriously.*" Consistent with their values, the company is also a living-wage employer. Kresse believes their approach brings commitment, enthusiasm and enhanced productivity—arguments most consistent to that outlined in Chapter 6 through the notion of resourcefulness.

Consistency in an organisation's brand values can also extend to the design of the physical fabric of buildings and offices. We were struck by the approach taken by Kresse to their premises in Tonge, Kent. The building is entirely consistent with their guiding values of reclaim, transform and donate. They have rescued a derelict 200-year-old water mill, restored the building to its former glory and, in Kresse's words, "*given it a chance of life for another century.*" The donation value is reflected not only in recovering the building for future generations, but also in restoring the wildlife habitat in the grounds. The area was previously home to rare water voles, and Elvis and Kresse have used old trees and reconstructed the landscape to provide a protected environment to support the voles' growth.

With a purpose-driven brand, authenticity is crucial. Consumers or employees pledging custom, loyalty and advocacy, will demand that the enterprise is truthful and authentic. Even the best advertising will not create something that is not there. Without authenticity, trust will not follow. Leslie de Chernatony refers to a brand as a 'promise'—an experience that must be delivered consistently and authentically over time—and a failed promise in any relationship will lead to loss of trust (de Chernatony, 2010). The Boston Consulting Group (2011) has highlighted enhanced brand reputation as a benefit of addressing sustainability. However, if sustainability credentials can build a company's image, those credentials can also be easily damaged. Companies that fail to live by a set of declared principles may get away with it for a while, but intense scrutiny and negative feedback from customers (facilitated by the instant nature of online communications between activists, bloggers and consumers) can bring a brand down. Unless reality matches rhetoric, making sustainability claims is a risky business. We assert that it must be authentic, credible and defendable.

For a purpose-driven brand, a key demonstration of authenticity is vested in the personal behaviour of managers and employees. Brands are delivered by people, and so the CMO leader, and indeed all directors and employees, should be a living manifestation of the brand values. We have, sadly, seen countless examples where the behaviour of executives has fallen short of appropriate standards, with significant implications for both the executive and the organisation's value. We personally remember two classic examples, which were broadcast on TV—and now preserved forever on YouTube—which highlight the point: in 1991, the jokes by

Gerald Ratner at the Institute of Directors Annual Convention, denigrated the poor quality of his products. And the statement in 2010 by BP CEO Tony Haywood, commenting, in the face of the worst oil spill in US history and the death of 11 workers, that he wanted 'my life back' (Reuters, 2010). For a purpose-driven brand, consumers, employees, suppliers and investors look to the organisation's leaders to be exemplary and consistent brand ambassadors. Any opposing or inconsistent messages damage consumer faith and trust.

Related to authenticity is the increasing need for ethical brands to prove their credentials. Transparency is important to enable traceability. Individual transparency is closely connected with corporate transparency as they continuously reinforce each other. Without transparency, secrecy creeps in, followed by manipulation and game playing and these lead to a toxic environment that can ruin brands and individual lives. The fashion sector is noted for its secrecy with IP and new designs and, in some cases, a desire to hide what might be happening in their complex supply chains. Consumers, however, often want to know how products get to market. Kresse believes passionately in transparency. "*We are a 100% transparent brand. We are vertically integrated. We manufacture almost everything ourselves, so we know where it is from. We can't make the zippers, but we source from YKK and they are covered by ISO14001 and so on, so we can trace and track.*" The transparency extends further for customers. Elvis & Kresse advertise an open invitation to customers and interested observers to "*visit our home at Tonge Mill*" to see how their products are made. They also offer an opportunity to engage in a hands-on immersion in the waste-to-product process: joining workshops where customers can design and make their own 'Fire and Hide' clutch bag, as well as share an evening with the business owners. This level of openness does not only confirm transparency it makes the abstract ideas of sustainable brand, values, long-term commitment to waste reduction a lived, observable and co-created experience. It offers a powerful example that an alternative way of being, working and leading is possible and achievable. It also conveys a strong 'can do' attitude and inspires visitors to review their own practices and make more responsible choices.

A consumer's perception of a brand emerges from a holistic experience. First, is the experience of the products, services and advertising messages that are laid out in front of them by brand owners. Second, is the lived experience of the brand: owning and using the product, listening to others about their experiences and engaging with the array of customer-company touch-points. Effectively, this holistic brand experience is a 'conversation'—an ever changing, continuous, literal and metaphorical dialogue between an organisation and its customers. As such, a brand experience needs to be continuously curated, narrated and maintained. With purpose-driven brands, where consumers have a stronger emotional connection and often seek to become a part of a community, the scale and depth of the conversation can increase. Kresse enjoys the interactions and the rewards, but admits her greatest challenge along the way is the *'relentless'* need for engagement: *"You can't stop for a minute, when you are dealing directly with customers. They expect availability and engagement all the time."* Although the leader's visibility and continuous connection with existing and future customers is important, inviting willing customers to engage more actively and act as ambassadors for the brand can enhance the impact of the brand, creating a ripple effect in communities and transferring the philosophy of Kresse to a broader range of possible initiatives.

If organisations are authentic about their missions, and the goal beyond financial sustainability is to drive social and environmental change, then partnerships and collaborations are more likely to be entertained. In working with partners, a purpose-driven brand can acquire networks and resources to extend their capability and capacity to achieve impact and change on a broader scale. Reflecting the arguments outlined in Chapter 7 regarding social innovation and the progression of social innovation with partners, Elvis & Kresse have recently announced a major partnership with the Burberry Foundation, a high profile and major corporate actor in the global fashion business. Elvis & Kresse had already embarked on its second mission to tackle the 800,000 tons of leather waste going to landfill, but the new partnership with Burberry is, according to Kresse, *"designed to super-charge' the rescue mission."* The Burberry Foundation has provided a grant to support Elvis & Kresse's work and to transform at least 120 tons of leather off-cuts from the production of Burberry products into a new range of accessories and homeware. The partnership *"aims to affect real change in the supply chain of the leather goods industry,"* provide apprenticeship and work experience opportunities for young people and reach thousands through public events, competitions and workshops (Elvis and Kresse, 2018). For Burberry, the partnership supports its new 'Responsibility' agenda, of which a key role is to invent new approaches to revaluing waste. Kresse has been cautious about joining partners in the past when they have challenged the values of the enterprise or when the motivations were for show rather than for real. A partnership has to be based on trust and similar values, otherwise consumers will see through it: *"We evaluate all prospective partners. Like in a marriage: do I trust them? Do I trust their motivations? We need partners who understand us and understand that sharing is a good idea."*

Reflections on Purpose-Driven Brand Leadership

Our expectations of brand leaders are changing. It is no longer enough to continuously increase shareholder value and financial dividends. Leaders are also expected to follow a higher purpose and engage the brand in deeply meaningful activities that bring good dividends to all stakeholders and contribute positively to pressing global issues. The socioeconomic, geopolitical and cultural-spiritual challenges of our time are interconnected

(Guattari, 2000). The enormity of these challenges requires a review of how humans relate to themselves, to each other and to the environment in a more responsible way (Obolensky, 2010). To address these issues we need a fundamental change of perspective. "Not only do we have to change things, but we have to change the way we see things" (Brabandere, 2005: xi). The power and responsibility of brand leaders are significant. Strong brands are, by definition, well known and they can significantly influence choices and behaviours. By expanding the values and visibility of the brand to pressing global issues they invite consumers to buy into and support the higher purpose behind products and services. As the case of Elvis & Kresse illustrates, a purpose-driven brand can educate consumers and organisations about collective and individual responsibilities for our planet, our communities and the legacy we leave for future generations.

We suggest that leaders need to have clarity about their personal values and purpose and fully and passionately commit to the needs and the potential good dividends of the brand. Without an authentic and virtuous character it is simply not feasible or likely to be able to lead and ignite the creative passion and drive in others. Good brand leaders guard the values of the organisation, support inclusivity, release the energy of people, enlarge the human and intellectual capital of employees, build a purpose-driven community and educate consumers and customers. According to Laloux "the level of consciousness of an organisation cannot exceed the level of consciousness of its leader" (2014: 239). Leaders project their views, values and beliefs onto an organisation. Consciously, and often subconsciously, they drive the organisation in the direction that is close to their personal views of the world. It is a great competitive advantage when the personal values and purpose of the leader are closely aligned with the underlying values and purpose of the brand. When there is a good fit, the leader passionately serves the interests of the brand. He/she will become one with the brand and protect its reputation with his/her whole being. Elvis & Kresse was built on the founder's passion for sustainability and waste reduction. This passion gave the leadership energy and made 'reclaim, transform, donate' not only the published, but also the 'lived' values of the organisation.

We opened with our personal reflections as educators engaged with developing future managers. Reflexively considering our examination of E&K and in particular Kress's leadership this has reinforced our conviction for the need for responsible management education. In particular in terms of giving far greater emphasis to value rationality in the curricula and initiatives to develop the whole person. By whole person we mean self-knowledge, personal values, opportunities for character formation, finding purpose and meaning. By whole person we mean battling with real life ethical dilemmas embedded in an understanding of the economic, social and environmental challenges that they will have to embrace. And reference to examples of brand leaders such as Elvis & Kresse can only beneficially impact on individuals, behaviours, values and choices of future generations.

10 Planetary Dividend
Leadership as Stewardship

Thomas Maak and Nicola M. Pless

The End of the World as We Know It—One Degree at a Time

"Seventy thousand years ago, *homo sapiens* was still an insignificant animal minding its own business in a corner of Africa. In the following millennia it transformed itself into the master of the entire planet and the terror of the ecosystem. Today it stands on the verge of becoming a god, poised to acquire (. . .) the divine abilities of creation and destruction" (Harari, 2014: 465).

The Israeli historian Yuval Harari closes his compelling history of *homo sapiens* with a rather grim afterword, questioning whether the Sapiens regime has a lot to be proud of. He asks whether we really have decreased suffering in, and of, the world, and doubts that we have used our accumulated power wisely. In fact, he argues that we have very little idea what to do with all the power and that "humans seem to be more irresponsible than ever" (p. 466). He then drops a final question: "Is there anything more dangerous than dissatisfied and irresponsible gods who don't know what they want?" (p. 466).

Looking back at the history of sustainable development and global economic growth over the past two decades or so, one must get the impression that the almighty homo sapiens are indeed torn between relentless growth to feed the "myth of the machine" (Mumford, 1967)—a highly integrated global economy—and her/his return to reason, perhaps in the form of sustainable development goals (SDGs), to save our planet and our communities she/he has mastered so inadequately. This chapter is about the reasons why we must put aside our differences and act in the interest of humanity's survival—and *the use of reason by leaders to help build sustainable futures.*

It is about time: "Oh men, oh mankind! Will you never become reasonable? Did our fathers and forefathers not wreak havoc enough, must we commit the same mistakes?" It was Goethe's main character Wilhelm Meister who made this timeless statement some 225 years ago at the end of his "wandering years", doubtful about his future in a world where men seem to repeat the same mistakes over and over again (Goethe,

1992: 954). And it was 45 years ago when E.F. Schumacher published a small but compelling book, entitled "Small is beautiful." His pledge for a purposeful, sustainable economy and lifestyle was labelled "new age economics" when it was first published but its core argument remains as timely as ever: "the modern industrial system, with all its intellectual sophistication, consumes the very basis on which it has been erected" (Schumacher, 1973: 21)—only at a much larger scale than in 1973.

According to the Global Footprint Network we currently use 1.7 Earths (2018)—see Figure 10.1. At a country level the figures are even more alarming with some countries consuming at a scale of 5 Earths. Hence, with an estimated rapid global population growth and the further rise of some Asian economies' sustainability seems to be moving further out of reach than ever—unless responsible leadership and action is being taken to curb this completely unsustainable development.

Schumacher also reminds us that "to talk about the future is useful only if it leads to action *now*" (1973: 21), urging a course correction at the individual, organizational and systemic level.

The good news is that we live in times where reason has evolved and normative truths exist. We may disagree fiercely on what that truth is, but were it not to exist we would have no reason to try to determine how to live—and thus to protect the planet we inhabit. Hence, while for some global warming is a left-wing conspiracy of green activists using the wrong data—some researchers try to use statistical data and probability mechanics to show that global warming is nothing but a myth (Green and Armstrong, 2007). For the majority on this planet, however,

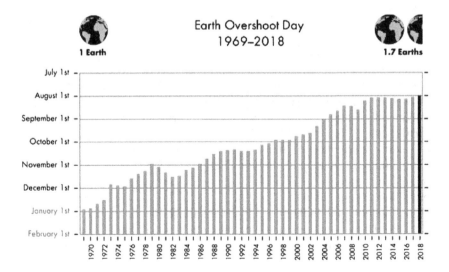

Figure 10.1 Earth Overshoot Day

Source: Global Footprint Network National Footprint Accounts 2018

global warming has become *the moral concern of our generation* and a question of survival for future generations to come—coral bleaching, extreme weather conditions, micro-plastic pollution of sea life around the world—being just some of the concerns.

Forty years ago the philosopher Hans Jonas argued that no previous generation had "to consider the global conditions of human life, the distant future, and indeed, human existence as such"—making the impact of our "technological civilization" on the planet an unprecedented ethical concern (1979: 28). Not surprisingly, many educated citizens find it ironic, some outright appalling, that we still debate the environment as if the past 40 years have not produced enough evidence of the moral urgency and indeed, *the need for a climate pact*.

Stephen Gardiner goes a step further; he predicts the "perfect moral storm" should we not finally start to take substantial action to protect our planet and our communities, calling it the "ethical tragedy of climate change" (2011). We know that humanity faces unprecedented climate change; we also know that we should do something about it; however, we don't seem to be able to engage in the concerted action to save and preserve this planet for generations to come. In other words, there is a *significant gap in the climate debate* between what we think we know about climate change and our activation of the human means at our disposal to do something about it (Chakrabarty, 2014). The *ethical tragedy* here is that the storm Gardiner envisions is unprecedented; that power is distributed unequally between affluent and developing countries, as well as between current and future generations; and we don't have robust theories to guide us (Gardiner, 2011: 7). The storm conditions are such that we risk being blown off course unless we engage in ethical action and overcome scientific and ideological differences.

However, as we said earlier, at least we give and respond to reasons and can thus elaborate on our differences. In a world without reasons, we would only follow our instinct and desires (Parfitt, 2011). It may not always seem like it, but humanity is better than that—we are part of one planet and indeed, a universe, that is starting to understand itself and as Derek Parfit points out, "we can partly understand, not only what is in fact true, but also what ought to be true, and what we might be able to make true"; adding that "what now matters most is that we avoid ending human history" (Parfitt, 2011: 620).

Hence, it is time to tap into the beauty of the human mind, leveraging its ingenuity, and unleashing the *moral willpower* to address the sustainability challenge. Closing the knowing-doing gap, however, requires responsible leadership at all levels, in organizations, communities and societies. When we speak here in this chapter of the planet we seek to be inclusive of the environmental and social dynamics. As outlined in Chapter 4 there is a strong systemic relationship between, for example, all of the following: climate change and migration, modern slavery and human rights, water and food security, famine and obesity, drought and flooding. Indeed, such issues impact in various ways across all communities that businesses are engaged with. The notion of "one-planet" (WWF) is concerned with global as well as very local dynamics. Because of the most central influence of climate change on the other grand challenges we shall give this priority attention in this chapter. However, we could have written the chapter in 10, 20 or indeed 30 different ways to explore the variety of the haunting challenges that face humanity and which are encapsulated within the planetary dividend. We have chosen to undertake an in-depth examination of climate change.

Our chapter is structured as follows. We will first elaborate in more detail on the idea of the planetary dividend. Given the unprecedented challenge of climate change we will then ask the question whether we face a "wicked problem" and what the role of leaders is in tackling it. Our argument is such that we propose an explicit stewardship ethos and will third, elaborate on why it is needed.' Finally, we address the question of unequal consequences and access to resources pertaining to current, disadvantaged generations in developing countries and future generations on this planet and hence the question of intra-and intergenerational justice Gardiner raises when he imagines the "perfect moral storm."

A Planetary Dividend

We contend that leaders have a *moral obligation* to engage in ethical reasoning processes on the future of this planet because they *share responsibility* for positive outcomes in areas pertaining to the sustainable development goals. In line with the overall objective of this book we suggest that leaders ought to entertain the idea of a *planetary dividend*— enriching and giving back to communities and the environment what they and their organizations have taken. Hence, at the heart of the planetary dividend lies the moral concept of stewardship.

The idea of stewardship is not new and yet, despite efforts to re-invigorate the stewardship ethos for leadership (Block, 1993; Maak and Pless, 2006a, 2009a), the notion that leaders must protect and enrich what they are entrusted with and that they should focus on the needs of future generations while serving the needs of the present, has yet to get the traction it deserves. The reasons for this are manifold: first, there is the built-in conflict of short-termism in business versus a long-term ethos; second, the moral conviction that leaders must contribute to sustainable futures often remains just that, a moral conviction and belief system in tension with the operational pressures of profit and short-term results; and third, sustainable management approaches are often driven by economic and technical considerations rather than the conviction that it is the right thing to do. This leaves sustainability vulnerable to changes in the operating environment in the absence of a clear sustainable purpose.

Although the empirical evidence for climate change can only be described as overwhelming, excuses for non-action remain omnipresent. More specifically, even if economists would come up with a cost-benefit analysis of welfare loss due to climate change—calculating the damage function from weather extremes, rising sea water levels, and human loss and displacement—the urgency and sheer magnitude of climate change is such that *we must accept the fact that the global climate system is changing in relatively predictable ways and action can be taken and managed by human ingenuity, moral motivation, and political will* (Weitzman, 2009; Chakrabarty, 2014). Thus, there is *no good reason* to wait—"we will never get a more exact estimate than we already have" (Edwards, 2010: 439). As John Maynard Keynes once famously said, "in the long run, we are all dead." The potential catastrophic rise of sea water levels and the resulting effect on global climate would throw economic calculations haywire (Chakrabarty, 2014: 5). Hence, economic cost-benefit analysis to tackle climate change leads to "cost-benefit paralysis" (Gardiner, 2011, ch.8)—leading to climate change inertia at a time when humanity arguably needs decisive action to secure its survival.

Concomitantly, the idea of a *planetary dividend* cannot be seen as an economic one but must be developed from an *integrative* perspective, coupling a stewardship ethos with practical consideration in regards to the social and environmental implications of one's actions. The idea of the dividend is a compelling one because it implies a *positive net result* rather than a neutralized impact on the environment, let alone the mere offset of emissions or pollution. In other words, the idea of the planetary dividend requires from leaders that they aspire and achieve a positive net impact of their organizations' social and environmental performance—*leaving both people and planet better off.*

Additionally, in Chapter 4 we have argued that organizations gain from the planetary dividend. By connecting the organization's sense of purpose with planetary and community needs there would be positive dividends to employee resourcefulness, as well as to the reputational and brand dividend of the organization. The systemic connection of the planetary dividend with the system of good dividends provides a deeply centred capitalistic reason for embracing the planetary dividend—argued in Chapter 2 as moral capitalism. But it is more than this.

Hence, we suggest considering the idea of a planetary dividend as an inherently *integrative concept*, is beyond mere economic calculations. This is not to say that such calculations of impact and net result are not helpful—they are in that they illustrate in tangible ways the actual impact of the Anthropocene on the natural environment. However, not everything that is important can be counted and not all things counted are important. In other words, just because something cannot be exactly measured doesn't mean that it doesn't deserve attention. That said, new forms of measurement can raise immediate awareness. For example, in 2015 the World Wildlife Fund (WWF) published a study produced in collaboration with The Global Change Institute at the University of Queensland and The Boston Consulting Group (BCG) valuing the ocean's value at 24 trillion US dollars, making it the world's seventh largest economy, albeit one that is rapidly diminishing because of overfishing and pollution risking to throw global climate off-balance. Already, the summer of 2018 appears to be one of the hottest on record in Europe, a clear sign for climate scientists that weather extremes are increasing as the regulatory function of the world's oceans diminishes, mainly because of global warming and rising sea temperatures. More specifically, "the ocean's value is quantified based on assessments of goods and services ranging from fisheries to coastal storm protection, resulting in an overall asset value and an annual dividend output (comparable to a GDP)" (WWF, 2015). Thus, the WWF works with the idea of a planetary dividend and we would argue these attempts to measure our socio-ecological footprint are helpful—if they are driven by the appropriate ethical concerns. The former is required to convince the naysayers, the latter to make it impactful and sustainable.

The integration of ethical concerns, moral drivers and practical action also addresses the aforementioned pertinent issue: the debate and actions pertaining to climate change suffer from *chronicle paralysis* at the interface of sustainability advocacy and climate change denial. Let us make an assertion: The conflict between believers and non-believers in climate change can only be overcome through integrative responsible leadership (Pless, Maak and Waldman, 2012; Maak, Pless and Voegtlin, 2016), driven by a moral commitment to sustainable futures.

We therefore agree with Gardiner that climate change is first and foremost an *ethical concern*, and not a technical, economical, or scientific issue. Of course, solving the climate crisis and saving our planet requires technical solutions, smart economics and advances in all relevant scientific disciplines; however, humanity will not be able to unleash advances in these areas unless there is political will and ethical motivation to make the necessary leaps. Indeed, Jonas (1979) argues convincingly that current generations must apply moral imagination to consider their *potential* impact on the future—just because we have not experienced the apocalypse, and thus lack the concrete evidence of what it's like, does not mean that we have an excuse to risk it!

Is Climate Change a Wicked Problem?

Moreover, there is increasing pressure from stakeholders (among them NGOs, consumers and the broader public) on business leaders to use their power and influence to take on more active roles as global citizens, beyond charitable action (Maak and Pless, 2009b); the role of business leaders, especially leaders of large corporations, is in enabling sustainable futures. Such leaders are not only asked to engage in environmental protection, but also to practice self-regulation and contribute to the production of global public goods. The call for business leaders to act as responsible citizens and statesmen (Chin, Hambrick and Trevino, 2013) mirrors the new political role of business in a globalized world (Scherer and Palazzo, 2011), and concomitantly that of top executives as decision makers who act on behalf of the corporation. Chief executive officers (CEOs) in particular shape the decision-making context for important strategic choices pertaining to the vision, mission and strategic direction of their organization, including sustainability and corporate social responsibility initiatives (Chin et al., 2013; McWilliams and Siegel, 2001). However, this book seeks to illustrate the opportunity for business wide activity, beyond the functional confines of CSR and sustainability departments, to undertake responsible leadership rather than the limited (but important) championing of the CEO and the CSR director.

The good news is that business leaders individually and collectively have made advances to address the grand challenge of climate change and align their actions with the ambitious but necessary agenda of the sustainable development goals (SDGs)—see Chapter 13 for an example of a small business that has done just this. The World Business Council on Sustainable Development may be the most prominent example.

Or, consider the consistent and far reaching route the world market leader in insulin production, the Danish company Novo Nordisk, has taken to integrate sustainable development goals and policies in its operations (Kingo and Stormer, 2011). What is interesting and perhaps telling about Novo Nordisk though is that the firm's commitment to SDGs is rooted in company values that date back to its founding more than 90 years ago. The founder's values, translated into 10 principles called "The Essentials", and a history of deep engagement with sustainability around the world, led to a relatively well integrated approach—merging ethics and concrete action based on technological expertise. However, the company also acknowledges the complexity of SDGs and climate change and consults with stakeholders on the requirements for positive change on a regular basis, more recently in a "Blueprint for Change Forum".

Indeed, it could be argued that the problems and challenges arising from climate change are "wicked", multi-dimensional, interconnected problems spanning sectors, organizations, countries, continents, disciplines and generations—past, present and future; affecting the Anthropocene, or human-centred world as a whole. As mentioned above, we don't know *exactly* how climate change will affect us—we know though that it will end badly if we don't act now; climate change affects richer and poorer countries in different ways—who should scale back at what rate and based on which criteria? Whatever we do will affect *future generations*—what are their rights in light of the fact what we have taken from the one planet we share across generations; and what is perhaps our responsibility towards our forefathers who have built and one could argue, sustained, the planet we inherited?

Chakrabarty (2017: 27) makes the point that if we stop looking at climate change as a linear, one-dimensional problem that can be solved through technological wit and market signals, but, rather, as a "complex family of interconnected problems" making up the footprint and ecological overshoot on the part of humanity—then we would see the urgency, complexity, and yes, *the wickedness of climate change*. We humans know what is at stake but we also know that we may not be able to solve the problem for good. What we know is that it affects rich and poor, north and south, current and future generations. Unlike in recent crises of global capitalism, however, "there are no lifeboats here for the rich and the privileged" (Chakrabarty, 2009: 221).

Keith Grint (2005), building on Rittel and Webber (1973), calls problems "wicked" when they are complex, intractable, not having a unilinear solution, often generating other "problems", having no right-or-wrong answer, but only better or worse alternatives. Wicked problems require leadership—leaders who ask the right questions and facilitate a collaborative process to generate the best alternative to tackle the problem (2005: 1473). In contrast, tame problems have a low degree of uncertainty (because they are not novel, but known), are complicated but "resolvable through unilinear acts" and thus can be managed through appropriate processes to generate a solution (such as, for example, integrating sustainability into the value chain based on a best-practice approach—see Chapter 8 for details on this).

Earth system science insights reiterate the need for a more integrated, encompassing view when it comes to climate change, a view that mirrors the actual complexity and interconnectedness of the problems (Reid et al., 2010; Liu et al., 2007). More specifically, it is suggested that action is taken on three trajectories: (1) understanding the non-linear dynamics of climate change or, more precisely, of coupled human and natural systems; (2) determine institutional, economic and behavioural changes pertaining to concrete and effective steps toward global sustainability; and (3) encourage technological, political and social innovation to achieve global sustainability (Reid et al., 2010: 917).

Therefore, *leadership for sustainable futures requires the willingness and ability to mirror the complexity of interconnected problems* and thus significant integrative qualities (Maak et al., 2016). At a very minimum one could appeal to the enlightened self-interest of present and future leaders. However, given the urgency of the matter and the necessity of concrete action, moral willpower and motivation is required embedded in an ethical perspective that spans generations, ideologies and overcomes short-term thinking. We contend that such a perspective is at the heart of a stewardship ethos applicable across all the challenges that face communities and humanity and will therefore elaborate on the idea of leadership as stewardship and its propensity to achieve planetary dividends in more detail in the following section.

Plunderers of the Earth or Planetary Citizens? Leadership as Stewardship

Leadership as stewardship is a powerful but underutilized concept. Stewardship is to hold something in trust—deriving its meaning from the historical role of the steward as someone who was entrusted with protecting a kingdom and its resources while the king or those rightfully in charge were away or still underage (Block, 1993). Indeed, the purpose of stewardship was quite often to govern for the underage king or queen. Hence, stewardship is a fitting metaphor if we consider the underage king or queen as the next generation(s).

A responsible leader as steward is someone who understands themselves as a custodian of social, moral and environmental values and resources, trusted with their protection and enrichment, and guided by the question "What am I passing on to (the) future generation(s)?" (Maak and Pless, 2006a: 108). Concomitantly, the steward becomes the *moral trustee*— and the *voice*—for planet and future generations. Thus, the stewardship ethos provides an important normative foundation for tackling the wicked problem of climate change and safeguarding the virtual interests of future generations.

Stewardship reflects a clear sense of commitment and duty to others, and future generations in particular, expressed by the explicit subjugation of personal interests to act in the protection of future generations' welfare (Hernandez, 2012). Inherent to the concept of stewardship are therefore a sense of moral obligation and a clearly espoused sense of other-regard directed at broadly beneficial ends in the sense of *future collective welfare* for generations to come.

While research on stewardship is limited and thus far mainly concerned with replacing the agency paradigm with a more pro-social concept (Davis, Schoorman and Donaldson, 1997; Hernandez, 2012), its intellectual appeal to address the pertinent challenges of the planet and in particular climate change is obvious. We argued earlier that an ethical perspective is required to overcome the uncertainties of climate change and the deficiencies and temptations of the economic system. A stewardship ethos does so in three ways: (1) because it is directed at the welfare of others, specifically the collective welfare of future generations, and where self-serving economic behaviour remains an exception rather than the rule; (2) stewardship entails a long-term perspective and outlook on the role of business and its impact on the environment and future generations, overcoming the prevalent short-termism in managerial decision-making; and (3) stewardship gives future generations and thus otherwise powerless stakeholders a voice and recognition.

In practice, the depth of moral conviction and the actual scope of engagement directed at sustainable futures will vary. Well-known examples include Dame Anita Roddick, founder of The Body Shop, who considered herself a "planetary citizen" and committed herself and her company to an extensive sustainability agenda (Pless, 2007, 2011); and the late Ray Anderson, CEO of the world's largest carpet manufacturer Interface, who embarked in the 1990s on what he labelled a "mid-course correction" (1998). Challenged by his managers to give them a sustainability vision he admitted to not having one at first, but then, while reading Hawken's *The Ecology of Commerce*, experiencing an epiphany of being "a plunderer of the earth." Hawken writes in his book about the "the death of birth", a fitting metaphor for the growing extinction of species. Ray Anderson subsequently not only developed a sustainability vision for Interface but he engaged the company in a profound transformation of its business from a "traditional polluter" to becoming an exemplary zero-emission business, exhibiting a clearly espoused and inspiring stewardship ethos. A lesser known, but equally compelling example, is Yvon Chouinard's leadership of apparel maker and outdoor company Patagonia—which has vowed to be a force to help solve the environmental crisis and stopped business growth when it became unsustainable as a victim of its own success (Chouinard, 2005). On closer examination we find steward leaders in all countries and economies and their leadership in enabling sustainable futures should give us hope that the idea of a planetary dividend will receive the attention it deserves.

The Justice Challenge

To design the planetary dividend as an inherently moral concept, and to propose a stewardship ethos as its driving force, is important in regards to key challenges arising for distributive and intergenerational justice.

We have argued above that stewardship is required for at least three reasons: first, to overcome the built-in conflict of short-termism in business versus a long-term ethos; second, to master the inherent operational pressures resulting from such short-termism and the fact that others may not care as much about communities, the environment and future generations; and third, to balance the techno-managerial framing of climate change with an ethical perspective and clear purpose for action. However, from a justice perspective the role of a stewardship ethos is arguably even more crucial.

Let's first consider the question of *intergenerational equity and justice*. At the heart of the debate on sustainable futures, as Anand and Sen (2000) have pointed out, is the basic belief that the interests of future generations *should* receive the same kind of attention and recognition that present generations claim for themselves. The "should" here connotes a clear sense of moral universalism such that "sustainability", at its core, is "a particular reflection of universality of claims—applied to the future generations *vis-à-vis* us" (Anand and Sen, 2000: 2030). Anand and Sen put it in simple prose:

> We cannot abuse and plunder our common stock of natural assets and resources leaving the future generations unable to enjoy the opportunities we take for granted today. We cannot use up, or contaminate, our environment as we wish, violating the rights and the interests of future generations.
>
> (2000: 2030)

Hence, from a justice perspective the questions of sustainability become one of equal rights and opportunities to assets, resources and enjoyment of our natural habitats requiring the *recognition of our shared claim to a life worth living*—at present and in the future.

Now, in light of the psychological distance between current and future generations, the fact that consequences of one's actions are temporally and physically removed from the decision maker, combined with the above mentioned operational pressures and the tendency of egocentrism (individual and organizational) inherent to economic activity, this moral claim would seem to have a hard time of getting traction (Wade-Benzoni, Hernandez, Medvec and Messick, 2008). Unless, that is, actors consider the ethical implications and indeed, the ethical need, of stewardship in addressing matters pertaining to sustainability.

Wade-Benzoni and colleagues (2008, 2010) and Bang, Zhou-Koval and Wade-Benzoni (2017) have investigated the role of stewardship in a series of experiments. Their findings confirm the key role of a stewardship ethos—implicit or explicit—in decisions pertaining to future generations. Individuals conscious of the ethical implications of an allocation decision will behave more generously to future others, such that highlighting intergenerational choices and their ethical implications encourages actors to think more about future others as well as their own legacies (Wade-Benzoni, Sondak and Galinsky, 2010: 29). Moreover, if the context elicits responsibility and stewardship concerned actors will tend to act in more pro-social ways to distant others (Wade-Benzoni et al., 2008), highlighting the role of both stewardship mindset and an organizational context conducive to sustainability. In a more recent study Bang et al. (2017) investigated the interplay of intent, outcome and feelings of stewardship stressing the role previous generations' intentions can play in strengthening actual stewardship.

What these experiments confirm is in essence the crucial role stewardship considerations play in making decisions pertaining to generations in the future. More specifically, claims of intergenerational justice are claims of moral universalism and therefore require leaders to reflect the socio-moral complexity of these claims through the appropriate moral thinking and motivation. At their heart lies the realization that we share a cultural legacy and habitat with past and future generations and *that we share a distinctive space* to whose creation no individual or organization has contributed more than any other—thus, "an *asymmetrical capacity to shape the natural world* is the source of future generations' legitimate expectations" (Risse, 2012: 169). Hence, the stewardship ethos embodies a boundary-spanning mental frame honouring the cultural accomplishments of previous generations *and* the legitimate moral claims of future generations, bridging and indeed, *linking past, present and future generations*.

In conclusion, in order to meet the emerging and legitimate needs of future generations and in light of the critical impact of humanity on many species and the natural environment it has become clear that we would need a form of *strong sustainability* to achieve our targets (Neumayer, 2000). The problem is, as we have explained above, that at best we have managed to endorse a notion of "weak sustainability" in which all forms of capital are substitutable—carbon offset schemes being just one example. A notion of *strong sustainability*, however, assumes that given the delicate balance of ecosystems some resources, goods, species are not substitutable for each other. Thus, to make sure that regenerative capacities remain intact, that species are protected, and that ecosystems can continue to function becomes a leadership challenge. For strong sustainability to work, however, leaders must not be distracted by the fact that values are contested and vague, but instead recognize the rightful moral claim of future generations as good reasons to act now, as their trustees and stewards.

Let's now consider the question of *intragenerational justice*. In contrast to questions and ideas of intergenerational justice, matters of *intragenerational* justice concern the present, not the future. They are at once more accessible and some may argue, more urgent. However, because they raise issues pertaining to distributional equity among current generations— north and south, rich and poor, developed and least developed—and make poverty alleviation and the inequitable use of resources at a global level a matter of sustainability, they are, by and large, even more contested claims. Put differently, we are not talking about our next of kin and their human capabilities in the future, but about human development and flourishing of others in the present.

More specifically, questions of intragenerational equity refer to the impact of climate change on the very poor and the role of the poor in the process of sustainable development. The World Bank has made it clear that poverty alleviation plays a key role in achieving global sustainability goals, an argument that since has been incorporated in the SDGs:

> The poor are both victims and agents of environmental damage. About half of the world's poor live in rural areas that are environmentally

fragile . . . and they rely on natural resources over which they have little legal control. . . . The very poor, struggling at the edge of subsistence, are pre-occupied with day-today survival. It is not that the poor have inherently short horizons; poor communities often have a strong ethic of stewardship in managing their traditional lands. But their fragile and limited resources . . . prevent them from investing as much as they should in environmental protection.

(World Bank, 1992: 30)

Sustainability was, and is, a global problem and challenge for future generations. What the World Bank argument stresses is that for sustainable development to work we must also consider it as *human development*. Indeed, human development should be considered an integral and key component of sustainable development: it enhances the capability of people, especially the poor and the very poor, to lead worthwhile lives and to be able to contribute to the SDGs in the first place (Anand and Sen, 2000). Hence, the leadership challenge of intragenerational justice is to acknowledge the moral responsibility of protecting and enhancing the well-being and livelihood of present people—at home and abroad. In other words, moral universalism demands from us to consider the poor and deprived at present *and* the well-being of future generations simultaneously. This involves some form of redistribution to the poor and very poor to improve their health and education and enable them to contribute to sustainable futures (Anand and Sen, 2000). As human beings we are naturally inclined to care more for our next of kin and "our grandchildren;" we also owe more to those we share a state with than to others in, say, the developing world. However, irrespective of the aforementioned moral obligation to the poor, from a "one planet" perspective we all share the same limited resources our global habitat has to offer and as a consequence both rich and poor are members of the same planetary community. By virtue of our common humanity and shared planetary membership we are bound by the same sphere of social justice (Young, 2011). This is why we owe each other at least *some* form of mutual support to lead a life worth living and subsequently mutual enablement to contribute to a sustainable world. Thus, from an intragenerational justice and development perspective we are asked to acknowledge the *moral obligation to assist the poor* in the pursuit of sustainable futures and to define our *social obligations towards others as planetary citizens*.

One Planet, One Purpose: Towards Dignified Sustainable Futures

We stated earlier that the idea of a *planetary dividend* must be developed from an *integrative* perspective, coupling a stewardship ethos with practical consideration in regards to the social and environmental implications of one's actions resulting in a *positive net result* rather than a neutralized impact on the environment—*leaving both people and planet better off.* In the last section we provided reasons as to why such integrative stewardship requires boundary-spanning intentions and capabilities, linking past, present and future (intergenerational justice) *and* involves concerns for adequate redistribution of resources and human development of the least privileged both at home and abroad (intragenerational justice).

Thus, leadership requires a clear sense of moral obligation and purpose. The purpose of leadership in striving towards sustainable futures is to make sure that the planetary dividend takes shape and concomitant goals are set. Given the urgency to act it is arguably one of the most important leadership projects to consider. And while many advances have been made in areas such as renewable energy, zero-emission business and smart technology, the world is deeply divided, ironically more than it was some 20 years ago, such that the prospect of fulfilling the SDGs anytime soon are slim.

Business leaders in particular have therefore a responsibility to advance sustainable development as stewards of their organizations. They have both the power and the means to overcome the global political divide: at least 69 of the world's largest economies are companies, not nation states (World Bank, 2016)—a number that is likely to increase in the near future. In 2018, Amazon.com has overtaken New Zealand, a hardly noticed but symbolic step towards an increasingly corporatized global economy. In light of the deep political divide on climate change this may not necessarily be a bad thing; indeed, it may provide a chance for corporations to push for more ambitious climate change targets provided they use their growing power in responsible ways, driven by a clearer sense of purpose and—as we have argued here—a stewardship ethos endorsing a notion of strong sustainability for the benefit of current and future stakeholders.

In Chapter 13 the argument for business leaders as stewards taking responsibility for advancing sustainable development is outlined. An in-depth examination of pursuing this responsibility to realise the planetary dividend is explored in the context of a small business. Luke Freeman applies the SDGs to his business by identifying which SDG aligns most closely to the purpose they are pursuing and which connects most strongly to the stakeholders of the business. Luke's case study should be seen as a companion and empirical explorations to the underpinning arguments we have outlined here.

Leading with purpose in the context of dramatic climate change means that business leaders must act as planetary citizens, making sure that their organizations generate planetary dividends and act as agents of world benefit—even if there is no immediate tangible gain from doing so. In the context of sustainable futures the benefit will always be directed at others, current and future generations. But that is what we as citizens and stakeholders should expect: business leaders who commit their organizations to purpose-driven, positive impact on their environment. Human dignity for many—at present and in the future—not profit, is the ultimate goal of a business (Donaldson and Walsh, 2015). Conceptualizing and enacting the idea of a planetary dividend will bring us a good step closer to achieving it.

11 The Leadership of Value

Leading the Leading Indicators for Good Dividends

Anthony Hesketh

Introduction

How are we to think about value in the twenty-first century? It is a question that has been increasingly preoccupying those charged with the responsibility of understanding, articulating and managing value in academic, financial and executive circles, respectively. The nature of capital, value and their relationships are changing as capitalism evolves. The accounting profession's conception of value has not yet aligned itself with these changing winds, leaving us with an emerging and increasingly material challenge. Could society's interests in the activities of our largest organisations be de-coupled from and more appropriately re-connected to new conceptions of financial value, or are we locked in an accounting-inspired Weberian iron cage from whence there is no escape (Weber, 1910)? Is the current state of affairs even sustainable without at least revisiting and reconstituting what value comprises for the different constituencies which make up the complex social and economic ecosystem of contemporary capitalism?

What follows begins from the premise that what society values about modern day organisations is changing and yet how we seek to understand, account for and lead these same organisations is out of step with the views of the wider society. Corporate thinking continues to be constrained and heavily distorted by approaches advocating the *transfer* of value to shareholders in the short term as opposed to enhancing and protecting value *creation* over a longer-term horizon (Bower and Paine, 2017). Tackling this lack of capitalist imagination is not without its problems. In the contentiously titled *The End of Accounting*, Baruch Lev and Feng Gu highlight how the reporting practices of modern accounting, although appearing to change in line with emerging contradictions, have remained obdurately static for 110 years and counting (Lev and Gu, 2016: xxv). The iron grip with which portfolio managers in our largest financial institutions hold on to their methodological assumptions of so-called 'leading indicators' says more about the 'masters of the universe' fear of the 'zero gravity' represented by change than the lack of any suitable alternatives they could grab onto should they release themselves from the good Star Ship *Deductive Short-termism*. We cannot underestimate what a monumental challenge—and problem—this leaves us with.

This chapter represents an attempt to at least outline the shape of the problem and to point to the very beginnings of a possible solution. First, I provide a tentative critique of accounting and its current understanding of new forms of value. In many ways I am pushing on an open door as the accounting profession itself is engaged—albeit tentatively—in a form of navel gazing in relation to emerging forms of value. The next section unpacks in some detail the four primary problems why accounting finds new forms of value so problematic, which is immediately followed by potential solutions to each of these 'knotty issues.' The role of leadership— and its specific responsibilities in relation to formal governance—is a knot tied so tightly requires most careful attention if the other knots are to be untied. The final section, which returns us to the discussion outlined in Chapter 5 on limited attention to intangible assets, explores what good dividends might look like in terms of new *modalities of strategic value*. I also present various data including new empirical financial evidence, which reveals that the greater the level of human capital disclosure, the seemingly higher the levels of performance a firm can secure, thereby representing a 'good dividend' from the moral leadership of capitalism espoused by Steve, Ken and Thomas (in Part 1 of this volume).

Problems, Problems, Nothing But Problems

The contemporary challenge of accounting and corporate reporting more generally is no longer limited to robustly capturing and reassuring investors as to the value of their holdings *in* listed firms. New conundrums of valuation are emerging from *without* as new entities of value become increasingly transparent and demand the extension of value calculations to the ways in which some of the largest firms across the globe shape— either directly or indirectly—the resources, opportunities and environments of large swathes of the globe's population.

The world's population can be described as either the owners of/ investors in *financial capital* or those selling their capability, skills and knowledge (*human capital*). Organisations can consume natural resources (*natural capital*) in the production of their goods (*manufactured capital*), which in part draws on the unique ingenuity of an organization's innovation and creativity (*intellectual capital*) and its capacity to differentiate itself through either price or brand value (*social capital*). (Please note that Steve, Ken and Thomas adopt a slightly different conception of these six capitals. I will return to that below). These six capitals in their current guise certainly leave a lot of other communities and interests disenfranchised. Thinking through their recombination in different ways to release wider benefits or 'good dividends' at least represents a starting point in challenging the orthodoxy of financial capital and the concomitant constraint they place around accounting.

The magnitude of global influence yielded by firms and their financial capital in shaping the distribution of the other capitals across stakeholder groups has grown to such an extent that concerns are now being raised over the way in which large multi-national corporations have acquired more financial power than the governments of many nations states (Clark, 2000; Zald and Lounsbury, 2010). For example, just 30 US based firms have issued over $1.2tn in cash, cash equivalents, marketable securities and investments, meaning they have more firepower in financial markets than most leading asset managers (Platt, Bullock and Skaggs, 2017). As this concentration of financial capital intensifies, we are left with the very real prospect of the administrations of troubled nation states and their financial institutions going cap-in-hand not to venerable institutions such as the International Monetary Fund or European Central Bank but, albeit indirectly, to the likes of firms such as Apple, Coca-Cola and Boeing for much-needed cash-injections.

These massive distortions are just one of the knock-on effects of large corporations prioritising the acquisition of *financial* value above all other considerations. Cynics have recently observed how these behemoths of lending have arisen not through choice but because firms cannot bring onshore the huge resources of cash they have located in overseas geographies. It was precisely for this reason that the Trump administration announced in 2017 a significant modification in corporate taxation policy to effectively repatriate the billions of dollars held overseas by US firms. As the European Central Bank considers whether to taper down its long-standing quantitative easing programme, one of the primary material factors shaping the decision revolves around whether this repatriation by US firms of their profits from the balance sheets of major European banks might indirectly lead to deeper problems of capital liquidity in Europe. And so the beat goes on.

It cannot continue like this. However, we have little in the way of alternative thinking when attempting to hold the biggest multi-national corporations to account. Moreover, this over-concentration of financial capital is but one isolated example in terms of the huge distortions caused by thinking of value solely in *financial* terms. We could just as easily raise the issue of how firms selling billions of products everyday leaves huge environmentally destructive footprints. Alternatively, we could begin to chastise those organisations for collecting, storing and selling-on our personal data without our knowledge or consent. And, of course, this says nothing of the impact on people when firms—or, more accurately, their leaders—are fixed to the iron cage of short-term financial thinking and simply eject large numbers of their workforces in order to meet payments to their shareholders.

It is not just financial capital that distorts our relationship with capitalism. Other capitals, be they *natural, manufactured, social* or *human* capitals, present in the examples above, are discarded with seeming routine alacrity without the perpetrators being held—quite literally—to account in anything other than conventional financial accounting terms. The march of margin nearly always trumps the social demand for 'good dividends.' Clearly, a new form of accounting for twenty-first century capitalism is required. This new form of articulating value would take into consideration the aspirations and expectations of a wider stakeholder base and its conceptions of what exactly constitutes value and the dividends such a wider conception might generate.

A different form of thinking is required to that which has brought us to this challenge. Underlining the scale of feeling, no fewer than 59 separate initiatives are investigating alternative frameworks for mitigating the continuing negative impact of large organisations on the vast majority of those whose lives they touch. (For transparency, I should disclose here that I am the sole academic currently working on the joint Coalition for Inclusive Capitalism/EY initiative on Long-Term Value, known as *The Embankment Project* (CIC/EY, 2017). I should also make clear that the contents of this chapter are based on my own musings and do not represent the views of CIC, EY, or any of the participating firms and regulators. I should also say I am very grateful to a number of Embankment participants, too numerous to mention here, for their generous support to and feedback on my research).

But something far more radical than the current *status quo* is required. If what people value about work and their interaction with firms is changing, should there not also be a corresponding sea change in the way we value *value*?

Accounting for Accounting's Failure to Capture Value

Value, at least certainly value of the enduring kind, is an elusive concept. Perhaps the classic example here is the accounting industry's continual grappling—somewhat unsuccessfully—with the conundrum offered by the rise of intangible value. Estimates vary, but even the most conservative of estimates offered by the largest accounting and audit firms, known as 'the big four' estimate only half of a firm's total value is now captured by accounting methodologies with the remaining value consisting of the difference between so-called accounting or 'book value' and market capitalisation (e.g. EY, 2016; Lev, 2000). Other estimates go further suggesting accounting covers as little as 16 per cent of total value (Ocean Tomo, 2016). Accounting's role in capturing value, then, oscillates between, at best, the flip of a coin. At worst, the Paretian notion of just 20 per cent of book value is somehow 'accounting' for the other 'missing' 80 per cent of the total value of a firm, holds sway. Making matters worse, some accountants confuse their independence and objectivity with seeming omnipotence over all things material, reflected by an apparently unshakeable faith in the capacity of minority book value to drive much bigger constellations of value across financial markets. For others, the rise in the significance of intangible value represents a direct challenge to the imperious status currently commanded in contemporary capitalism by accounting (e.g. Lev and Gu, 2016). The creeping seepage by intangible value onto the balance sheet in the form of goodwill, brand and intellectual capital is, for some hawkish accountants, tantamount to letting water into their finely tuned balance-sheet engines (Penman, 2009). The adage that you cannot 'eat,' or 'bank' intangible value has bred an accounting industry deeply circumspect of anything it cannot materially wrap its arms around. The Einsteinian notion that not everything that counts can be counted, or even that not everything that *can* be counted, counts, is not good enough for the 'queen of the managerial sciences.'

This turning up of its collective nose by the accounting profession at the rise of intangible value has been far from helpful. The daily price of shares is certainly subject to the wilful movements of short-term oriented traders and the not insignificant fact that (most) boats rise and fall broadly in line with overarching market tides. The seeming melting away almost overnight of the value accounted for in firms like Autonomy or Carillion to name two recent high profile examples of accounting methodology failure, is not just cause for growing concern, but stands as a direct challenge to the materiality of the accounting profession itself. Prosaically speaking, if the audit industry, on its own admission, can only account for at best one dollar in every two, how can we take its definitions and audit of what constitutes material value seriously? The old adage attributed pejoratively at marketing now appears to equally apply to accounting: we know that one half of the value of a firm is based on voodoo, bluff and pseudo-science; we just do not know which half.

Executives may not be pushing for the intangible value to be value but they are certainly interested in managing and leveraging its value, even if accountants are not. All this means that three decades after the publication of Johnson and Kaplan's (1987) devastation of the relevance of accounting for those charged with the responsibility of leading our organisations, Lev and Gu can still conclude, 'based on our evidence, we grade the ubiquitous corporate financial report information as largely unfit for twenty-first century investment and lending decisions' (2016: xiv). The rise of intangible value is very much one of the driving forces of this problem.

If the arcane and impenetrable world of accounting and financial reporting fails in its primary task of informing the investment community of the direction of travel of value creation, or even its location on the balance sheet, should we find it surprising that shareholders, and the wider investment community underpinning them, focus on the tangible half of value they can materially get their hands on? Would an alternative view of value help us to begin to unpack the role of the firm—and the value it both creates and protects as well as releases—in a different way? Tackling this knotty problem requires our being aware of the constituent parts comprising the knot in the first place.

Unravelling Value's Value From Accounting

This knot comprises four major strands all tightly intertwined together.

Strand #1—Short-Termism of Accounting Practices

The link between accounting profit and shareholder returns appears to have become disconnected. Research by Merchant and Sandino (2009) claims only 2–10 per cent of changes in shareholder returns can be explained by corresponding changes in reported profits. The criticism of accounting's retrospective view amounting to executives effectively driving their firms' strategies via the rear-view mirror is a long-standing one. Nevertheless, precious little has changed as Lev and Gu's (2016: 2–12) comparisons of the income statements and balance sheets of United States Steel Corporation from 1902 and 2012 palpably reveal. They claim the capacity of corporate accounting information to drive stock prices has halved since the 1950s (Lev and Gu, 2016: Figure 3.1: 31). The primary reason for this lies in contemporary accounting practices still failing to convey the implications of future revenue or expenses by limiting analysis to short-term operating costs, business investment and profitability with very little motivation for recognition of internal value creation extending beyond the current financial year's end. Accountants have to set the parameters of reporting periods at some point in time. The challenge lies in the capacity of different stakeholders to transcend these parameters in order to recognise today's investments are tomorrow's returns. Efforts by a firm to articulate its intention to invest in the architectures of underlying value represented by the internal, deeper and intangible strategic resources and assets (Hesketh, 2014, 2018) beyond the immediate or short-term (via market updates) are routinely ignored by financial markets. This limits recognition of these internally generated assets by accountants and subsequently encourages incumbent executives to focus on short-term gains. For example, a firm's investment in making future cash flows more predictable actually yields an increase in short-term operating costs without accounting for the longer-term value released via reduced cash-flow risks. Firms are effectively punished in the present for making long-term investments that will be realised in the future. Both meanings of 'discounted' are in play. Accountants discount future returns by applying a discount rate to tomorrow's projected returns from today's investments. They also discount—ignore—tomorrow's returns by pricing in today's results irrespective of tomorrow's returns. One in the hand is always worth two in the bush.

Strand #2—The Nature of Value

With recent research by NESTA (2015) calculating the growth of intangible value in 1990–2011 at approximately three times the rate of tangible, physical assets, and investment in intangible assets running 50 per cent higher than investment in tangibles, contemporary accounting practices continue to discard assets that slide down the accounting hierarchy of tangible to intangible value, which runs synonymously with market prices. Firms who generate their intangible value are doubly penalised by not being able to offset the investment in developing their own intangible value nor book its value on the balance sheet as an internally constructed asset has never been 'priced' by the market.

Debate is still raging as to whether the rise of 'softer' assets is down more to their invisibility—hence speculation and distortion—than intangibility, but there is no mistaking the transition from a knowledge-*based* economy to knowledge-*valued* firms (Hesketh, 2014). Contemporary accounting convention loses its lustre not to mention aura of calculative invincibility when companies such as Facebook are prepared to pay $19 billion for a company (in this case WhatsApp) with just 55 employees run on as little as $60 million of funding. Whilst the traditionalists dominating the accounting profession point, quite understandably, to the speculative bubbles fuelled by intangible value which have emerged and exploded in relation to sub-prime property, technology, global regions and social media, the growing disconnect between market capitalisation and book value, 'undermines the perceived accuracy of, and confidence in, the reporting process' (EY, 2016: 8). The powerful link between executive strategic imagination and best owner has never been more material or unaccounted for.

Strand # 3—Sustainable Long-Term Value, Really?

While a growing number of investment houses acknowledge their wider social responsibilities falling under the aegis of what in financial circles is described as environmental, social and governance factors—or 'ESGs'—more focused empirical research continues to reveal how portfolio managers routinely overlook such factors in favour of the financial elements they regard as more material to the short-term value of the funds they have under management (Hesketh, 2014). We appear to be in the contradictory position of being inundated with a number of examples of leading investment houses queuing up to take their place in requiring the firms they invest in to take a more responsible approach to their long-term futures (see Chapter 12), only for this initial enthusiasm to be met with inertia from the wider markets for a number of complicated, financial and mindset aspects (e.g., PRI, 2018). Make no mistake; money is certainly beginning to shift, and in relatively material amounts as new ESG-related products are being built. We have yet to be crushed by the rush of portfolio managers to the doors of ESG-inspired asset products. The extent to which ESG factors have, or perhaps more accurately, can, become a 'leading indicator' of value—that is to say success in environmental and social factors foreshadows subsequent economic performance as firms enjoy 'good dividends' from the impact of wider investors who screen for opportunities using ESG factors as a signal of outperformance—is, as we shall see below, beginning to emerge from the fog of analysis. (See Chapter 12 for a related discussion on ESG from a governance perspective). The nascent form of this analysis needs greater encouragement through more extensive disclosures of relevant information by firms and, as we shall also see, clearer methodologies of accounting for newly emerging forms of value. There is, then, a need for leaders to lead the construction of new leading indicators. This leads nicely to the fourth strand in our knot: the role of governance—this is such an important strand of the knot as it can help unravel the rest.

Strand #4—Governance: Leading the Leading Indicator Debate

For all the apparent rhetoric of environmental and social factors shaping the investment decisions of leading asset managers—the recent declaration by Blackrock chief executive Larry Fink being the latest manifestation of this meandering road to Damascus, which is being taken by leading financial firms—there has not been as much progress as advocates of change demand. As Paul Polman of Unilever, arguably the chief executive more than any other who serves as the lightening rod between a more socially oriented view of business and the capitalist establishment encapsulates the problem, we have 'a clash between people who think about billions of people in the world and some people that think about a few billionaires' (Polman, cited in Edgecliffe-Johnson, 2018). Far from representing a coherent aspect of business activities, ESGs appear to represent a contradictory impasse between environmental and social factors on the one hand and governance on the other. Here, the theoretical strands recently advocated by Steve, Ken and Thomas (Chapter 2) and Bower and Paine (2017) appear to converge in the space of the fiduciary duties of those leading and, in its widest sense, investing, in the world's largest organisations. Whilst continuing data appear to underline increasing stakeholder demand for a more responsible approach to capital accumulation, governance at national and international level has not kept pace with developments.

The cacophony of noise from pressure groups, NGOs and the end-less number of business-led initiatives set up with the primary intention of calling capitalism to account has succeeded only in increasing the complexity of the picture. This complexity consequently limits possible solutions to unravelling the knot that is represented by widening social disparities and environmental damage, which stem largely from the operations of our global corporations. The latter maintain their innocence. They are aided, in part, by a lack of agreement on how any causal impact can be established with competing 'index-superiority' with ESG-related products instead of enabling the enhanced-transparency that a more enlightened capitalism requires.

Governance, then, might be seen to represent the strand that unravels the knot as a whole. The problem of short-termism can be addressed through a combination of moving away from quarterly reporting with far more emphasis—and by this we mean subsequent investment as well as evaluation—being placed on value creation and protection articulated over a longer term; and moving to on a more sustainable basis than simply relying on temporal sleights of the calculative accounting hand at a particular point in time to achieve short-term gains through value transfer. For example, Paul Polman's decision to dispense with quarterly reporting on becoming chief executive of Unilever in 2006 did not just change convention. But he arguably represented a transformation of the business model at the heart of long-term strategy by shifting emphasis away from near-term margin *enhancement* to long-term margin *sustainability*. The initial response by markets to Polman's move was a rapid draining of market capitalisation. Later vindication of the veracity of a longer-term strategy was subsequently forthcoming, culminating in the way Unilever successfully defended itself from a hostile takeover bid in 2017 by the combined forces of Warren Buffett's Berkshire Hathaway, 3G Capital and Kraft. Nevertheless, as Polman has since conceded, this war was won while conceding territory in the battles of greater returns—read value transfer—to shareholders through a €6 billion share buy-back. There was also a declaration of future margin aspirations, which Polman had previously hoped to avoid being publicly turned into targets he and his team were compelled into delivering in the near-term at the cost of their longer-term aspirations (Edgecliffe-Johnson, 2018).

Unilever's example is but a blip in the history of how we ensure the transparency and accountability of our executives, which, despite Polman's and others' efforts, continues to perpetuate short-term thinking. The convention of quarterly reporting dominates the reporting cycles of many of our largest firms with an over-reliance on near-term financial performance. Such thinking is likely to remain unbroken until there are alternative financial indicators that can simultaneously reveal short-term performance and long-term value orientation, if you know where to look.

Governance plays a key role in determining not just the *when* of financial reporting, but the *what* of the value being reported. Even amongst the Big Four accounting firms there is an emerging view that, 'too often we are measuring and reporting the wrong things' (EY, 2016: 7). Establishing the variables which matter requires our taking a long hard look at both the dependent as well as independent sides of the performance equation. This knot is arguably the tightest of all at the heart of unravelling a more long-term oriented capitalism. On the dependent side of the equation, how we begin to understand, articulate and measure value is critical. This stems from the 'leading the leading indicators' conundrum. On the one hand, investors are reluctant to advocate even the measurement, let alone the importance, of alternative variables capturing different conceptions of value other than in financial form. Their reading of their own fiduciary duty to the consumers of their products advocates an unrelenting focus on securing the returns and meeting expectations, which normally means equalling, or preferably exceeding, wider market performance. Anything detracting away from securing this primary focus is treated with a high degree of caution or even disdain. Moreover, the rhetoric of fiduciary responsibility enables asset managers to defend any rejection of alternative versions of value in the name of protecting the long-term and conventionally framed *financial* interests of their consumers. This is exacerbated on the independent side of the equation by the so-called 'hunt for margin' or what drives *alpha*—the measure of a stock's expected return that cannot be attributed to overall market volatility—leading asset managers and their research teams to seek out leading indicators of *alpha*. We are left with the circular argument of there being no measures to unpack the signalling potential of outperformance (aka *alpha*) of wider ESG factors because their inclusion is precluded by their not being acknowledged as 'leading indicators' in the first place.

What if that which determines *alpha* lies beyond finance? That some *extra-financial* variable materially shaping the value of firms lies beyond conventional quantum reporting forms? Clearly, this is a state of affairs academics, regulators and the leaders of our largest organisations urgently need to address. However, given these different stakeholders rarely talk to, let alone agree with each other, the size of the task is all the more daunting.

A wide array of research points to how the decisions being taken by the leaders of our largest organisations are out of step with wider stakeholders' perceptions of what counts as valuable. The problem is the research usually stops at this point. We understand little in terms of what is valued and why, let alone the direction of travel of these new and evolving forms of value. We do know that younger generations are less interested in financial value than their parents or grandparents; but the extent to which there can be a reconciliation between a more virtuous form of capitalism with tomorrow's workforce and today's wider consumers has still yet to be adequately worked through. This was in part what Lev and Gu were trying to resolve in their *The End of Accounting* as they pointed to the appetite of analysts on quarterly earnings conference calls for more information relating to what they label the 'strategic (value creating) assets' of the firm than for the traditional accounting measures of earnings, sales, tangible assets, and so on (I will return to this in the next section).

The leading of leading indicators, then, requires our regulators, business leaders and major investment houses to create a new form of governance with, at its heart, a new economy of market information enabling wider stakeholders of capitalism to judge the performance of firms in ways other than financial capital, thereby creating alternative leading indicators. These, in turn, will materially move financial markets as portfolio managers begin to unpack and devise strategies to deal with evolving consumer behaviour shaped by society's perceptions of the performance of firms against this new economy of long-term *or supererogatory value*. This 'build it and they will calculate' approach takes us neatly to evolving theories of value and its new manifestations in the form of good dividends.

Good Dividends as New Modalities of Strategic Value

How, then, are firms to disclose their journey from a short-term, value transfer orientation to one advocating a long-term approach to value creation and protection? Any addition to the requirements of financial reporting is nearly always greeted with a negative response from firms who view such modifications as adding to the regulatory burden they already face, not to mention the increased management distraction and increased audit costs (e.g. Walker, 2009; Kay Review, 2012). This negative response looks increasingly unsustainable on at least two counts.

First, a tipping point appears to have been reached where those firms not voluntarily disclosing information deemed important by wider constituencies are placing at risk their brand value and subsequently competitive advantage in the market place. The well-publicised examples of several high-profile firms failing to meet deadlines and the requirements of compulsory disclosure in the UK regarding the pay of men and women in their firms has led to their losing ground in the eyes of the key talent pools in which they are seeking to recruit.

Second, not just the social, but the *economic*, case for wider and deeper disclosures across a number of different factors beyond financial capital appears to be gaining ground. In advocating their *company-centred model*, which focuses more on the firm's long-term health as opposed to short-term wealth, Bower and Paine (2017: 58) outline the challenge more cogently than most:

> In a free market system, companies succeed only if customers want their products, employees want to work for them, suppliers want

them as partners, shareholders want to buy their stock, and communities want their presence. Figuring out how to maintain these relationships and deciding when trade-offs are necessary among the interests of these various groups are central challenges of corporate leadership.

At face value, the majority of business academics, practitioners and regulators would certainly maintain that the current state of affairs in accounting procedures and corporate law more than meets the architectural requirements for the smooth operation of the relations described by Bower and Paine above. There is, however, a subtle, more emotional shift taking place in the underlying elements of value that shape what stakeholders really want from their engagement with firms. This turns not just on functional factors such as access to requisite economic resources and desired products, but also turns on the availability of information revealing a greater level of transparency on deeper, more life enhancing relationships, enabling consumers to realise their supererogatory goals of securing high quality products and services while simultaneously making a positive social impact (Almquist, Senior and Bloch, 2016).

Critically, those constituencies in wider society, and certainly beyond the financial communities, with which the leadership of many global firms usually engage, demand far more in the way of information. We appear to be moving from an expectation of *comply-or-explain* to one of *disclose-or-firefight* as consumers demand evidence-based authenticity in the purpose and activities underpinning a firm's contribution to supererogatory value. They seek what Bower and Paine outline above but, critically, their affinity and concomitant likelihood to economically engage with a firm turns on a new and underlying complex set of elements resembling multi-dimensional building blocks of social preferences.

A 'healthy approach' is not simply about celebrating the upside, but about recognising, mitigating and disclosing the impact of the negative externalities produced by a firm's activities. Unilever's Sustainable Living Plan does such. A focus on long-term value, then, requires the formulation and contribution to a higher purpose, which modern firms must articulate and make transparent to the variety of stakeholders their operations touch. A consensus as to what purpose comprises has yet to be reached, but there is agreement that a more expansive, human-centred, aspirational definition of purpose seems to be emerging (e.g. Kempster, Jackson and Conroy, 2011; Robinson, Hickman and Sorenson, 2014). Again, Polman's Unilever has put in motion a clear policy of reporting on the wider material factors outside the usual financial fundamentals its consumers seek information on. These new social fiduciary fundamentals have hardly become commonplace, but they represent the beginnings of a new economy of options open to firms to make more transparent what their purpose comprises and the progress they are making against the wider, healthier goals the organisation has set for itself beyond the creation and protection of its shareholders' wealth.

These new *modalities of strategic value* represent a transformation in our understanding of the way in which a firm's *structural capital* (associated with Integrated Reporting, IIRC, 2013) —as opposed to capital structure—forms new constellations of value through the recognition and deployment of strategic assets and resources, which themselves require a new form of financial accounting and reporting (Hesketh, 2014; Lev and Gu, 2016; Hesketh, Sellwood-Taylor and Mullen, 2018). Optimising the combination between these factors enables firms to increase both customer loyalty as well as revenues. As Steve, Ken and Thomas articulate in Chapter 1 and Chapter 2, purpose is about so much more than simply results. A new lexicon is required to capture these new modalities of strategic value, which takes us to the heart of how we articulate and capture the new forms of value or 'good dividends' in relation to alternative concepts of capitals offered by others.

Table 11.1 presents an overview of the commonality across the concepts offered by varying perspectives on the elements comprising the different forms of value represented by capitals, dividends or modalities. The notion of differential reward for those firms who outperform across these different elements in the eyes of stakeholders is as old as the hills (for the latest examples of descriptions in formal accounting terms, see Gleeson-White, 2014; De Villiers, Rinaldi and Unerman, 2014). Examining different elements through a more contemporary lens raises significant pointers to continuing discussion and future research in the generation and recognition of the good dividends advocated in this volume. These new elements require new forms of codification or modalities, which enable emerging forms of value to be captured and comparatively examined by different stakeholders. Markets require information to breathe, and, as new modalities of value become established, new market places— or economies—will be created as firms compete over scarce resources differentially allocated by various stakeholders. These can range from capital investment from shareholders, through to potential employees, as they weigh the different economies of experience made available to their skillsets, or to society as it weighs in the balance—and allocates the cost of capital accordingly—new economies of (negative) impact. These new economies are clearly only in nascent form and will develop over time. Some examples might prove useful here.

Economies of Materiality

The notion of financial dividends at first seems straightforward, but it does not take long for the transformative element of finance to reveal itself and its underlying complexities. Recent research has pointed a way forward to overcoming such variations (Barton, Manyika and Keohane Williamson, 2017b). Significantly, *most* of the variables used in

Table 11.1 The New Modalities of Strategic Value, Capitals and Good Dividends Compared

IIRC Structural Capitals	Financial	Natural	Manufactured	Social	Human	Intellectual
Good Dividends	Financial	Planet and Communities	Operations	Brands	Human	Social Innovation
CIC Long-Term Value Framework	Financial	Society	Consumer		Human	
Strategic Modalities of Value	Economies of materiality	Economies of impact	Economies of reciprocity		Economies of experience	
Examples	• Investment • Earnings quality • Margin growth	• Externality accounting • Environmental benchmarking	• Internality accounting • Supply chain scrutiny • Partner constellations • Virtuous communities		• Employee engagement • Investment in R&D • Human capital architectures • Human capital asset	

computations are publicly available in the financial information reported by firms. For example, we can examine the *investment* orientation, or otherwise, of firms by calculating the ratio of capital expenditure to depreciation. Increasing levels of depreciation relative to investment, financially speaking, suggests a greater emphasis on yesterday than tomorrow. In addition, by examining *earnings quality* in terms of the share accruals' command of revenues enables us to establish how long-term oriented firms generate earnings reflecting cash flows not accounting decisions. *Margins*, too, will grow in a way depicting a steady cadence as opposed to short unsustainable bursts to reach short-term targets. Relatedly, long-term firms do not get caught on 'performance treadmills,' which demand ever-linear growth in earnings, opting instead to miss quarterly targets and setting realistic future goals. Similarly, those firms over-indexing on earnings per share (EPS) ratios could be returning residual value to their shareholders, or burning investment in generating long-term *EPS growth* by redirecting funds back to shareholders who are seeking higher returns in the short to medium term.

Using these five indicators (investment, earnings quality, margin growth, quarterly management and EPS growth) Barton and colleagues observed how the 164 US firms meeting these benchmarks during 2001–2015 outperformed the remaining 451 US firms, by 47 per cent in average company revenue growth; 36 per cent in average company earnings; 81 per cent in average economic profit growth; and by $7 billion in average growth of market capitalisation. The numbers, then, certainly begin to look like they are stacking up. Extrapolating from these findings, Barton and colleagues estimate that had all US companies taken a similar approach, 'public equity markets could have added more than $1 trillion in asset value, increasing total U.S. market cap by about 4%. And companies could have created five million more jobs in the United States— unlocking as much as $1 trillion in additional GDP' (Barton, Manyika and Keohane Williamson, 2017a: 67). Clearly, in terms of financial capital alone, the *material* case for long-term value can be seen to generate a number of fundamental financial gains for firms advocating this approach. Significantly, we do not have to deploy the notion of dividend in order to simply allude to its symbolism of capitalism (Kempster, Maak and Parry, this volume in Chapter 2). On the contrary, it would appear we can have the best of both worlds. Moreover, these new *economies of materiality*, acting as modalities of strategic value through which material financial returns accompany long-term principles, provide an incentive to firms to disclose more information regarding their activities in order to reveal additional financially accretive good dividends.

Economies of Impact

These alternative modalities of strategic value present themselves in relation to other elements. As new and innovative ways of measuring a firm's utilisation of natural resources become available, firms are being held increasingly to account by their business partners, as well as customers, to at the very least monitor, if not manage-down, their ongoing rate of natural resource consumption. The overarching expectation, however, is one of assuming responsibility for the internalisation of these negative externalities in financial as well as social form (e.g. KPMG, 2014). This new process of internalising and subsequently accounting for the external impact of firms of their environmental footprints represents one of the primary challenges to regulators, accountants and researchers as debate over how best to quite literally account for environmental impact moves on from the periphery to more mainstream discussion of the criteria used by stakeholders of many types to differentiate between firms in a new *economy of impact*. Differential impact across our 'planet,' identified by Steve, Ken and Thomas, will clearly result in differential returns to firms should the cost of capital be increased through legislation for those firms who disproportionately and negatively impact natural resources. This is much more easily elucidated than achieved as reaching consensus on the views of wider stakeholders is far from a straightforward process. It is precisely this thorny issue that governments, executives, academics and accountants must engage with if we are to make progress. Significantly, the nascent state of these variables should not preclude their disclosure or any attempts to initiate new forms of value calculations. Variables that remain unverified should not be discarded. Research by financial analyst communities themselves reveals this important stakeholder is not averse to additional information being disclosed if its utility can be articulated (CFA, 2013).

Economies of Reciprocity

Similarly, we see other market places opening up in other modalities of strategic value as the supply chains and manufacturing processes used by firms are more closely scrutinised, upstream as well as downstream, creating new data points as firms are judged by their actual resource-based footprints as opposed to their capability to 'greenwash' their operational footprints through outsourcing processes. Examining how these activities drive brand value on the one hand, and how being associated with other less well-performing firms for example impact problems in upstream or down stream supply chains creates new *economies of reciprocity* as firms are judged, not just by their own performance in elements of value of importance to stakeholders, but also by the performance of the firms they serve. As the examples in Table 11.2 illustrate, billions of dollars in value are shifting on the basis of these new and emerging modalities of value, as they combine thinking around capitals with good dividends to form new ways of understanding the implications of the utilisation of a firm's strategic resources and assets, together with the calculative possibilities of extending long-term value into new forms of assets on the balance sheet.

Table 11.2 The Financial Impact of New Modalities of Strategic Value

Modality of Value	Company	How value is changing and why
Economies of impact	Swiss Re	Swiss Re, one of Europe's biggest insurers, recently announced it is moving its $130bn investment portfolio to new ethically based benchmark indices in a bid to provide incentives for companies to change and consider the wider factors of economic and social governance (ESG). The Chief Investment Officer, Guido Fürer, described the move as, 'more than doing good—it makes economic sense,' as the firm was seeking to protect sustainable value by limiting downsides rather than relentlessly pursuing upside potential.
Economies of experience	Unilever	The Unilever Sustainable Development Living Plan captures the discretionary effort of employees motivated by reducing the environmental footprint of a company selling 2bn products a day worldwide. Consequently, the firm has created a new human capital asset through its employee value proposition underpinned by the purpose of 'doing well by doing good.' Target recruitment groups now rate Unilever as the number one employer of choice in 32 countries.
Economies of reciprocity	Axa	Axa announced in 2016 it was selling its investments in particular sectors and was quickly followed by other financial firms including Aviva, AMP Capital, Calpers, Scor and Sweden's AP4 pension fund. In all, some $4bn has moved with more companies considering the move. For Axa, it is no longer just about how you do business but *with whom* you do business. 'We won't cover [certain sectors'] manufacturing plants and car fleets,' says Alice Steenland, the insurer's head of corporate responsibility. 'This is fairly specific to Axa—we consider it a form of financing.'
Economies of Materiality	EY	The Big Four accountant, EY, together with the Coalition for Inclusive Capitalism (CIC), asset management firms with over $25 trillion under management, and a number globally significant firms, are developing a new financial reporting system offering insight into how organisations create value over the long-term; communicate the value of their strategic assets; and provide a wider set of information relevant to stakeholders to rebuild trust; and simplifying reporting to enable all stakeholders to make informed decisions as to who they invest in, do business with, or even who to work for, thereby capturing new elements of longer-term value conventional accounting fails to capture or provide assurance.

Source: Hesketh et al. (2018: 7)

Clearly, these examples alone underpin how leadership with purpose is having a financially material impact on a global scale.

Modalities of value do not operate at the firm level alone. For example, there is increasing competition between firms for human capital when employees seek greater alignment with their own values and identities as they seek 'good work' with firms offering them superior employee value propositions in the new and emerging *economies of experience.* These are closely related to the opportunities that firms offer for development leading to the development of competition between firms for those employees who can convert their human capital into new forms of what Steve and Minna Halme (in Chapter 7) label social innovation, subsequently building the firm's intellectual capital, which does appear on the balance sheet. There are, then, clear opportunities for the development of new internal and underlying *architectures of value* (Hesketh, 2014, 2018) within firms, which focus less on MacIntyres (1985) notion of external, economic and transactional returns of activities, but more on the generation of internal goods or good dividends developed by Steve, Ken and Thomas in Chapter 2.

This distinction between internal and external goods takes on greater significance when we recognise how Generally Agreed Accounting Principles (GAAP) steadfastly refuses to recognise the value represented by modalities of strategic value arising out of the economies of experience. Put another way, this represents not just a failure to account for the intangible value represented by human and intellectual capital, but, in MacIntyre's view, effectively 'destroys' or 'eliminates' the very long-term value good dividends seek to capture, develop and extend, as firms and accountants deny the asset value of human capital from its rightful place on the balance sheet (Hesketh, 2013, 2014). In addition, new forms of value represented by emerging modalities of strategic value represent a clearer line of sight into the 'productivity puzzle,' where modern forms of capitalism continue to underestimate the required investment in human capital (the denominator), thereby inflating the earnings or return on investment (the numerator) as the underlying asset value represented by workforces is consistently underestimated and consequently under-invested. The data presented by Steve Young and colleagues in Chapter 5 speaks loudly to this point. This does not have to be the case, but the combined forces of accounting and wider investment communities continue to fight any change in financial reporting, which leads to a downgrade in their return from assets, even if it means literally cashing-in at the expense of investment in our people over the long term.

Leading the Leading Indicators: Human Capital Disclosure

If the relationship between large-scale firms and wider society is under strain how are we to fix it? One obvious place to start might be with the relationships between people and their firms. As an example, were a firm to buy a new piece of machinery for $10 million, its presence would be discernible on both the income statement in the form of cost of goods sold (COGS) and, in future years, on the balance sheet. As a fixed asset, the value of the machine would be depreciated on a straight-line basis, by, say an arbitrary amount of 10 per cent or $1 million each year, over a 10-year period. Moreover, analysts would subsequently be able to compute the return on investment from such an asset by estimating and then discounting future value generated by the investment over the long term. No such transparency in a US firm would be afforded to a potential employee. Not only can we not calculate what the possible return on our investment in talent might be; we would not even be able to establish what the firm in question invests in its employees (see Chapter 5 for an overview of the limited reporting on such investment).

It is staggering to think that in contemporary capitalism, an individual cannot consider before committing to what could be a working relationship stretching over half a century, the firm's approach to people management via the financial evidence published in a firm's annual accounts. In 2017, just 75 firms out of the S&P 500 published their total people costs (Ernst and Young, 2018). The generation of supererogatory value requires a similar openness and commitment beyond the legal minimum to engage in supererogatory disclosure. Interestingly, of the 75 firms who did undertake this voluntary disclosure in the US, the majority are to be found in the top 20 per cent of performing firms as measured by earnings before interest and taxation.

Moreover, supererogatory disclosure appears to signal outperformance when comparing firms on a value-creating and value-transferring basis (Figure 11.1). Reading from left to right, firms disclosing their human capital costs perform strongly in value creation, whereas those firms not disclosing their costs offer their shareholders higher rates of returns, but not significantly so. Claiming human capital disclosure causes firms to outperform their peers in relation to value creation is problematic. Suggesting those firms who are transparent and take the time to disclose information they view to be important to their stakeholders on a supererogatory basis, might also be well run and consequently high performing, does have an appealing logic—at least to me.

This logic for the positive performance of disclosers gains even more support when examining firms in the UK's FTSE 100 (Figure 11.2). Using a human capital reporting index devised by the author, comparison of the financial return generated by employees for every £1 spent on salaries, bonuses and benefits reveals those firms that are disclosing more information about their human capital (e.g. turnover, training and development, engagement, etc.) secure a significantly higher level of productivity than those in the lower reporting quartiles. Again, the case for the causality of human capital reporting on the financial performance of firms is

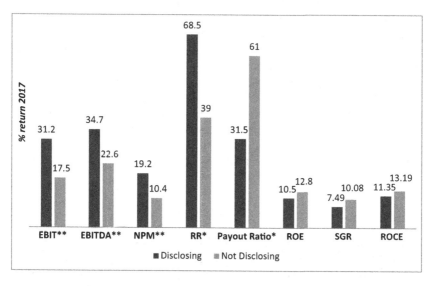

Figure 11.1 Value Creation and Value Transfer by Human Capital Non-disclosure.
Source: S&P, Compustat & firm publications, Analysis by the author

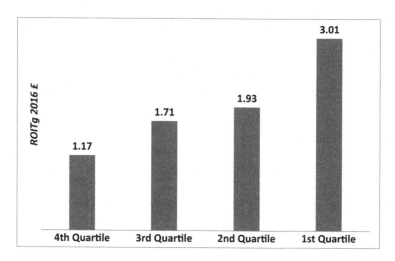

Figure 11.2 Employee Productivity by Human Capital Reporting Index.
Source: FTSE, & firm publications, Analysis by the author

not a straightforward case but the capacity of those firms who honour Steve, Ken and Thomas's moral leadership—and engage in supererogatory disclosure—do appear to enjoy differential results, or, using Steve, Ken and Thomas's language, good dividends. Perversely, just at the point when we should be encouraging US firms to disclose more information relating to their investment in their people, the UK's leaving of the European Union puts at risk the adherence to European law by UK domiciled firms of their disclosure of their total workforce costs and individual categories of spend broken down across salaries and bonuses, pensions and other benefits. At the time of writing, the climate in US regulatory circles evinced by the aversion to quarterly reporting puts at even higher levels of risk disclosure of non-compulsory elements such as human capital. The extent to which leaders of US and UK firms will lead the leading indicator discussion in this highly volatile context will be an interesting area of future research of direct interest to the assets that drive the value of all other assets: people.

Conclusion

In this chapter I have sought to demonstrate three primary challenges in accounting for good dividends. First, drawing on recent research, we have seen how the relevance of accounting information to understanding the value managed and created by firms is fading. Second, this accounting fade has been exacerbated by the falling out of kilter between accounting convention on the one hand, with changing expectations in the new relationships people seek, with organised capitalism on the other. Third, we have seen, albeit in their very early stages, how long-standing notions of the capitals represented in conventional accounting approaches can be translated into new modalities of strategic resource and value.

We are very much in the foothills of developing new forms of value that capture the elements of that which wider stakeholders and constituencies hold dear. These very stakeholders and constituencies require extending with new forms of recognition for their interests as firms compete to demonstrate the value of their underlying purpose or 'social licence to operate.' The building blocks through which these social licences will be granted still require a substantial element of calculability and material 'bones' to be developed around the intangible 'flesh' of the new and evolving forms of value that currently lie beyond current conventions. It is to this future challenge that firms, leaders, future scholars—and even accountants—must turn if they are to calculate capitalism's good dividends.

Part 3

12 The Good Dividends and Governance

A Leadership Perspective

Randall Zindler

Leaders Facing the Issues

A group of about a dozen current or former CEOs or Chairpersons, all Young President Organization (YPO) members from a variety of sectors, gathered for a dinner discussion in Vancouver, in March 2017. We all travelled from the far corners of the Earth to be there—not out of obligation, but passion. It was my job to steer the discussion and so the below letter was sent to the participants a few days previous.

> Humanity is increasingly concerned with issues of sustainability, climate change, pollution, technologically driven change and the impacts of business on society, particularly a sense of growing inequality in many dimensions. This interest and level of engagement is seen across YPO membership and trends point to this only being on the rise.
>
> The issues of: Community Engagement, Sustainable Business, Humanitarian Efforts, Public Policy and Diplomacy, Environment and Wildlife, and Philanthropy provide avenues of engagement for YPO membership. The influence that YPO members are having on issues related to these themes is significant and with huge opportunity before us to make more of a difference.
>
> As the first Millennials come into YPO they bring growing interest as to how exponentially accelerating technologically driven change is impacting society. The YPOer community may benefit but many people around the world will feel significant dislocation as artificial intelligence expands, again, exponentially. The Social Impact Networks of YPO have big opportunities to be influential in responding to such rapid societal change: a place of relevant learning and thought-provoking ideas exchange.
>
> (Excerpt from the pre-read materials for the leaders of YPO social impact networks, in 2017, RZ)

A very rich discussion ensued as we grappled with these grand challenges and explored opportunities. Each of these leaders were engaged in bringing positive social impact through their businesses and were convinced that *doing well and doing good* is the way forward—for business and society. These were the leaders and governors of their firms therefore the examples, models and practices they put into play would be the guide-posts for how their firms would function, the impact they would have and the legacy they would leave.

These leaders felt first hand the business benefits of looking beyond what economist Milton Friedman proposed in 1962, in *Capitalism and Freedom*. His statement is well known: 'There is one and only one social responsibility of business—to use its resources and engage in activities designed to increase its profits so long as it stays within the rules of the game, which is to say, engages in open and free competition without deception or fraud' (1962: 112). Whether one agrees or disagrees with all or parts of this statement it is clear that the times have changed since it was written. Corporations have become enormous. There has been a huge shift in political power, climate change is a real threat, the word 'exponential' is often used to describe areas of innovation and business growth, and technology (when compared to 1962) has become a total game changer. In the midst of this millennials are showing interest in things other than the quest for profit. Today's context is clearly different from Friedman's world of the 1950s and 1960s. But let's not throw the baby out with the bath water—his suggestion to operate within the rules and without deception and fraud are good things. These are some of the foundational elements of good governance. Nearly 60 years previous G.K. Chesterton wrote: 'When you break the big laws you do not get freedom. You do not even get anarchy. You get small laws' (*Daily News*, 29 July 1905).

The Sarbanes-Oxley Act of 2002 was a reaction to the corporate scandals of Enron and Worldcom. Those firms did get the first part of Friedman's statement—to seek profit. But they missed the second part about obeying the rules. The reaction has been to increase regulation with more 'small laws' for non-executive directors and their firms to comply with. The administrative burden from this has crept into all sectors. While the regulations may help to provide necessary boundaries for business, they are indeed burdensome and that burden does come with a cost. Some of that cost is budgeted and known and some of it shows up in the form of more time needed for making decisions, or the stress carried by staff, and the effort needed for reporting. Perhaps there is an issue here about the mark that we as leaders set for ourselves through our internal regulations, practices and culture as something different to those put on us by external bodies.

When Steve approached me to consider writing a chapter on the good dividends I was enthusiastic and then cautious. Most of my career has been in leadership roles rather than academia. I was pleased with Steve's encouragement to draw on my experiences and connections in the business world, and position the chapter from a leadership practitioner's perspective of governance situations and frameworks, rather than an academic commentary on governance. I shall not provide a comprehensive review of governance models, but rather select those that I think resonate deeply with the thesis of the good dividends. So, in this chapter I seek to offer a simple examination of the governance duty from two governance models: the Anglo-Saxon model and the Continental Europe. The narrative of the chapter is to illustrate an increasing questioning by leaders of the dominant Anglo-Saxon model and increasing attention to the Continental Europe model. The questioning is with regard to broader aspects of governance that reach beyond profit in the pursuit of purpose and alignment of purpose to a range of stakeholders. In this way I seek to explore the relationship of governance to the good dividends, and indeed the realisation of the good dividends through governance. And this is done through the perspective of leaders reflecting on governance challenges.

The chapter is structured as follows. First, I offer a personal account of governance with regard to control and with regard to achieving excellence. Second, I briefly summarise the two dominant governance models— the Anglo-Saxon and Continental Europe. Although the Anglo-Saxon is dominant with its emphasis on the fiduciary duty to the shareholder, I explore the increasing trend towards the growth of the Continental stakeholder model. Inter-related to this trend is the increasing attention to environmental, social and governance (ESG) measurement and reporting. To understand more of how money is following this trend I next examine the perspective of an investment banker and the focus on impact investment and the leadership orientation of the businesses they invest in. I shall then explore how family businesses interact with the concepts within the good dividends. Finally, I shall look at two models of governance that may have much resonance in how the Continental European model can be advanced and applied for the realisation of the good dividends: namely employee ownership and BCorps. I shall do this through two leadership case studies. I conclude the chapter with offering a set of principles that may be useful to guide governance direction towards establishing good dividends.

Governance Striving for Excellence: Together With Control and Compliance

I recall landing in El Geneina, West Darfur, Sudan some years ago. As the CEO of Medair, one of the lead international humanitarian agencies in the region, I went to better understand the humanitarian and security situation, visit the affected areas, meet those who we were serving, engage with staff, and see officials and various partners. As the plane approached I saw some camels and a few Land Rovers near the airstrip. Walking off the plane I was met by our local driver. I should say here that there were only a few vehicles in town (no traffic at all), the roads were mostly sand (slow driving) and wide (few obstacles). I jumped in and was ready to move toward the office. The driver said 'I am sorry but we cannot leave yet,' to which I replied 'ok, why not.' He replied 'because you have not attached your seat belt.' I was quick to respect the role and authority of our driver and do not recall feeling uncomfortable or irritated at all. I felt that he showed the same genuine concern for me as he did for all his passengers. Later, while speaking with one of our auditors he shared a similar experience and said 'it's the small things that matter.' I am not sure but I do not think that safety practice was something enforced by the government—it was however a serious protocol within the organisation.

These were not isolated incidents. Years previous the governing board made a decision to become ISO9001 certified worldwide and set out to articulate what we will insist on with regard to issues related to safety, security and of course many other areas. I specifically remember working with the board as we crafted the organisational vision, which included these words: 'staff will know they are cared for.' This was informed by the culture that had been established by the good leaders that came before. However, the new strategic direction led to objective setting, training and finally habitual seat belt buckling at points far away from the boardroom. Local leaders were essential in contextualising the mission, vision and values, and seeing through policy compliance. Their spirit was not about what the minimum standard we must comply with was, but rather how we strived for excellence—and in this case how we cared for our people. We did not always get it right but I share this example to show how decisions in the boardroom play out throughout the organisation, bringing several good dividends, and not in a way that avoids breaking the rules set by government. While this story is hardly headline newsworthy we will never know the crisis (and media attention) that has been avoided by the cascade effect of good governance.

Broken Rules or Broken Capitalism?

In a conversation with Marcello Palazzi, which I will share later in this chapter, he spoke of capitalism, as it is commonly known, really being *broken-capitalism*. If that is the case, if it is indeed broken, can it be fixed? Enter the good dividends. Perhaps this is a good time to revisit Figure 4.1 in Chapter 4 of this book (see page 44). This model is not a simple expansion of the over-used used cliché, 'win/win,' as we describe the upside of a deal we may be pursuing. The good dividends model acknowledges multiple wins for all stakeholders.

For the purposes of this chapter, the model shows the critical role that good governance plays. While it may look like the role of governance is to exercise control and hold it all together, and while there is some truth to that, there is more. In this chapter we will read of leaders who have a governing role as owners, chairman, or shareholders. We will try to see the world through their lens. In some cases we will read of regret—where some of the aforementioned dividends were not realised. In other cases we will read of leaders who are driving transformation in their organisations, and beyond, to see more engagement with stakeholders in their dealings—to strive for more positive impact (than just the financial bottom line). We will also look at the implications of governance on organisational culture and how governance is exercised through investors, family members and corporate governing structures.

Governance Models

Winston Churchill told the House of Commons, in 1947, that '*[m]any forms of Government have been tried, and will be tried in this world of sin and woe. No one pretends that democracy is perfect or all-wise. Indeed it has been said that democracy is the worst form of Government except for all those other forms that have been tried from time to time. . . .*'

Many agree that this idea did not originate with Churchill; nevertheless, his speech helped to encourage reflection and debate on various models of government. While Churchill was speaking on the governance of nations, we will take his prompt to explore some of the various approaches of governance for organisations. If democracy is said to be the best of the worst for governing nations, is there a comparison for governing organisations?

The Cadbury Commission defines corporate governance in this way.

> *Corporate governance is the system by which companies are directed and controlled. Boards of directors are responsible for the governance of their companies. The shareholders' role in governance is to appoint the directors and the auditors and to satisfy themselves that an appropriate governance structure in place. The responsibilities of the board include setting the company's strategic aims, providing the leadership to put them into effect, supervising the management of the business and reporting to shareholders on their stewardship. The board's actions are subject to laws, regulations and the shareholders in a general meeting.*
>
> (Cadbury Committee Report on the Financial Aspects of Corporate Governance 1992: 14)

Ahmad and Omar (2016) recently undertook a systematic review of basic governance models. Using their report I will look closer at two basic models, the Anglo-Saxon and the Continental European. There are many other models and many names used for the same models but most will have very strong commonalities to either of these two basic models.

Anglo-Saxon is the dominant model globally. It is often referred to as the American model or the Shareholder model and is also the model widely applied in the UK. However, in the UK where separation of the executive and non-executive is mandatory, the CEO cannot be the Chairman. This is not the case in the US where it is commonplace to see a title of 'President and CEO.' The model is based on shareholder theory and stresses that the role of management is to maximise the wealth of the shareholders (owners).

The Continental model is based on Stakeholder Theory where the 'manager's' fiduciary duty is to safeguard the legitimate interests not only of shareholders, but also of a broader group of internal and external stakeholders, such as employees, customers, suppliers, management itself, government, political and social groups, environment and society at large (Ahmad and Omar, 2016: 77). An excerpt from their research provides this side-by-side comparison of the two models illustrated in Table 12.1.

While the Anglo-Saxon model is dominant (and is embedded within neo-liberal capitalism—outlined in Chapter 2) trends may be pointing

Table 12.1 Dominant Corporate Governance Models

Aspect	Anglo-Saxon (USA-UK)	Continental European
Corporate purpose	Corporate purpose: maximisation of shareholder wealth	Maximisation of stakeholder wealth
Background	The separation of ownership from control	Different styles of management
Corporate control	Shareholders controlling the managers	Stakeholders controlling the managers
Rights and interest	Protect the rights and interest of shareholders	Protect the rights and interests of stakeholders alongside shareholders
CEO duality	Permitted	Not permitted
Nature of management	Management dominated dominated	Controlling shareholders
Management boards	One-tier board	Two-tier board
Capital related	Dividends prioritised	Dividends less prioritised
Appointment of independent auditors	By independent audit committee	By supervisory board
Disclosure requirement	Limited in 10-K filing, details in proxy reports	In annual reports
Proposition	Market efficiency	Social efficiency of economy
Governance problem and cause	Agency theory; shareholder do not have enough time	Absence of stakeholder involvement; governance failure to represent stakeholders' interest

(Ahmad and Omar, 2016: 94)

to a strengthening Continental model, which seeks to consider the issues of a much wider stakeholder perspective. Looking through the column for the Continental model it does to me have a striking similarity with stakeholder or moral capitalism and from my reading of Chapters 1 and 2 a significant overlap with the good dividends. This chapter will seek to suggest that for the realisation of the good dividends leadership attention needs to be made towards the development of governance that reflects many of the principles outlined in the Continental European model.

Power, Money and Governance

To begin exploring the movement towards the Continental stakeholder orientation let's follow the money and specifically to activist shareholders. Jillian Popadak is Assistant Professor at Duke University's School of Business where she researches governance. Her work, published by the Brookings Institute in 2016, looks at the role of governance and culture in creating value. More specifically she looked at the role of activist investors and how they are increasingly exercising shareholder governance. She claims that 'stronger governance and activist firepower are not always the best remedy for corporations' shortcomings' (2016: 10). The aim of shareholder governance is to enable investors to secure the best returns on their investment by making strategic changes. Popadak claims that in the case of hedge funds it can go so far as to demand divestitures and raise dividends with the aim to improve return on investment. Her work focuses on the implications of shareholder governance on organisational culture and concludes that this practice is often value destroying. The example she gives is of the once giant American retailer, Sears Holdings, and said that it 'was beating the market by 18% in the year after hedge fund investor Eddie Lampert took a major share of the company. But a single-minded concentration on achieving (financial) results changed the firm's culture to such an extent that two years after the acquisition, profits had dropped by 45% and sales gains had vanished' (Popadak, 2016: 1). It seems that when those who exercise governance authority do not look beyond the short-termism of the balance sheet they can bring undue risk to the organisation—the argument outlined by Ant Hesketh in the proceeding chapter. And this points to the opportunities (that are being taken) for investors to drive changes with other objectives—as seen when looking at ESG investing.

A December 2017 Boston Consulting Group (BCG) report claims that 'research reveals a positive correlation between a company's environmental, social and governance (ESG) ratings and its financial results. Firms with higher ESG scores tend to produce greater profit margins with less risk. Driven by investor demand for both sound corporate practices and solid returns, the market for responsible investing grew from $18 trillion in 2014 to $23 trillion in 2016' (2017: 1). Ant Hesketh (Chapter 11) has explained why this might be so. In a similar explanation to Ant the BCG suggest that large investment funds and institutional investors often address a company's governance differently than how they approach its social and environmental practices. While investors actively seek changes that will create value they may 'refuse to buy or may get rid of shares in businesses that do not meet their environmental or social criteria. Alternatively, if investors worked closely with a firm's executives to address social and environmental concerns like carbon dioxide emissions, they could improve the firm's financial performance and reduce its negative impact on society' (2017: 1). This is of course the central thesis of this book and the good dividends. Boston Consulting Group suggest the following actions for institutional investors:

1. **Build an integrated approach to ESG assessment**—Incorporate the ESG evaluation into the risk management process, rather than allocating to a department.
2. **Define priorities for engagement**—Decide the ESG factors that matter the most.
3. **Categorise portfolio holding**—Decide which companies are likely to benefit from outside influence and which are easiest to guide.
4. **Develop a plan for engagement**—Engage management, create an action plan.
5. **Set up systems to track ESG progress over time**—Quantify the impact of ESG being incorporated into the financial results.
6. **Be willing to divest**—If companies do not achieve ESG targets, define the exit plan.
7. **Pilot, test and learn**—Walk before you run. Start small, listen, learn and practice ESG engagement—then grow.
8. **Spread the word**—Broadcast the approach and impact widely.

Drawn together these eight elements point toward leadership commitment and competence to integrating ESG throughout the business as integral to the business model. In this way the notion of impact return on investment (ROI) comes to the fore. Impact investment seeks to bring positive social impact as an outcome of its activities, as it brings financial return to investors.

Through the Lens of One Impact Investor

In a conversation with Florian Kemmerich, Managing Partner at Bamboo Capital in Geneva, I wanted to find out more about what they look for in the companies, including the leadership orientation, for whom they invest in. He started the conversation by differentiating various approaches to impact investing. This must be placed into the context of the upsurge of activity in the values-based investing sector. Rather than a 'commercial first' approach to investment Bamboo Capital is pioneered initially with private equity 'impact first' in emerging markets. This distinction is not intended to highlight ROI or to say one is better than the other. Rather, it states a general approach on impact investing, which guides board decision making. For instance, as a lead investor if they see a company in which they have invested is not meeting their targets they could step in and engage in change management—nothing unique there. However, impact investors may consider such a decision even if they are performing well financially—but are not performing on social and environmental impact measures.

Florian says that Bamboo has learned a lot over the years and they have been a key player in the wave of impact investing for the low-income population in frontier markets. Collaboration across many stakeholders has been and will continue to be key. This comes with a cost as it can increase complexity. Partnering with government bodies or NGOs may go very well but complications may arise at time of exit. Bamboo needs to exit to redistribute the funds to its investors, but some stakeholders may want the investment to continue. These are challenges they learn from and consider for future initiatives. Florian comments that socially minded companies come to Bamboo Capital because they know from the board down into the organisation they are about being impact first, which requires a multi-stakeholder dialogue, and it means that finance does not trump everything else. Bamboo focuses on scalable social impact as an output of their investment and demands quarterly reporting along the way.

Such structured governance requirements place clear demands on an organisation to deliver impact in the form of ROI through managers acting as agents serving a broader fiduciary duty—one that strongly resonates with the Continental European model.

Within family businesses the owner-managers are placed in a different context and a potentially different set of governance needs. The family business and indeed the owner-manager led business dominates as the most common business format (see Chapter 13 for more details on the SME sector). As such I want to give a brief review of the governance issues of family business.

The Family Business

'There has been growing discussion regarding the potential of family firms to embrace practices of corporate sustainability—the tendency to behave in economically, socially, and environmentally responsible ways in a manner that benefits all stakeholders and the community at large' (Le Breton-Miller and Miller, 2015: 26). Miller and Miller suggest that the governance model of family businesses exhibit governance according to three categories: ownership structure, the qualities of its executives and the nature of the board of directors. They argue that each of these categories can play a role in whether or not a business will seek a broader path of responsibility for society, the environment and other stakeholders. With regards to structure they suggest that if the business carries the family name it may be more inclined to behave responsibly to protect the family brand. Family firms often see their future in terms of generations and often have a longer view with regards to decisions and strategic planning. They claim that family firms will engage in more sustainable behaviour when ownership remains in family hands and can look radically different when a family firm goes public.

With regards to the characteristics of the family executives, they must have the ability and willingness to engage in long-term initiatives across many stakeholders. These skills may or may not exist in the family. Family members that can engage in this way have an advantage as they are more likely to behave in a way that protects the family reputation. It can take years though to groom the next generation 'family' executive to take on the leadership role. It is this long-term basis, associated with developing the next family executive that creates the context for a close association with sustainability being firmly on the agenda. This is because of the intent to pass on the business to the next generation (for a useful review see: Le Breton-Miller, Miller and Bares, 2015; Le Breton-Miller and Miller, 2006). Such a long-term orientation invites a willingness to invest in the future of the firm, often by forming win–win relationships with stakeholders. This, in turn, can encourage hiring, training and rewarding of good people, nurturing trust-based relationships with customers, building firm reputation, and embedding the business in the community via good corporate citizenship.

I should emphasise here that the family business has all the latent potential for sustainability to be in the DNA of the business; but this of course may not be realised as a consequence of leadership orientation. If leadership and governance structures do not embrace the win–win stakeholder orientation, the family business may not be capable of being passed on through many generations. The succession model may be a paradox. The need to be a family business requires the family to remain in control. Yet much success of the family business requires a greater involvement of employees in the governance to enrich the quality and diversity of the leadership that often cannot be found through family members. In essence, why should non-family talent remain in the business if there is no progression to leadership? A difficult governance task then, to balance family and non-family members, in the interest of sustaining the family business.

This long-term DNA of the family business and the broader latent responsibilities that become connected with this orientation are potentially very different to the owner-manager investor business. In the next section I explore a governance structure that enables employee ownership and the benefits that may flow from employee ownership in terms of realising the good dividends. There is much potential for the family business in this route, yet of course much challenge in terms of sustaining the pre-eminence of the family interest.

Leaders Leaving a Legacy: Exploring the Governance Transition Process From Founder to Employee Ownership

The rain was falling on a brisk day on the Isle of Skye. Sitting around a glowing peat fire two Scots nursed their glasses of single malt. They had first met in the late 1980s and though walking down different paths in life they were brought together by their common passion of farming in the ocean. Ian Anderson had climbed his way from a sales assistant in Lancashire to becoming a rock legend as leader of the band Jethro Tull. Dennis Overton had studied agri-business in Edinburgh and eventually founded Aquascot. Ian and Dennis built two businesses in parallel, in the Highlands and Islands of Scotland.

The discussion that day was transformative for Dennis. Ian shared that he just heard that the acquirer of the salmon products business that he sold a few years previous was closing its doors to the main processing plant, which employed more than 300 people in Scotland, and the operations were shifting to another part of the country. Dennis stared into the fire and decided that Aquascot would take a different path.

That was 2003. Now, in 2018, Dennis reflects on the eighteenth century and how bonded labour and slavery was so acceptable. He feels that in a hundred years social scientists will be looking back and asking how people could really buy and sell businesses with such little engagement from those that did so much to create the wealth—the employees. Employees essentially have no say in the matter.

Two years after that fireside chat, Dennis and his business partner began to develop plans for change. Aquascot was doing well. Was this really a time to change? Clearly, it was. They drafted what became their roadmap toward an employee ownership trust. The trust was to buy 100 per cent of the equity over the period 2008-2016. This used free cashflow-generated (pre-tax) funds from trading activities. They asked a couple of professional services firms to recommend an EBIT multiple, which were then compared with their own views of fair value and in this way the valuation of the firm was determined. Growth and profitability were taken into account in the formula.

The deal was approved by Her Majesty's Revenue and Customs (HMRC), which is the department of the UK Government responsible for the collection of taxes by individuals and businesses. This meant that Dennis and his partner would receive a huge tax break. UK laws provided the incentive toward such a model by requiring Dennis and his business partner to pay no tax on the gains from the business since their initial investment 25 years earlier. This in a way is a good dividend—good in the sense that any other approach toward an exit would have brought a huge tax liability; and the additional good dividends were more about the future and about impact. Clearly both are necessary if all stakeholder value is to be generated.

Aquascot is in the aquaculture sector. It is the fastest growing form of food production (both plants and animals) in the world today. They farm, process and retail salmon, and are in one of just a few countries in the world that has been successful in farming salmon. Aquascot has recently opened a seaweed farming division. Shore, as it is called, is set out to start a whole new industry in Europe. This business is in rural Scotland where companies of this size are very rare. The business is now over 30 years old and the employees are global experts in the field of aquaculture. In many firms this is the stage of business where the founders would be looking at a liquidity exit. Dennis's thinking process in all of this included reviewing what became of other business that chose to take the other path—the path his friend Ian took. He found that in most sectors it meant consolidation and a move south within five years. This is not what will happen to Aquascot—its future, embedded in the community and to the employee's interests, is far more secure.

The Aquascot Trust has one purpose—'to act in the long-term interest of the beneficiaries.' So, instead of a 'dividend' the company pays a partner bonus to the partners/employees each year based on organisational performance, the first £5,000 is tax-free. This last point is due to a new piece of legislation by the UK government, which acknowledges the value of such a model. Dennis says that 'Aquascot is a practical prescription against the rising tide of inequality.' He adds that the process has really driven employee engagement and in a time where disengagement of employees seems more like the norm. There is a powerful sense of purpose aligned with ownership.

So, what are the employee-owners seeing so far? To date their firm has had nine years of partial turnover to the employees and two years of complete turnover. The employee attrition rate is low relative to the industry norms as is the rate of absenteeism due to sickness. Productivity, earnings and innovation rates are all upper quartile in the sector. A Partnership Council sits alongside the Management Team and Company Board. So, while the business is run in a professional way the Partnership Council can have a voice into the business. What this means is that passionate millennials who are interested in sustainable sources of food will see Aquascot as the employer of choice. The benefits include much more engaged staff who are more aligned to organisational strategic aims, and behave like the responsible owners that they have become. But the impact of all this is moving beyond Aquascot.

Dennis and others have learned from this experience and have created a vision for employee ownership in Scotland. According to the Employee

Ownership Association, firms engaged in EO enjoy a 6–8 per cent superior value when compared to models that are more traditional. Dennis desires a future where 'Scotland becomes recognised internationally as the country which over indexes when it comes to employee ownership. Consequently, there is a more proactive approach to tackling the corrosive effects of inequality and lack of inclusion. Long-term thinking enables more mid-sized businesses to develop. The employee ownership business population impacts disproportionately on Scotland's productivity and also on the innovation indices. Employee ownership as a governance model roots business in Scotland and reduces the potential for operations to be re-located and jobs lost. The children that work in employee owned businesses have a better life and a set of better life outcomes than the national average.' Dennis says that 'it is a life affirming process packed with long-term purpose.' Dennis has shared his story with his peer members of the Young Presidents Organisation (YPO), and in so doing encourages his peers to explore and debate (governance) roads less travelled.

The story here is not just with Aquascot. Many years ago Dennis met Nicholas, a PhD student from Rwanda who managed to get out of the country when it was all coming apart, in 1994. Their friendship developed and after completing his PhD in agriculture sought to start an agribusiness back in his home country. Dennis decided to engage, then invest and became Chairman of the start-up called Ikirezi. Now in its twelfth year it is growing in size, sales and positive social impact. It has been a complex start-up says Dennis. He comments:

> Complex start-ups in the deep countryside, with potential to scale are still rare. Even rarer, businesses with the dignity of countryside people at the heart of their purpose. This year the business will produce seven species of essential oil plants, extracting those oils at distillation centres which are now running 24 hours a day to keep up with the agriculture. We have successfully installed the first hectare of solar powered drip irrigation, which I believe will be transformational to the agriculture. The philosophy is organic throughout, so I've been delighted to see the cow herd grow to produce 30% of our dung requirements; a rabbit enterprise started with urine collection for fertilising; a trial vermiculture (worms) operation scaling up to produce brilliant compost, orange sweet potato being used as a break crop, producing premium organic crops, much in demand in Kigali and 15 beehives now established, producing Rwanda's only (we think) certified organic honey. All of this translates to life changing outcomes for those who work with us. Yesterday, I visited 3 new houses and was proudly escorted round them by their owners.

Dennis is Chairman of the board and has been an important funder in Ikerezi. However, he sees the development described above happening on other regions and sectors in the country. This is so heartening to me. I worked in Rwanda in 1994 as part of the relief and recovery effort immediately following the genocide. Dennis's story is an example of how the authority and vision of a Chairman has great influence across all the elements highlighted in the good dividends. Perhaps we can even add another dividend—the joy felt by leaders that invest themselves in this way, and the joy felt by those watching—knowing what it was like before.

The final section explores an emerging new governance structure of the Benefit Corporation that holds much promise for start-ups, established small and medium businesses and indeed for the corporations. It draws heavily on the Continental model and perhaps beyond. It certainly has much potential to realise the good dividends.

An Entrepreneur Connects with the BCorp Movement

Entrepreneurship has been in the blood of Benoit Greindl since an early age. Soon after university, in Belgium, Benoit and some friends started a real estate business. The organisation began to scale and became a success. Several years on, and with his wife and four children, he decided to sell everything and move to China. They settled in Shanghai where Benoit began another real estate venture. His business was growing from strength to strength when his cousin who was skiing the backcountry of Switzerland contacted him. He was touring well off the marked pistes when his ski bindings broke. The only way out of the situation was to trudge through the snow to a small hamlet called Commière. There was something very alluring about this place—where time seemed to be forgotten. Perched high up in the Swiss Alps, near the French and Italian borders, there were less than a dozen residents when Benoit first travelled back from China to have a look. Walking around the derelict stone barns a vision developed and something very different to his previous real estate initiatives. The idea was to create a place where leaders could really get away, reflect and reconnect.

As Co-Founder and CEO of this new venture, *Montagne-Alternative*, a business charter was drafted, which includes a number of commitments: to the local community and other stakeholders they strive to develop and maintain honest and lasting relationships. To their customers they provide a comfortable environment, which seeks to be in harmony with nature and local traditions. For the environment, they strive to preserve the ecosystem through the use of existing and local materials as well as using innovative approaches for insulation and energy production. The business aims to grow in profits while 'maintaining the balance between the community, customer expectations, employees, suppliers and shareholders, in order to make a positive contribution to the wider society in which we live.' As the shape of the business developed Benoit became familiar with the BCorps Movement and this did play a key role aligning the Shareholders and as well as the many other Stakeholders.

Richard Stammer is the former President and CEO of Cabot Creamery Cooperative, based in Vermont. His *Harvard Business Review* article in December 2016 highlights the reasoning of Cabot Creamery to become BCorp certified. The Benefit Corporation (BCorps) 'are businesses that meet the highest standards of verified social and environmental performance, public transparency, and legal accountability to balance profit and purpose. B Corps are accelerating a global culture shift to redefine success in business and build a more inclusive and sustainable economy (Benefit Corporation, 2018).' They are a community of leaders, now with more than 2,300 companies that have been certified and many others that have undertaken the B Impact Assessment (www.cultivatingcapital. com/completing-the-b-impact-assessment/) as a starting point, which probes into five sections:

- Governance: Standards related to mission, stakeholder engagement, governance structure and controls, and transparency.
- Workers: The standards in this section look at how a company treats its employees, including the compensation practices, benefits, training, worker ownership and work environment.
- Community: This section covers the company's impact on external community stakeholders, including suppliers, distributors and the local economy and community, as well as the company's practices regarding diversity, job creation, civic engagement and charitable giving.
- Environment: Standards related to your company's direct and indirect environmental impacts.
- Customers: Standards related to the impact that your business model has on your customers and whether you serve underserved populations.

Stammer writes 'when the marketing team suggested that Cabot become a certified B Corporation, I was sceptical.' He assumed they were already self-monitoring enough. He then learned that customers were putting more scrutiny on their impact and that something with more teeth would be needed. They completed the BCorps certification process in 2012. Stammer writes:

> To my surprise, certification not only addressed the questions posed by our retail partners but also delivered value beyond our expectations. B Corp certification encouraged more "whole-systems thinking" around our social and environmental practices, which led Cabot to develop even more robust customer and consumer programs, cut operating costs, and strengthen our brand reputation as a sustainability-minded company.
>
> (Stammer, 2016: 3)

Cabot leaned on the findings of the Nielsen survey, *The Sustainability Imperative*, which reveals the willingness of consumers to pay more if they feel the product and firm is aligned with the social good (for an elaboration of this see Chapter 9 on purpose-driven brand dividend). Cabot saw improvements in waste management, operational cost saving, attractiveness as an employer and the ability to benchmark with others who have joined the movement. Their scores are posted online.

In my conversation with Benoit he shared how the BCorps movement opened up advantages for the business as well as challenges. From a marketing perspective his business would be the first BCorp certified member in Switzerland. But it was to the challenges of meeting the criteria of the assessment for certification, outlined above, that significant value was gained from a leadership perspective. Addressing the assessment criteria gave a strong structure that aligned with the purpose of the business as well as alignment of stakeholders to the business. The five assessed areas enabled structured governance processes to focus on realising value for the stakeholders in a way that the business leadership could engage, oversee and control all that the business was doing. It gave Benoit the confidence to pursue the notion of doing well and doing good in a systematic and measurable way. Moreover, it was an overt tool of leadership in the boardroom to avoid distractive issues. Benoit was able to manage his board, structure employee engagement and embrace the community by reporting on the activities of the business framed by the five areas of assessment. His final comment on the advantages was the opportunity for engaging in a common governance model that was part of a trusted network of business managers and owners—the opportunity to develop a learning and supporting community.

I had the opportunity to discuss B-Corps with Marcello Palazzi. Marcello is the founder of B-Lab Europe, the governing structure for business becoming B-Corp certified. He manages the B-Lab National Offices across Europe and has recently been appointed Global Ambassador for B-Lab.

Marcello offered up strong evidence that the tide is turning from shareholder capitalism (the Anglo-Saxon model) and firmly towards stakeholder capitalism (the Continental model). He emphasised that more and more companies are recognising the need to take a more inclusive approach to doing business—where stakeholders voices are heard, where the issues of the environment are taken seriously, which seeks to bring positive impact to society, and where there are felt benefits by staff—while making and indeed increasing profits. Much of his time is spent connecting leaders to those that can help them in this journey. The businesses he speaks with range from multi-billion dollar multi-nationals, to Montagne Alternative. Size is not an impediment for embracing this inclusive approach, and he spoke convincingly of how governance models like B-Corps, employee ownership and other forms, such as cooperatives, will become most prominent and perhaps, just perhaps, the dominant governance models.

Conclusion

We opened this chapter by joining a meeting where CEOs gathered to discuss the changing times, grand challenges and to explore opportunities that would bring positive impact on society. We then looked at the cascade effect of governance from shaping values and vision in the boardroom and how that translates into responsible behaviours by staff throughout the organisation—and not just seeking to comply with minimum standards, but as an extension of values. We then revisited the good dividends model as we see its bridge to the practice of governance. The two basic governance models most common today were put on the table for us to identify the areas with the most affinity for the good dividends. The alignment of the Continental model to the good dividends was most striking. The notion of impact and investor ROI pursuing ESG was explored. This offered us encouragement that aligning a business to stakeholder interests further resonates with where investor money is trending. We explored governance of family businesses and how the long-term orientation offers up much scope to connect with the principles of the good dividends. Finally, we looked at some real examples of governance case studies that were akin to the Continental model through the leadership examples presented.

The good dividends argument has resonance with the Continental model and more specifically the values-based model that has grown out of that. I would stress the importance for the realisation of the good dividends that leadership makes this connection most salient. In the way that responsible leadership enables the good dividends, then governance overseas and controls the realisation of the good dividends.

As a means of summarising the key aspects of the chapter and the thrust of my argument, I offer a set of four statements that reflect principles of governance that would speak to an organisation that is realising the good dividends:

#1—The behaviour of the Chairman, Board, Founder, Owner or CEO can have profound implications with regards to the societal impact of the firm. If you are in one of these roles consider the legacy you would like to leave, as an individual and as an organisation. Knowing the importance of board composition, consider how the female voice is heard in your boardroom.

#2—Moving from shareholder focus to stakeholders requires a wide-angle lens and new skills in managing different relationships previously not considered. So consider if there are stakeholders that require your time and attention; and consider how to be more inclusive of young leaders in direction setting.

#3—Governors within organisations can find incredible meaning and purpose in their roles by leading in new ways, through innovation and strategic change. They also have a role to play in ensuring their firm's purpose is clear and compelling throughout all levels in the firm. Consider the level of purpose and meaning felt by the staff around you—is there a need to lead the change?

#4—New models, partners and frameworks such as the Benefit Corporation Movement (BCorps) and the Sustainable Development Goals (SDGs) are gaining purchase. Consider your level of knowledge of these initiatives and consider if your organisation can contribute and benefit from engagement in such initiatives—and consider the risks of ignoring these opportunities.

Then, as a final footnote, watch this space as millennials, who generally carry a strong interest in organisational purpose, social impact and equality, continue to develop businesses. They will see this argument perhaps as the common-sense Steve described in the opening chapter of his son's opinion of the good dividends because they would not wish to pursue governance according to those who in hindsight appear quite flawed.

13 Applying the Good Dividends to a Business

A CEO's Reflections

*Luke Freeman, Steve Kempster
and Stewart Barnes*

Introduction

This chapter applies the good dividends concept to a multi-disciplined small-medium-sized enterprise (SME) in order to enhance this organisation—that is to generate good dividends. Attention is given to the planetary dividend (as outlined in Chapter 4 and Chapter 10), an aspect that had not been considered before within the case organisation, and in particular to draw on United Nations (UN) Sustainable Development Goals (SDGs), as a means for understanding and measuring the planetary value to an SME. The chapter explores how stakeholders were engaged to distil areas of value and how such areas of value could be measured in the context of the business. The chapter highlights different orientations of stakeholders to the good dividends; most notably the enthusiasm of employees in contrast to the owners of the business and the suppliers. We conclude the chapter with a conversation with Luke reflecting on beginning to implement the good dividends in his business. The conversation centres on a fundamental question: how can engaging with the SDGs add value to small businesses?

Small-medium-sized enterprises (SMEs) account for 99 per cent of the UK business population, generate 48 per cent of GDP and employ 60 per cent of people. Globally these figures are representative of other nations. SMEs are embedded in local communities in terms of employment, supplier and customer relationships. Collectively SMEs are a most important contributor to local, regional and national well-being. Moreover, the influence of the owner-manager(s) to the orientation of SME activity and practice is significant (Barnes, Kempster and Smith, 2015). In essence, by working with owner-managers considerable change within SMEs can be enacted. Accordingly, SMEs and owner-managers can be an important arena in which the challenges of society identified in Chapter 2 can be addressed.

Stoian and Gilman (2017) argue that businesses are neither responsible for the world's problems, nor do they have the resources to solve them all. However, they go on to assert that by careful prioritisation of the needs of stakeholders, companies can focus on those needs that make most strategic sense. They argue that SMEs need to focus on CSR activities that contribute to their competitive advantage and hence enhance firm growth. Stoian and Gilman (2017) contend that SME firms which implement CSR activities related to the community, the workforce and the environment are likely to grow faster than if they were to focus singularly on the marketplace. This is of course the central argument of this book, and it is helpful that Stoian and Gillman connect this argument to the SME context as a strategic orientation for growth.

This chapter focuses on the case of the M F Freeman Group (MFFG). The group turnover in 2017 was £25m and it employs 100 people. The business operates in the area of the West of England in the UK, near Ross-on-Wye. Luke Freeman is Joint Chief Executive Officer (JCEO) of MFFG, which operates a diverse portfolio of divisions across residential and commercial property development, groundworks and building contracting, plant hire, farming, forestry and leisure. The case study focuses on the housing division, called Freeman Homes (FH).

Steve and Luke met during a workshop being run by Stewart exploring the good dividends (GDs) in the context of SMEs in December 2016. Luke, together with three other businesses, formed an action learning set to explore how to realise value from the GDs. Luke was keen to understand where value could be realised and connect the same to various stakeholders of the business. Although aware of sustainability and CSR discourses this had been at arm's length to the everyday activity of the business. A perception that CSR was more of a nice thing to do but was framed as a cost and negative impact on profitability.

To give a context to the sector Luke operates in, globally the land, real estate and construction sector contributes 30 per cent of greenhouse gas (GHG) emissions (the largest amount among all business sectors). In addition, it consumes 40 per cent of energy and resources with a heavy reliance on finite natural resources such as water, primary aggregates and timber amongst other building materials (Construction and Real Estate Sector Supplement, 2011). As a consequence, the construction industry is most influential globally when it comes to impacting the health and well-being of people and the environment from a local and indeed a global perspective. Herweijer and Combes (2017) suggest that sustainable products and services represent a growth market, because they are backed by the commitment of governments globally with regard to the 2015 Paris Agreement for Climate Change (United Nations, 2015) for a low-carbon economic transition by mid-century. Herweijer and Combes (2017) go on to suggest that responding to the SDGs could realise meaningful returns in the short- and medium term, where novel technologies become cost competitive quickly, or sustainable goods and services simply provide a better user experience (see, for example, home smart metres).

Reflective of Luke's previous perspective, Unruh et al. (2016) comment that many company executives embrace the neo-liberal conventional wisdom that little weight is given to environmental, social and governance (ESG) metrics. The prominent context, highlighted in Chapters 5 and 11, is that many listed companies still give little reporting attention to aspects such as ESG metrics. Unruh et al. argue (along with Ant and Randal in Chapters 11 and 12) that there has been a movement by investors to give greater weight and emphasis to the value of ESG metrics by recognising that sustainability-related activities are material to the financial success of a company over time. This view is further supported by the apparent shift of policy in major property development companies such as Singapore's largest developer (CDL, 2017), India's major builder (Tata Group, 2015) and one of the largest housebuilders in the UK (Berkeley Homes, cited in Pless and Maak, 2011). These organisations established their sustainability statements many years ago and since the 2015 Paris Agreement for Climate Change (United Nations, 2015) appear to have given more attention to setting clear direction and robust ESG goals and metrics to guide them to 2030, aligned to the target date of the SDGs.

Encouraged by the foregoing, Luke is seeking to steer FH to consider the benefits of a transition from a neo-liberal business focused mainly on profit to one that embraces moral capitalism by adding value to all elements that it touches, interacts with and impacts: generating purposeful social impact profitably. By seeking to explore an overt social purpose, a series of questions emerged: can the business become known as an innovator and beacon of forward thinking for sustainable practices, disrupting traditional methods that exist within the sector, particularly for SMEs? Additionally, how would such an approach impact on the business employees and customers? Would it have any significant impact on supplier relationships? And could a focus on the SDGs be a useful step in enabling the business and in particular employees, customers, supply chains and the Board, to engage with the GDs approach? This ambitious final question links with the established purpose of the business captured in its mission statement 'Building for a Better Future'.

But to be clear, Luke highlights the importance of the business as doing good in terms of engaging in the SDG's as long as it can be demonstrated that by doing such adds value to the business. Luke advocates that if the project is approached in this way then this is most likely to create greater engagement levels from the range of stakeholders, most particularly his board.

The chapter is structured as follows. First, we contextualise the case study. SMEs have received very little attention with regard to implementation of sustainability and CSR, most notably in the construction sector. Yet SMEs are most significant to economies, employment and community impact. A gap that needs addressing, and one that is unlikely to be addressed without engaged owner-manager leadership. Second, we outline the case research undertaken by Luke to identify which SDGs would add value to the business and to stakeholders. This embraces a leadership lens of an owner-manager seeking to embrace stakeholders to engage with the GDs through attention to the SDGs. The result of Luke's approach is explored and it highlights very different stakeholder responses. Of particular interest is the difference between the board and employees. The results illustrate how the SDGs can be tailored to the specific needs of an SME and aligned through measures to the GDs. The final part of the chapter draws on an interview with Luke to understand the leadership agenda in light of the emerging outcomes of implementing GDs through attention to the SDGs.

Purpose and Profit in the SME Construction Context

One of the SDG targets (12.6) cites the benefits of sustainability reporting and encourages companies to integrate sustainability information into their reporting cycles. According to the KPMG Survey of Corporate Responsibility Reporting (2015), 92 per cent of the world's largest 250 corporations report on their sustainability performance and 74 per cent of these use GRI standards to do so (Global Reporting Initiative, 2011). Yet, research has reported a lack of follow through from integrated reporting and change in behaviours and practices (see Chapter 5). The 9,500 UN Global Compact (United Nations Global Compact, 2017) participants, the majority of which are SMEs, are required to report annually on their sustainability impacts. It is very unclear from such reporting how value is generated from such activity and for whom. Certainly, there is a dearth of attention to how SMEs could frame engagement in sustainability and CSR in a manner that gives clarity on value generation. Indeed, methods of measurement are similarly thin on the ground. The absence of clarity and direction regarding evidence of value add, and few approaches to guide such work became the catalyst for Luke's engagement outlined below.

Of the little guidance that is specific to the construction industry, the work of Hartenberger (2015) is helpful in identifying seven areas that fuse aspects of sustainability and CSR (and in this case the principles of GDs) intended to enhance a construction business. The list has strong resonance to a number of the GDs (emphasised by italics):

1. Demonstrate *[financial] responsible business* commitment through communication of their strategies, policies and integrated reporting.
2. Increase *brand value* and reputation as a leader on environmental, social and corporate governance issues.
3. Reduce *operational, supply chain* related and reputational risks by complying with regulatory requirements and industry standards.

4. Reduce *[operational] supply chain* related risks by securing consistent and long-term access to high quality raw materials and products.
5. Maximise *human capital* through improved working conditions and increased well-being.
6. Optimise *operational resource efficiency* by enabling bottom line cost savings (e.g. energy, water, waste efficiency, fewer raw materials used).
7. Contribute to overall *social equity* and stability thus creating a stable investment environment.

The similarity of these seven aspects to the GDs gave Luke a sense of confirmation that the ideas are worth investing effort into. Not that Steve is necessarily a dangerous optimist, but the business stakeholders need taking along a journey, particularly a journey that questions taken-for-granted assumptions. As such it was useful and encouraging to view independent arguments that are complementary. To give further encouragement the arguments of the GDs reflect closely the work of Adams (2017) who aligns the SDGs with the 'capitals', discussed in Chapter 1. Adams offers her five-step process:

1. Understand sustainable development issues relevant to the organisation's external environment.
2. Identify material sustainable development issues that influence value creation [for the business].
3. Develop strategy to contribute to the SDGs through the business model.
4. Develop integrated thinking, connectivity and governance.
5. Prepare the integrated report.

She refers to her five-step model as being able to 'maximize value creation and enhance knowledge of the impact of business activities on sustainable development. It can assist organisations in reducing risk, identifying opportunities and delivering long-term, innovative solutions and technologies for addressing sustainable development' (Adams, 2017: 7). While this five-step model shows good progression in the maturity of application of SDGs, for Luke it lacked rigour and a level of granularity to make it a powerful tool that can be practically applied by SMEs. Although mention is given to risks and opportunities that exist for businesses who are willing to embrace the SDGs, little detail is offered on this. Luke's concerns related to the vague and opaque attention to the process of undertaking the five steps and how value is generated for the business and for other stakeholders. There is a leadership necessity to be clear on processes for value realisation and measurement of value, and for whom value is generated.

Giving emphasis to 'measure what matters' (which complements 'what gets measured gets done') points leadership attention to a sense of a forward-thinking goal. There is an abundance of possible ways to measure the SDGs and the GDs. There is the need to be selective. In this way Luke's focus was not about uncovering metrics and objectives, but to understand how to choose from those metrics that are available and which are directly applicable to his business and will resonate with stakeholders. He comments that 'focusing on value adding impact to the business is a much easier sell to stakeholders such as employees, and board members.' He extends the argument that 'the easier it is to sell this concept, and its change, the better the impact and the results.'

Drawing on these principles and the notion of 'measure what matters' he applied the following four leadership steps:

1. Conduct a board level strategy session to consider the relevance of the SDGs to the business, identifying opportunities and risks.
2. Benchmark current and future planned activities against the outcome of the board strategy and define corporate goals, key performance indicators and implementation plans in line with priorities identified.
3. Establish board and senior management oversight to support integration into decision making and action.
4. Disclose sustainability impacts and progress on the SDGs, and integrate sustainability information into the business reporting cycle.

These four steps provided a useful catalyst to enter into the space of engaging with the SDGs. The remainder of this chapter explores step 1. Steps 2 and 3 have begun and Luke explores early issues on these steps within the interview at the end of the chapter.

To enable engagement with the SDGs, greater granularity was needed than was offered in the documents of the SDGs and related sub-targets. The SDGs are far too expansive and wieldy for the size, capability, applicability and ambition of an SME. There is insufficient specificity toward a particular business and context. The orientation of the SDGs is primarily for large organisations (large businesses, NGO's, local and national governments) in terms of how much impact can be brought to bear on delivering a particular goal. However in the SME context, arguably the relationship between SME and the SDGs should be considered the other way around if it is to have traction, and value. That is, what value can the SDG have on the business? Further, there are few concrete examples of the application of the SDGs to an SME from which modification can be discerned. Finally, if stakeholders find it difficult to relate the output or impact of the SDGs to the business they are unlikely to engage.

Luke set about seeking to identify a set of potential objectives that were related to the SDGs, but importantly anchored to the business model of the GDs that were specific to the business needs of FH. These would subsequently be tailored to stakeholders through a filtering process. The three objectives were:

1. Create a baseline of how FH are currently operating with respect to GDs, thus defining how '"Goodly" FH are?' in order to inform what is required to make progress.
2. Identify what objectives can be set, which will support the delivery of GDs in order to design a strategy. To add maximum value for least effort it is necessary to identify objectives which when realised will deliver GDs.
3. Understand the desired and necessary future state with respect to GDs in order to provide visible and realistic targets for all FH stakeholders, and to provide means to measure performance.

To be instructive for others we briefly describe the method Luke employed to achieve the above objectives.

Methods to Measure What Matters

Rather than seeing the three objectives as separate disconnected parts (marbles) Steve and Luke sought to situate the objectives into a systemic hole (the bird's nest). Using systems thinking (outlined in Chapter 4, where the bird's nest and marbles are elaborated!) FH is imagined as a business system that generates good dividends in order to provide a better future by building the right houses in the right places to enhance their community. The system activities became:

- Increasing the *human resources dividend* through empowerment, engagement and training of employees to grow the organisation to build for a better future.
- Increasing the *social innovation dividend* by creating communities which have a sense of place and are enjoyable, rewarding and sustainable places to live.
- Increasing *the planetary dividend* by ensuring that we build sustainable developments which are carefully designed with the highest regard for the environment and sustainable communities.
- Increasing the *operational dividend* through innovation programmes into improved production techniques that minimise the use of resources. Also test new approaches to design, technology, materials and construction techniques to enhance the planetary dividend.
- Increasing the *brand dividend* through excellent customer service and stakeholder consultation during the development process.
- Increasing the *financial dividend* through engaging understanding and support of the owners/stakeholders in building for a better future.

With this system stated, Luke sought to understand how the SDGs as a first step might enable all of the above GDs to be enhanced and hopefully aligned to create a whole greater than the sum of the parts. The SDGs were seen as a focal area to stimulate implementation and measurement of the GDs within FH. The steps undertaken were as follows:

1. *Derive metrics for FH based on relevant SDGs from prior research undertaken by PWC (2017)*: PWC identified which of the 17 individual SDGs are most relevant to different sectors of business and developed a tool—enter an industry sector (the construction sector) and it shows the most relevant SDGs.
2. *Map SDG metrics to GDs, thus finding the relationship between SDGs and GDs*: A questionnaire was created to gain insight into the level of relevance of each of the 68 objectives to each of the six GDs. This showed the association of the five SDGs and the six GDs with respect to FH. The questionnaire was completed by Luke and Steve, and also Stewart Barnes, who has worked with Luke for over two years as a leadership development coach. The least fit related to the social innovation dividend. Luke chose to drop this from the process because of the potential ambiguity and difficulty for stakeholders to engage in this dividend related to the SDGs.
3. *Evaluate each of the SDGs to see which is most relevant and impactful to FH*: A score was created where the objectives were ranked based on this scoring system to identify which ones were strongest in their mapping to each of the GDs.
4. *Select the objectives based on relevance and effort to measure*: First, a rough order of magnitude of how much effort it would take to assess progress of an SDG objective, or more importantly measure a metric of performance that is associated with an SDG. The second part was to understand how relevant the SDG sub-objective is to FH. A scoring system was constructed which combined the relevance to FH with the effort to measure performance. Twelve of the SDG measures were removed, leaving 52 sub-objectives that warranted further investigation.
5. *Derive the stakeholders that add value to FH*: Working with Head of Organisational Development for FH, Luke identified activities within the business and associated stakeholders engaged in these activities. A total of 17 stakeholders were highlighted. Through dialogue they identified the six most important stakeholders. Each of these stakeholders were aligned with the remaining 52 SDGs.
6. *Create a score for SDGs alignment to FH value generation*: Consultations with the stakeholders explored the relevance and value-adding nature of the respective SDGs to their stakeholder interest and to FH. The earlier questionnaire was adapted to suit respective stakeholders. It became a basis for conversation as well as a document to be completed. It provided a stakeholder estimate of which SDG sub-objective would give most value to FH and to themselves.

The final two steps in Luke's approach are explored in the interview. For completeness these steps were: #7: *Propose which SDGs, and aligned GDs, to focus on to add value for FH and the stakeholders*; and #8: *First actionable steps*.

The Results

There appeared to be much scope for FH to align its activities to the GDs and the SDGs. Through Luke's first six steps he has become assured that value can be obtained and measured. The data presented in Table 13.1, which Luke has compiled, give a glimpse into this:

Table 13.1 Summary of Analysis of Replies per Stakeholder

Stakeholder	No. Replies	Mean	Std. Dev
Internal managers	6	7.6	1.9
Board	2	4.2	0.9
Marketing Team	3	8.5	1.2
Finance Team	4	4.0	2.2
Customers	0	No Data	No Data
Subcontractors	1	2.9	0.0
Employees non mgmt.	20	7.3	2.5
Press	0	No Data	No Data

Luke provides a brief explanation of the columns:

> *Mean*—the average score that the respondents gave across all their questions between 0–10. A higher score shows they thought the objectives would add value; *Std. Dev*—How much of a spread in the questionnaire answers. A score of 0 means they all agreed completely on their answers, a higher score suggests more disagreement.

Although the numbers are not statistically significant in the meaning of statistics they are significant to Luke and his business context. The table highlights some very interesting insights with respect to the stakeholder attitudes. For example, the marketing team was most positive about the SDG sub-objectives related to their area of expertise. They could see how they could add value. The only external group consulted, the subcontractor group, thought that there would be little value add from the SDG sub-objectives connected to their area. This might relate to the nature of the industry and to the highly contractual cost-based structure of the relationship, and thus find it difficult to interpret how value for them, and perhaps FH, would be created. The employees and management team were confident that value would be added; a sense of appreciating the scope and opportunity that may enrich their employment by engaging in the SDGs. However, the board and the finance team saw little value. This is most striking, and we shall explore this and the other stakeholder views in greater depth in the interview with Luke.

For Luke, taking the data as instructive of stakeholder insight to add value, effort and capability to measure, as well as a pragmatic guide of where the energy in the business may sit for engaging with the SDG objectives, he progressed to a final sift. A final 12 SDG sub-objectives were identified—two from each of the six stakeholders. It reflected a leadership judgement: the most likely to add value, least difficult or costly to measure, most relevant to FH, and are most likely to be positively received by respective stakeholders. These are illustrated in Table 13.2.

Table 13.2 Best Two Value-Adding Objectives as Defined by Each Stakeholder

Best from each Stakeholder

		1st		*2nd*
Internal managers	9.1	Upgrade *Freeman Homes* infrastructure (buildings, heating systems, construction processes, plant) to use less energy & fuel, create less waste and to be more respectful to the environment	11.1	Create community engagement strategy for all new Freeman development sites
Board	9.8	To use strategic business planning to innovate and employ disruptive business models	11.4	Ensure that all *Freeman Homes* social and environmental impact strategies have a governance process and policy in place (such as ISO14000)
Marketing Team	8.15	Develop a programme to support the training and employment of young persons and new starters	13.2	Ensure skillsets exist in *Freeman Homes* to manage the effect that climate change could have on the business (operations, supply, distribution and logistics)

Best from each Stakeholder

		1st		*2nd*
Finance Team	13.11	Initiate an action group of companies or become a beacon through our own actions, with relation to sustainability	13.1	Sign up to industry bodies related to business in climate action
Customers		No Data		No Data
Subcontractors	8.7	Implement policies and programmes to reduce workplace injuries and accidents	8.8	Implement policies and programmes to avoid work related disease e.g. chemical handling
Employees non-mgmt.	11.2	Ensure that all divisions have flexible working policies and measures e.g. flexi time	9.4	Become involved in building UK infrastructure in partnership with the government

Making This Happen Through Measures Associated With Good Dividends

From a leadership perspective, if Luke wished to achieve his desire for a GD system to be realised through engagement with the SDGs then the measures should be anchored to the GDs. The intention was for performance measures to be used internally, and externally (suppliers), as visible and transparent means to connect the SDGs with the GDs approach.

The 12 SDG sub-objectives were mapped back to the GDs using the mapping previously discussed with the top three scoring objectives for each GD selected. This is again anchored to the stakeholder-identified orientations. The objectives that were adopted for FH are shown in Table 13.3:

Table 13.3 Objectives Related to Good Dividends

Good Dividend	*SDG Objective/Metric ID*
Human Resources	8.7, 8.15, 8.8
Planetary	11.3, 11.1, 11.13
Brand	11.6, 11.1, 13.2
Financial	9.4, 13.1, 13.11
Operational	9.6, 9.8; 11.4,

The range of measures across the five GDs (i.e. social innovation was dropped earlier) gives scope to enable the business to commence along the journey of engaging primary stakeholders with the GDs implicitly, through the explicit legitimacy of engaging with the SDGs. Further, legitimacy is similarly associated with using the measures that draw from the work of PWC (2017). As such the notion of the SDGs speak to a discourse that other organisations are beginning to embrace. Using the SDGs as strategic focus, as well as using the measures associated with the SDGs, offers scope for Luke's business to engage and communicate with a range of stakeholders—internally and externally—on a topic and language that is legitimised through association with the United Nations. For example, the customers of the business, who have thus far not been part of the stakeholder engagement, may embrace the business's approach that illustrates a commitment to the SDGs (in actions and communications). As a consequence, the business has the potential to enhance its reputation (extend the brand dividend). It is possible that the action on the range of SDG's could be readily communicated between the employees and the customers—reinforcing the sense of purpose that FH is engaged in and highlighting why the business is engaging in the SDGs and potentially stimulate or align with customer interest on aspects of sustainability. The enhanced reputation has spin off benefits with regard to relationships with communities in which FH undertake activity. Often customers of FH are drawn out from immediate communities in which the housing developments are situated. FH are considering using external promoter measures to examine customer reactions to such conversations. The employee–customer conversation similarly reinforces the employee sense of confirmation of the purpose for which the business is engaged through pursuing the SDGs. Luke will be measuring the anticipated human resource dividend through his employee survey (to include net internal promoter scores) but also aspects such as attrition, sickness and staff injuries.

The process devised by Luke gives a strong sense of being logical. It engages the business stakeholders in a manner that is low risk. Luke's leadership approach is not to act in a zealous and evangelical manner. He has not sought to implement a comprehensive set of SDGs and related proliferation of measures. Rather these actions and measures draw on recommendations of stakeholders as aspects that are considered of low risk but of greatest value to the business and to themselves. This politically savvy and responsible leadership approach is all the more necessary in light of the relatively lukewarm (excuse the pun) response from the board and finance stakeholders.

What Happens Next?

The final section of the chapter is a conversation between Stewart and Luke on his leadership thus far in terms of progressing the development of the GDs.

Luke, Let's Start at the Beginning. Why Did You Want to Embrace the GDs Through the SDGs?

I liked the simple idea: if you maximise your capitals you will maximise profit. And the fact it is a business model is most appealing—it makes sense to me. The GDs are not about sustainability . . . they are a way of doing business profitably. But it does do something very different, which is challenging, but I like it—it makes you think of your purpose as central to the business and the business model. I should say though that the GDs concept is new and there is little background on it. However, there is more granularity in the application of SDGs to organisations and a greater maturity of SDGs in terms of businesses applying the concept. There are similarities between the SDGs and GDs and there is much in the former that can be applied to the latter. The SDGs encourage businesses to carry out their activities in a more sustainable and responsible manner. What can your business do to enable the SDGs? So I do like them as a framework and the way it links to the GDs. But here's the thing; I think the GD business model approach turns this round and asks 'what can taking action on the SDGs do for the business?' I like that.

It Was Interesting the Board's Reaction to You Pursuing the GDs. What Was Your Response to the Relatively Low Level of Enthusiasm of the Board?

'The literature said it was a typical response so I expected this reaction from the board. Yes, I was disappointed but it wasn't surprising as the overall purpose of the business is to make profit. We operate in a very competitive market and there was probably a worry that the GDs would be like sustainability related work and could affect us in financial terms making us less competitive. The perception is commonplace in our industry and CSR activities are often seen as philanthropic activities and not value adding. We need to prove the benefits. We need to measure what can be done and show the results. Show enhanced profitability. So it's understandable. But I guess that's my leadership role—managing stakeholders and in particular this important stakeholder.

Picking Up on the Leadership and Board Aspects Could You Speak About How the GDs Impacted on Governance Processes—for Example How Are the Measures Being Reported?

Our good dividend journey is one of continuous improvement. It will be a long journey and, although we have just commenced, we have already made significant steps by engaging our stakeholders to embrace the concept of the GDs. We have started reporting on goals and metrics related to the GDs and these are used to add value across the organisation in many ways. This includes, for example, promoting our strategy and progress of the GDs concept to improve our brand dividend, which in turn adds value by improved customer perception of the organisation. This in turn improves the attractiveness of the business thus improving sales.

Other examples include the adoption of technology such as smart meters in the homes we develop to reduce energy usage.

The goals and metrics related to the GDs can be used in line with the GRI integrated reporting standard.

Our vision is to continue to roll out these initiatives and report the benefits in our governance processes. Reporting on the goals and metrics will allow us to recognise the difference we are making and this will ensure that we make the most of embracing the opportunity to add value.

It is our vision to create a culture which has the concept of GDs embedded at its core.

How Have These Been Rolled Out?

The roll out of the goals and metrics are in progress. We have a methodology. We've engaged stakeholders, reflected on the responses and have gone back out to our stakeholders.

We have refined the process, re-surveyed everyone who was involved previously and we have increased the sample size plus undertaken further face-to-face follow up interviews.

To What Levels?

We are trying to engage as wide a spectrum of different stakeholders as is practically possible. We produce and publish a triannual 'Lifestyle' magazine which goes out to thousands of potential homebuyers and within this we feature articles highlighting the various ways MFFG, and in particular FH, contributes positively to the community. We shall add some detail on the SDGs'. Please delete 'towards GD's and SDGs. We regularly update our websites to communicate about our recent projects. We discuss GDs at meetings with potential investors as we believe there will be an increase in responsible investment. We are positioning ourselves as a beacon company for ethical investors to work with who value responsible leadership and sustainable development.

So What Has Happened Since You Commenced This Project?

Five years ago, I would have viewed GDs as a cost. Due to the project I now think differently. My personal awareness has improved of the challenges facing the planet, communities and humanity. My mindset has changed to embrace the GDs and SDGs.

There are organisations out there who use CSR as 'greenwash'. People can see through that. GDs addresses CSR in a deeper and more meaningful way. I am leading GDs across the company. Yes, it is top down, but it is change and it needs to be led.

GDs are filtering through the organisation. The awareness of the concept of GDs is being embedded in the organisation. It is at an early stage but I feel it is becoming part of the culture of the organisation. A conversation has kickstarted in the company. People see GDs as an opportunity, not as an obligation. Employee engagement has improved because our staff are seeing initiatives that they are engaged with and playing a big part in instigating ideas and taking the lead. These are being completed throughout the company. It's exciting. Seeing our people engaged with this, sense of purpose, exciting.

I also believe the understanding of the Board and Finance team has improved and their perception has shifted because they no longer see the concept of the GDs purely as a philanthropic activity. They recognise it has the ability to add value. Perhaps still sceptical, but that's OK.

Looking at What's Happened So Far. What Have Been the Leadership Challenges?

I think the challenge for my leadership has been to grasp the enormity of the climate change issue that faces us all. My improved understanding of the challenges that face humanity mean that I have reconsidered what my purpose really means and how I can use my leadership to make a difference and drawing people into conversations around purpose, aligning these—not everyone has to share a single purpose—but getting this much more tangible and part of everyday conversations and delivering on our purposes.

Other leadership challenges include, finding the time for such an initiative. Time in an SME is always at a premium. Another is the mindset of philanthropy associated with CSR. Also, getting customers to see the value of what we are doing, see the value in enhanced and more sustainable products and paying for such value.

Steve spoke to us about moral outrage. More moral outrage needs to be encouraged . . . a crisis to initiate change and meet the 2030 climate change targets. The credit crunch of 2008–2009 put sustainability back 5–10 years. When is the next recession? It will undoubtedly have a negative impact. If we lose a few more years then there is not much time left before 2030.

When I spoke to my brother about these challenges and after he absorbed the enormity and perceived requirement for moral outrage to create change, he responded by saying that he found it quite depressing. This made me think about approaching the issue differently because there was a danger that people would switch off and disengage from the problem. I realised that I needed to reposition my communication and highlight the opportunity rather than the problem. I believe this approach to addressing the issues is the way forward to engage stakeholders in the business to make a difference. As I said earlier, this cannot be 'greenwash'. We, the leaders, need to be able to demonstrate clear business benefit so that we create the drivers for rapid change.

The climate change issue is a ticking time bomb and we need to react on a greater scale and at a faster pace. This is a once in a lifetime opportunity to engage workforces around the planet, to innovate to solve the world's problems and at the same time add value to their organisations across the spectrum of the GD concept.

Why would we not do this?

So, my leadership challenge is to engage as many people as quickly as possible to make a difference. I find this exciting, engaging and I recognise this is the moment when I am able to use everything I have learned about leadership over my career to make a difference.

What Did You Expect From Moving Into This Space?

I expected resistance from the board and sub-contractors. Whilst my board is well-educated, awareness at the board level was low. I was quite naïve in not recognising this sooner.

I knew I'd be fascinated by the literature on responsible leadership and the GDs. The depth of literature available and excellent evidence of sustainable practices being adopted exceeded my expectations.

And the Unexpected?

The complexity of introducing new ideas on responsibility and sustainability. Much is written but it's often contradictory and there is nothing out there that SME business leaders can pick up quickly to engage the company and that addresses the key question, '*How can the SDG's add value to small businesses?*'

You Mentioned Excitement Earlier. So What Has Excited You?

Leaders can now go one stage further and ask themselves, '*How can each of the six GDs add value to my business?*' It is at this level of granulation where the GDs concept really excites me as actions can be agreed with people and teams taking responsibility for their tasks. By doing this, GDs will change the DNA of the business . . . if you can change the DNA?!

Although this sounds over grand, I'm also excited about playing a part in solving the world's problems whilst at the same time creating improved alignment with MFFG's overarching purpose of *'Building a better future'*.

So I Must Also Ask What Has Disappointed You?

Perceptions of capitalism. I am not sure many people understand the benefits of doing things differently. Profits are a good thing as they drive matters, but what hasn't come through yet is that by embracing responsibilities and sustainability you can improve profitability.

What is needed is a shift in perception.

But that can be very difficult. For example, consider the deforestation of Mexico. Villagers are hungry and have no money to buy food. Why would they not take a job in the logging industry?

The enormity of the issues facing humanity makes me sad and disappointed that not enough has been done in the past.

Most of the Conversation so Far Has Been Focused Internally. Have You Extended the Scope to Customers and Communities?

We have engaged customers as stakeholders, but did not include the wider community within the scope of the project due to time constraints. We do plan to engage with all stakeholders of the business to discuss the concept of GDs.

Previous work has in some ways enriched customers and communities, but I feel we have been simply scratching the surface and there is so much opportunity to work with them to add more value.

In our housebuilding division, we play a key part in the development of new communities acting as a developer. We have the ability to make a real difference and it is our desire to work more closely with our stakeholders to create developments that have a sense of place and add value to the community.

As a result of GDs, we have improved our public consultation events to ensure that we capture more of the richness of the input from our stakeholders in the process.

In our leisure division, for over a decade we have owned a village pub and restaurant, which sit at the heart of the community. There has been a mind-shift as a result of GDs. We no longer give money to community activities. Rather we work with the community to create the change and benefits. For example, we would rather support local suppliers, repair the church roof, or fill the potholes in the road as opposed to giving monies to someone else to do it. We run the local pub as the heart of the community. We are considering a different governance of the pub—a community pub, perhaps a B-Corp—let's see.

Looking Ahead What Do You Hope Will Occur Going Forward?

I hope that we continue to enrich the organisation by making a positive contribution to society whilst being truly aligned to our purpose and that we will have enjoyed a positive financial result through increases in engagement and productivity.

I would wish we will be viewed as a beacon company in the responsible way we approach things and the sustainability of our actions amongst SMEs, recognised as a pioneer and leading the change where the work carried out continues to positively impact the SDGs and the GDs. That we have inspired other firms to implement similar initiatives in their organisations, that would be so rewarding for us all at FH.

I'd like our work with GDs to be recognised at national level within our industries, e.g., winning the Gold Award at WhatHouse for best small housebuilder. This will help deliver our vision of being a beacon company for raising awareness of sustainability challenges and the opportunities available to business.

Finally, and Looking Back Over What You Have Done so Far What Would You Do Differently?

If I knew what I know now, I would have started applying the concept of GDs much sooner. The moral outrage must happen now and the way I see this happening is to raise awareness so that people are conscious of the current situation. This would then accelerate companies to understand the enormity of the challenge and the resulting opportunities where business can benefit. We all must get on with this.

14 Final Thoughts

Building the Evidence Base Through a Research and Learning Community

Steve Kempster and Thomas Maak

There are three good reasons for this last chapter. First, we did not want 13 chapters and the risk of bad luck! Second, we wanted to restate the central argument. And, third, to outline an agenda for research, to develop a strong evidence base for the good dividends, illustrating application and outcomes in a variety of contexts.

The central argument of the good dividends is a most simple one; it is a business model that seeks to utilise all six capitals of an organisation to realise the six good dividends—financial, human, social, brand, operational and planetary—and subsequently replenish the capitals. Why would any organisation not do this most obvious approach? This is where we started the book and of course is where the complexity lies: how can each of the dividends be realised, and realised systemically? The prevailing assumption of neo-liberal capitalism ties the capitals of a business into a metaphoric Gordian Knot—seemingly incapable of being unravelled. The dominance of the responsibility for financial maximisation through the use of operational capital over the short term, and having limited or no intent to address broader responsibilities restricts utilisation of human, social, reputational and planetary capitals. The notion of intent gives weight to the importance of leadership and it calls for a new theory of business rather than a theory of the firm (Donaldson and Walsh, 2015). The firm is, and always will be, an artificial construct based on the assumption that the owners of the firm are best served when managers maximise financial value. The problem of course is, and always has been, that this leads to an artificial reduction of business complexity resulting in all types of 'externalities' at the expense of the firm's multiple stakeholders. Re-framing this biased narrative from the good dividends perspective opens up the possibility to *mirror business complexity* and to add value(s) in all areas pertaining to a business's constituencies. Shifting gears towards the six capitals though requires responsible leadership.

More specifically, we have sought to suggest that it is through responsible leadership focused on a purpose-driven agenda that the fiduciary duty can be reclaimed from the paradigmatic givens drawn from neo-liberal capitalism. The intent of leadership then is all-important. The debate Robyn Remke and Steve offered in Chapter 6 illustrated the manner in which 'the greatest asset' of people has for the most part been underutilised because of the neo-liberal influence. The consequence of which manifests as the management and the control of people as human resources. They argued that the dividend from people is generated through enabling and leading resourcefulness—and offered the term Responsible HRM. Steve Young and colleagues reinforced this point with the empirical data on financial reporting that gives no weight to the value of human resourcefulness; Ant Hesketh captured the financial leaderships' inability to value human capital, and the other intangible capitals. He offered that it is not beyond the wit of leadership to do such. Rather it is to intent. Ant outlined a clear structure for realising intangible value. The intent of Kresse's leadership was described palpably by Malcolm and Katalin. Through the focus on a purpose-driven brand the business of Elvis & Kress has been able to realise the brand dividend by maximising the use of all the capitals: Natural (the waste of old fire hoses), reputational, human, social, institutional and financial. The case showed leadership intent and the realisation of the good dividends. The two Steves (Eldridge and Kempster) argued for operations management to embrace value realisation rather than cost minimisation, and do such with a clear eye on linking traditional operations management with sustainable ops and behavioural ops. The example offered of applying lean thinking to homicide police investigations illustrated how leadership in a non-traditional setting for operations management can embrace the underlying principles of responsible leadership and realise the operational dividend. Similar leadership intent was outlined by Steve and Minna with regard to social innovation. Three cases illustrated the ambition of the respective leaders. Each was dealing with the historic realities of neo-liberal expectations; yet each leader pursued an agenda to realise good dividends as this was common sense. For example, in UPM it made complete sense to do something with the waste products; the paper industry was in decline and they had to innovate. To quote the CEO: '[R]esponsible business can be efficient and profitable. The shareholder reaction and education to the business model speaks to this.' The intent of leadership in governance structures to realise good dividends from all the capitals was outlined by Randall. He gave the narrative of a local business once sold being relocated away from the community in which the employees were embedded and the devastation that followed. In response to this Randall described the intent of the owners to create employee ownership governance because this made good business sense; all the capitals have been utilised and replenished, and the profits have greatly increased. The example offered of Mika Antttonen (CEO of St1) in creating a 'carbon-sink' in the Moroccan Sahara as an expected profitable social innovation highlights the good dividends including the planetary dividend. The leadership intent here—as well as with Kresse, with Jussi Pesonen, CEO of UPM, with Lea Rankinen, VP Sustainability, SOK Finland, with Andy Webster, Head of Public Protection at Lancashire Constabulary, with Luke Freeman, CEO of Freeman Group, with Dennis Overton, founder of Aquascot, with Benoit Greindl, founder and CEO of Montagne-Alternative, Florian Kemmerich, Managing Partner at Bamboo Capital and with 'Pernille' at the Scan-Dan Bank, speak to the need for organisations to profitably embrace the moral role of business leadership—a role that connects the responsibilities of the business to communities, society indeed humanity. In Thomas and Nicola's chapter on the planetary dividend they speak of the importance of understanding climate change as an urgent ethical challenge, possibly an ethical tragedy, unless business leaders take action. The latter must be driven and motivated by a stewardship ethos, overcoming the shortcomings of managerial myopia and technocracy—both of which are dominant approaches of so-called 'sustainable development'. Responsible leaders must think of themselves as stewards and planetary citizens and act accordingly.

So responsible leadership with a purpose-driven intent appears a realistic and most plausible approach to maximise the fiduciary duty. But we need a greater evidence base.

We hope that readers of this book are not just our researcher friends and families! We hope that organisational leaders—senior, middle and junior managers of for-profit and not-for -profit, as well as owner-managers of small and medium businesses and students and academics of course—are drawn toward the notion of the good dividends and purpose-driven responsible leadership. Although we cannot point to a comprehensive research study of some thousand plus organisations from a range of sectors, we anticipate that you would resonate with the arguments and may have ambitions and intent to start an activity or indeed build on the actions you have under way.

This is the research (and learning) community we have in mind. Not academics distant from the realities of leadership activity and seeking to generate the next big leadership theory; but rather academics drawn from a range of disciplines (akin to the approach in this book) engaged with leaders pursuing a common agenda with aligned purposes. Steve and Robyn along with Eric Guthey (Guthey, Kempster and Remke, 2018) have advocated such an approach. They suggest a form of (mini) social movement of responsible leadership that seeks to develop collective knowledge of use for: leaders in developing the good dividends; for academics in pursuing evidence of impact; and for both and many others to generate knowledge and activity that enhances the human condition—the moral outrage we described in Chapter 2 that by necessity requires collective organisational attention.

To that end Steve along with Stewart Barnes have established a website as a platform to help build such a research and learning community.

Perhaps understandably the URL is: gooddividends.co.uk (a fundraising platform had already bought gooddividends.com! Makes money for Schools . . . nice). At the time of writing we are still building this. There is a high-level introduction to the good dividends. However, more important is an evaluation tool. The intention of the tool is to allow leaders (and perhaps others in the business) to assess their organisation against the six dividends and against responsible leadership. On the one level, we hope that the tool would stimulate inquiry by leaders to the areas in which they could take immediate action—provide a base line of current orientation and a frame for benchmarking future orientation. On another level we hope that as leaders complete the evaluation tool and indicate sector and size of business we can begin to construct a database. And on a third level we hope the evaluation will lead to relationships becoming established. Such relationships are between us and the leaders, but also we seek to set up the platform for leaders to connect up. As these relationships develop we shall seek to enrich the database with case examples of methods of engaging, challenges overcome and outcomes achieved. Through time a comprehensive body of knowledge would be developed as a repository for access and guidance for enabling any organisation to pursue purpose-driven, responsible leadership and realise good dividends—we hope so.

In this way the research community would become a form of collaboratory. In a chapter elsewhere, with Eric Guthey and Mary Uhl-Bien (Kempster, Guthey and Uhl-Bien, 2017), Steve unpacks the notion of a collaboratory as a portmantua word made up of collaboration and experimentation. The most famous collaboratory is that of the CERN project—the international science establishment in Switzerland where approximately 75 per cent of the world's particle physicists are engaged in a variety of aligned projects. Collaboratory is an organised future-oriented approach to tackling complex problems—such as the grand challenges that face humanity and form the basis for the SDGs (described in Chapter 2 and Chapter 10). A collaboratory seeks to draw on many people, with many insights, multiple experiments in many locations, and through aligned action, progress towards understanding the particular challenge and offering insight to one or more questions.

We envisage the growth in purpose-driven responsible leadership should address the question, leadership for what? Inquiry and action should follow together. The leadership research field will become the richer for such an approach. The field might just provide a valuable contribution to humanity—one that has been sadly lacking over the last 50 years or so. The same question of course is of even greater significance for leaders. The purpose of this book has been to hold to the notion that leadership is the most influential mechanism for social change on the planet. Communities, humanity and the planet have never needed leadership to be so influential as it does now. As we write these final words there are wild fires all around the world (notably California, Portugal, Australia and even the UK) and floods of biblical proportions (Japan—where over 2 million people fled their homes—and Kerala, in India, where 120 inches of rain have fallen since June and sadly 329 people have died) as the planet experiences perhaps the first glimpse of the effects of global warming on our everyday lives. Of course the knock-on impact of such climate change to water and food security, to disease and famine, to displaced people and modern slavery, to geo-political conflict and the increasing rise of nationalism in response to migration and globalisation, to the impact on unemployment through the growth of artificial intelligence and spectre of ever increasing inequalities, place communities and societies in great tension.

Leadership at all levels needs to come together. At an inter-governmental level, the Paris agreement is under threat from the US withdrawal. Wise heads though, we are sure, will hold together. But it is to everyday leadership that action will deliver the necessary planetary dividends. We assert that it is to the responsible leadership of organisations and the pursuit of purpose that a significant redirection in the footprints of humanity are most likely to emerge. We collectively need to acknowledge that the grand challenges humanity is facing today are first and foremost ethical challenges requiring moral willpower and vision translated into purpose. Just imagine a collective global community of leaders and their organisations pursuing the good dividends. If the particle physicists can come together to convince governments to fund the CERN project to discover the explanation for gravity, perhaps, just perhaps, organisations can come together with such collaborative weight to lobby for inter-governmental action to align with the everyday good dividends shaping and enriching our planet and our communities. We do hope so, and we hope you do as well.

Although we started the book with the idea that the good dividends are common sense, the application is of course complex. Quoting President JF Kennedy: 'We choose to go to the moon and do the other things, not because they are easy, but because they are hard.' For no less a reason than for humanity to flourish we need collective responsible business leadership.

References

Association of Chief Police Officers (England & Wales). (2005). *Practical advice on core investigative doctrine*. Wyboston, UK: NPIA.

Adair, J. (1984). The Hawthorne effect: A reconsideration of the methodological artifact. *Journal of Applied Psychology*, 69, 334–345.

Adams, C.A. (2017). *The Sustainable Development Goals, integrated thinking and the integrated report*. Retrieved from www.integratedreporting.org. (Last accessed 20th June 2018).

Adams, R., Jeanrenaud, S., Bessant, J., Denyer, D. & Overy, P. (2016). Sustainability-oriented innovation: A systematic review. *International Journal of Management Reviews*, 18(2), 1–26.

Ahmad, S. & Omar, R. (2016). Basic corporate governance models: A systematic review. *International Journal of Law and Management*, 58(1), 73–107.

Albert, S., Leon, J.X., Grinham, A.R., Church, J.A., Gibbes, B.R. & Woodroffe, C.D. (2016). Interactions between sea-level rise and wave exposure on reef island dynamics in the Solomon Islands. *Environmental Research Letters*, 11(5), (Online journal—Viewed 15th February, 2018).

Almquist, E., Senior, J. & Bloch, N. (2016). The elements of value. *Harvard Business Review*, 94(9), 13.

Alvarez, A. (1988). Martin Luther King's 'I have a dream': The speech event as metaphor. *Journal of Black Studies*, 18(3), 337–357.

Anand, S. & Sen, A. (2000). Human development and economic sustainability. *World Development*, 28(12), 2029–2049.

Anand, V., Ashforth, B.E. & Joshi, M. (2004). Business as usual: The acceptance and perpetuation of corruption in organizations. *Academy of Management Executive*, 18(2), 39–53.

Anderson, R. (1998). *Mid-course correction*. Atlanta: Peregrinzilla Press.

Archer, M. (1995). *Realist social theory: The morphogenetic approach*. Cambridge: Cambridge University Press.

Avini, A. (1995/1996). The origins of the modern English trust revisited. *Tulane Law Review*, 70, 1139–1163.

Bang, H.M., Zhou-Koval, C. & Wade-Benzoni, K.A. (2017). *It's the thought that counts over time: The interplay of intent, outcome, stewardship, and legacy motivations in intergenerational reciprocity*. Working paper: Duke University.

Barlow, J., França, F., Gardner, T.A., Hicks, C.C., Lennox, G.D., Berenguer, E., Castello, L., Economo, E.P., Ferreira, J., Guénard, B., Gontijo Leal, C., Isaac, V., Lees, A.C., Parr, C.L., Wilson, S.K., Young, P.J. & Graham, A.J. (2018). The future of hyperdiverse tropical ecosystems. *Nature*, 559, 517–526.

Barnes, S., Kempster, S. & Smith, S. (2015). *Leading small business: Business growth through leadership development*. Cheltenham: Edward Elgar.

Barnosky, A.D., Hadly, E.A., Bascompte, J., Berlow, E.L., Brown, J.H., Fortelius, M., Getz, W.M., Harte, J., Hastings, A., Marquet, P.A., Martinez, N.D., Mooers, A., Roopnarine, P., Vermeij, G., Williams, J.W., Gillespie, R., Kitzes, J., Marshall, C., Matzke, N., Mindell, D.P., Revilla, E. & Smith, A.D. (2012). Approaching a state shift in Earth's biosphere. *Nature*, 486, 52–58.

Barton, D., Manyika, J. & Keohane Williamson, S. (2017a). The data: Where long-termism pays off. *Harvard Business Review*, 95(3), 67–67.

Barton, D., Manyika, J. & Keohane Williamson, S. (2017b). Finally, evidence that managing for the long term pays off. *Harvard Business Review*, Boston, MA (pp. 1–11). Retrieved from https://hbr.org/2017/02/finally-proof-that-managing-for-the-long-term-pays-off#comment-section (Last accessed 11th July 2018).

Bass, B.M. (1999). Two decades of research and development in transformational leadership. *European Journal of Work and Organizational Psychology*, 8(1), 9–32.

Bass, B.M. & Avolio, B.J. (1990). Developing transformational leadership: 1992 and beyond. *Journal of European Industrial Training*, 14, 21–27.

Becker, G. (1964). *Human capital: A theoretical and empirical analysis with special references to education* (1st ed.). Chicago: University of Chicago Press.

Bendoly, E., Croson, R., Goncalves, P. & Schultz, K. (2010). Bodies of knowledge for research in behavioral operations. *Production and Operations Management*, 19(4), 434–452.

Bendoly, E., Donohue, K. & Schulz, K. (2006). Behavior in operations management: Assessing recent findings and revisiting old assumptions. *Journal of Operations Management*, 24(6), 737–752.

Benefit Corporation (2018). *About B Corps*. Retrieved from https://bcorpora tion.net/about-b-corps (Last accessed 7th June 2018).

Berners-Lee, M. & Clark, D. (2013). *The burning question: We can't burn half the world's oil, coal and gas: So how do we quit?* London: Profile Books.

Bernstein, A. & Beeferman, L. (2015). *The materiality of human capital to corporate financial performance*. Investor Responsibility Research Center Institute (IRRCi). Retrieved from https://lwp.law.harvard.edu/files/lwp/files/pension_paper_materiality_of_human_capital_042015.pdf (Last accessed 8th April 2018).

Block, P. (1993). *Stewardship*. San Francisco: Berrett-Koehler.

Boston Consulting Group (2010). *The 'embracers' seize advantage*. MIT Sloan Management Review Research Report, Winter 2011, MIT.

Boston Consulting Group Report (2017). *How big investors can have a bigger societal impact* (December). Retrieved from www.bcg.com/publications/2017/big-investors-societal-impact.aspx. (Last accessed 9th August 2018).

Bower, J.L. & Paine, L.S. (2017). The error at the heart of corporate leadership. *Harvard Business Review*, 95(3), 50–60.

Boxall, P. & Purcell, J. (2011). *Strategy and human resource management*. Basingstoke: Palgrave Macmillan.

Brabandere, L. de (2005). *The forgotten half of change: Achieving greater creativity through changes in perception*. Chicago, IL: Dearborn Trade Publishing.

Bratton, J. & Gold, J. (2015). Towards critical human resource management education (CHRME): A sociological imagination approach. *Work, Employment and Society*, 29(3), 496–507.

Brown, M.E. & Mitchell, M.S. (2010). Ethical and unethical leadership: Exploring new avenues for future research. *Business Ethics Quarterly*, 20, 583–616.

Brown, M.E. & Trevino, L.K. (2014). Do role models matter? An investigation of role modelling as an antecedent of perceived ethical leadership. *Journal of Business Ethics*, 122(4), 578–598.

Buchholtz, A.K. & Carroll, A.B. (2012). *Business and society: Ethics and stakeholder management* (8th ed.). Andover: South-Western Cengage Learning.

Byford, L. (1981). *The Yorkshire Ripper case: Review of the police investigation of the case*. HM Inspectorate of Constabulary (unpublished).

CFA (2013). *Global market sentiment survey 2015: Detailed survey results*. Retrieved from https://www.cfainstitute.org/Survey/gmss_2015_detailed_results.pdf (Last accessed 15th July 2018).

CDP (2016). *Global forests report 2016*. Retrieved from https://www.cdp.net/en/research/global-reports/global-forests-report-2016 (Last accessed July 12th 2018).

Cadbury, Sir A. (1992). *Committee on financial aspects of corporate governance*. London: Gee and Co. Ltd.

Cameron, K. (2011). Responsible leadership as virtuous leadership. *Journal of Business Ethics*, 98, 25–35.

Chakrabarty, D. (2009). The climate of history: Four theses. *Critical Inquiry*, 35(2), 1–23.

Chakrabarty, D. (2014). Climate and capital: On conjoined histories. *Critical Inquiry*, 41(1), 1–23.

Chakrabarty, D. (2017). The politics of climate change is more than the politics of capitalism. *Theory, Culture & Society*, 34(2–3), 25–37.

Checkland, P. & Scholes, J. (1999). *Soft systems methodology in action: A 30-year retrospective*. Chichester: John Wiley and Sons Ltd.

Chesbrough, H. (2012). Open innovation: Where we've been and where we're going. *Research-Technology Management* (July–August), 20–27.

Chin, M.K., Hambrick, D.C. & Trevino, L.K. (2013). Political ideologies of CEOs: The influence of executives values on corporate social responsibility. *Administrative Science Quarterly*, 58, 197–232.

Chopra, S., Lovejoy, W. & Yano, C. (2004). Five decades of operations management and the prospects ahead. *Management Science*, 50(1), 8–14.

Chouinard, Y. (2005). *Let my people go surfing*. New York: Penguin.

City Developments Limited (2017). *CDL future value 2030*. Retrieved from http://cdlsustainability.com/pdf/CDL_ISR_2017.pdf

Clark, P. (2000). *Organizations in action: Competition between contexts*. London: Routledge.

Construction and Real Estate Sector Supplement (2011) *Sustainability reporting guidelines and construction and real estate sector supplement*. Retrieved from https://www.globalreporting.org/resourcelibrary/G3-1-English-Construction-and-Real-Estate-Sector-Supplement.pdf (Last accessed 6th August 2018).

Crouch, C. (2011). *The strange non-death of neo-liberalism*. Cambridge: Polity Press.

Davis, J.H., Schoorman, F.D. & Donaldson, L. (1997). Toward a stewardship theory of management. *Academy of Management Review*, 22(1), 20–47.

de Chernatony, L. (2010). *From brand vision to brand evaluation*. Oxford: Butterworth-Heinemann.

Deming, E. (1982). *Out of crisis*. Cambridge, MA: Massachusetts Institute of Technology, Center for Advanced Engineering Study.

DeMott, A. (1988). Beyond metaphor: An analysis of fiduciary obligation. *Duke Law Journal*, (5), 879–924.

DeRue, D.S., Sitkin, S.B. & Podolny, J.M. (2011). From the guest editors: Teaching leadership issues and insights. *Academy of Management Learning & Education*, 10(3), 369–372.

Detert, J.R., Trevino, L.K. & Sweitzer, V.L. (2008). Moral disengagement in ethical decision making: A study of antecedents and outcomes. *Journal of Applied Psychology*, 92(2), 374–391.

De Villiers, C., Rinaldi, L. & Unerman, J. (2014). Integrated reporting: Insights, gaps and an agenda for future research. *Accounting, Auditing and Accountability Journal*, 27(1), 1042–1067.

Diffenbaugh, N.S. & Field, C.B. (2013). Changes in ecological critical terrestrial climate conditions. *Science*, 341, 486–492.

Donaldson, T. (1982). *Corporations and morality*. Englewood Cliffs, NJ: Prentice Hall.

Donaldson, T. & Walsh, J.P. (2015). Toward a theory of business. *Research in Organizational Behavior*, 35, 181–207.

Draper, S. (2013). *Creating the big shift: System innovation for sustainability*. London: Forum for the Future.

du Gay, P. & Morgan, G. (2013). Understanding capitalism: Crises, legitimacy, and change through the prism of The New Spirit of Capitalism. In D.P. du Gay & G. Morgan (Eds.), *New spirits of capitalism? Crises, justifications, and dynamics* (pp. 1–42). Oxford: Oxford University Press.

Eccles, N. (2017). *Overcoming constraints imposed by fiduciary duties in terms of tackling 'Leadership challenges that matter'?* Paper presented at the 4th Responsible leadership conference, 15–16th March, Pretoria University, Johanseburg.

Economist (2002). Is global inequality really getting worse? A new study says no. Retrieved from www.columbia.edu/~xs23/papers/worldistribution/Economist.htm (Last accessed 11th June 2018).

Edgecliffe-Johnson, A. (2018). Unilever chief admits Kraft Heinz bid forced compromises. *The Financial Times* (27th February).

Edwards, P.N. (2010). *A vast machine: Computer models, climate data, and the politics of global warming*. Cambridge, MA: Harvard University Press.

Eisenhardt, K.M. & Martin, J.A. (2000). Dynamic capabilities: What are they? *Strategic Management Journal*, 21, 1105–1121.

Elvis & Kresse (2018). *The burberry foundation partners with Elvis & Kresse*. Retrieved from www.elvisandkresse.com/blogs/news/the-burberry-foundation-partners-with-elvis-kresse

Enderle, G. (2016). How can business ethics strengthen the social cohesion of a society? *Journal of Business Ethics,* 150(3), 619–629.

Engelen, E., Erturk, I., Froud, J., Sukhdev, J., Adam Leaver, A., Moran, M., Nilsson, A. & Williams, K. (2011). *After the great complacence: Financial crisis and the politics of reform*. Oxford: Oxford University Press.

Equalities Act (2010). *Gender pay gap information & regulations 2017*. Retrieved from www.legislation.gov.uk/ukdsi/2017/9780111152010. (Last accessed 12th June 2018).

Ernst & Young (2016). *Accounting and reporting for the long term*. London/New York: Ernst & Young.

Ernst & Young (2018). *Embankment project for inclusive capitalism*. New York: EY/CIC.

Fernando, M. (2016). *Leading responsibly in the Asian century*. New York: Springer International Publishing.

Financial Reporting Council (2014). *Guidance on the Strategic Report*. Financial Reporting Council: London. Retrieved from www.frc.org.uk/getattachment/2168919d-398a-41f1-b493-0749cf6f63e8/Guidance-on-the-Strategic-Report.pdf. (Last accessed 24th February 2018).

Fourcade-Gourinchas, M. & Healy, K. (2007). Moral views of market society. *Annual Review of Sociology*, 33, 285–311.

Francis, R. (2013). *The Mid Staffordshire Foundation Trust Enquiry*. London: The Stationary Office.

Frankl, V.E. (1959/2004). *Man's search for meaning*. London/Sydney/Auckland/Johannesburg: Rider.

Freeman, R.E. (2000). Business ethics at the millennium. *Business Ethics Quarterly*, 10(1), 169–180.

Friedman, M. (1962). Capitalism and Freedom, with the assistance of Rose D. Friedman. Chicago: University of Chicago Press.

Friedman, M. (1970). The social responsibility of the corporation is to increase its profits. *New York Times Magazine*, 13th September.

Fukuyama, F. (1993). *The end of history and the last man*. New York: Avon Books.

Gallup (2018). *The state of employee engagement in 2018: Research on employee engagement practices from over 700 HR professionals*. Retrieved from https://info.glintinc.com/2018_03_WP_State_of_EE_PPC. (Last accessed 10th September 2018).

Gambardella, A., Raasch, C. & von-Hippel, E. (2016). The user innovation paradigm: Impacts on markets and welfare. *Management Science*, 63(5), 1450–1468.

Gardiner, S.M. (2011). *A perfect moral storm: The ethical tragedy of climate change*. Oxford/New York: Oxford University Press.

Gates, B. & Gates, M. (2014). *3 Myths that block progress for the poor*. Retrieved from www.gatesfoundation.org. (Last accessed 11th June 2018).

Gino, F. & Pisano, G. (2008). Toward a theory of behavioral operations. *Manufacturing and Service Operations Management*, 10(4), 676–669.

Gleeson-White, J. (2014). *Six capitals: The revolution capitalism has to have: Or can accountants save the planet?* Sydney: Allen & Unwin.

Global Footprint Network (2018). *Ecological footprint*. Retrieved from www.footprintnetwork.org/our-work/ecological-footprint/ (Last accessed 14th September 2018).

Global Reporting Initiative (2011). *Sustainability reporting guidelines & construction and real estate sector supplement*. Retrieved from www.globalreporting.org/resourcelibrary/G3-1-English-Construction-and-Real-Estate-Sector-Supplement.pdf (Last accessed 18th May 2018).

Goethe, J.W.V. (1992). *Wilhelm Meister's Wanderjahre: Werke Band 4*. München: Artemis & Winkler.

Goodman, J., Korsunova, A. & Halme, M. (2017). Our collaborative future: Activities and roles of stakeholders in sustainability-oriented innovation. *Business Strategy and the Environment*, 26(6), 731–753.

Gould, R.W. (2012). Open innovation and stakeholder engagement. *Journal of Technology Management and Innovation*, 7(3), 1–10.

Grachev, M. & Rakitsky, B. (2013). Historic horizons of Frederick Taylor's scientific management. *Journal of Management History*, 19(4), 512–527.

Green, K. & Armstrong, J.S. (2007). Global warming: Forecasts by scientists versus scientific forecasts. *Energy and Environment*, 18(7/8), 995–1019.

Greenleaf, R.K. (1977/2002). *Servant leadership: A journey into the nature of legitimate power and greatness* (25th Anniversary ed.). New York/Mahwah, NJ: Paulist Press.

Gregson, N., Crang, M., Fuller, S. & Holmes, H. (2015). Interrogating the circular economy: The moral economy of resource recovery in the EU. *Economy and Society*, 44(2), 218–243.

Grint, K. (2005). Problems, problems, problems: The social construction of leadership. *Human Relations*, 58(11), 1467–1494.

Grint, K. (2007). Learning to lead: Can Aristotle help us find the road to wisdom? *Leadership*, 3, 231–246.

Grugulis, I. (2017). *A very short, fairly interesting and reasonably cheap book about Human Resource Management*. London: Sage.

Guattari, F. (2000). *Three ecologies*. London: The Athlone Press.

Guthey, E., Kempster, S. & Remke, R. (2018). Leadership for what? In R. Riggio (Ed.), *The Problems with leadership* (pp. 272–292). New York: Routledge.

Hafenbrädl, S. & Waeger, D. (2017). Ideology and the microfoundations of CSR: Why executives believe in the business case for CSR and how this affects their CSR engagements. *The Academy of Management Journal*, 60(4), 1582–1606.

Hajer, M., Nilsson, M., Raworth, K., Bakker, P., Berkhout, F., de Boer, Y., Rockström, J., Ludwig, K. & Kok, M. (2015). Beyond cockpit-ism: Four insights to enhance the transformative potential of the Sustainable Development Goals. *Sustainability*, 7(2), 1651–1660.

Hall, J. & Wagner, M. (2012). Integrating sustainability into firms' processes: Performance effects and the moderating role of business models and innovation. *Business Strategy and the Environment*, 21, 183–196.

Halme, M. & Laurila, J. (2009). Philanthropy, integration or innovation? Exploring the financial and societal outcomes of different types of corporate responsibility. *Journal of Business Ethics*, 84, 325–339.

Halme, M., Lindeman, S. & Linna, P. (2012). Innovation for inclusive business: Intrapreneurial bricolage in multinational corporation. *Journal of Management Studies*, 49(4), 743–784.

Hansen, E.G. & Grosse-Dunker, F. (2013). Sustainability-oriented innovation. In S. Idowu, N. Capaldi, L. Zu & A. Das Gupta (Eds.), *Encyclopaedia of corporate social responsibility* (Vol. 4, pp. 2407–2417). Heidelberg, Germany: Springer.

Hanson, S., Nicholls, R., Ranger, N., Hallegatte, S., Corfee-Morlot, J., Herweijer, C. & Chateau, J. (2011). A global ranking of port cities with high exposure to climate extremes. *Climatic Change*, 104, 89–111.

Harari, Y. (2014). *Sapiens: A brief history of humankind*. London: Vintage.

Harris, J. & Freeman, R.E. (2008). The impossibility of the separation thesis. *Business Ethics Quarterly*, 18(4), 541–545.

Hart, S.L. (2005). Innovation, creative destruction and sustainability. *Research-Technology Management*, 48(5), 21–27.

Hart, S.L. (2010). *Capitalism at the crossroads: Next generation business strategies for a post-crisis world* (3rd ed.). Upper Saddle River, NJ: Wharton School Publishing (Pearson Education).

Hartenberger, U. (2015). RICS: Royal Institution of Chartered Surveyors. *Advancing responsible business practices in land, construction and real estate use and investment.* Retrieved from www.unglobalcompact.org/docs/issues_doc/RICS/ GC_RICS_Resource.pdf. (Last accessed 4th May 2018).

Hayes, R.H. & Wheelwright, S.C. (1984). *Restoring our competitive edge: Competing through manufacturing.* New York: Wiley.

Helbing, D. (2013). Globally networked risks and how to respond. *Nature, 497,* 51–57.

Hernandez, M. (2012). Toward an understanding of the psychology of stewardship. *Academy of Management Review, 37,* 172–193.

Herweijer, C. & Combes, B. (2017). *Innovation for the Earth: Harnessing technological breakthroughs for people and the planet.* Retrieved from www.pwc. com.uk/services/sustainability-climate-change/insights/innovation-for-earth. html. (Last accessed 12th May 2018).

Hesketh, A. (2013). *Valuing your talent: Resourceful assets?* Discussion paper. London: UK Commission for Employment and Skills.

Hesketh, A. (2014). *Managing the value of your talent: A new framework for human capital management.* London: UK Commission for Employment and Skills.

Hesketh, A. (2018). Architectures of value: Moving leaders beyond big data and analytics. In P. Sparrow & Sir C. Cooper (Eds.), *A research agenda for human resource management.* Cheltenham: Edward Elgar.

Hesketh, A., Sellwood-Taylor, J. & Mullen, S. (2018). *Boardroom capital: The new currency for practicing leadership in the boardroom.* Working paper series: Lancaster University Management School.

Hewlett, S.A. (2007). *Off-ramps and on-ramps.* Boston: Harvard Business School Press.

Hönisch, B., Ridgwell, A., Schmidt, D.N., Thomas, E., Gibbs, S.J., Sluijs, A., . . . Williams. B. (2012). The geological record of ocean acidification. *Science, 335,* 1058.

Hörisch, J., Freeman, R.E. & Schaltegger, S. (2014). Applying stakeholder theory in sustainability management links, similarities, dissimilarities, and a conceptual framework. *Organization & Environment, 27,* 328–346.

Howie, G. (1968). *Aristotle.* London: Collier-Macmillan Ltd.

Huselid, M. (1995). The impact of human resource management practices on turnover, productivity, and corporate financial performance. *Academy of Management Journal, 38,* 635–672.

IIRC (2013). *Capitals: Background paper for IR.* London: IIRC.

Interbrand (2018). *Best global brands 2017.* Retrieved from www.interbrand. com/best-brands/best-global-brands/2017. (Last accessed 18th April 2018).

Johnson, T.H. & Kaplan, R.S. (1987). *Relevance lost: The rise and fall of management accounting.* Boston: Harvard Business School Press.

Jonas, H. (1979). *Das Prinzip Verantwortung.* Frankfurt am Main: Suhrkamp.

Juntunel, J.K., Halme, M., Korsunova, A. & Rajala, R. (2016). *Powering sustainable innovations: Strategies for collaborating with deviant partner.* 32nd EGOS Colloquium 'Organizing in the Shadow of Power', 7–9 July, Naples, Italy.Kay Review (2012). *Kay review of UK equity markets and long-term decision making.*

Retrieved from www.gov.uk/government/uploads/system/uploads/attach ment_data/file/253454/bis-12-917-kay-review-of-equity-markets-final-report. pdf. (Last accessed 23rd October 2016).

Kazadi, K., Lievens, A. & Mahr, D. (2016). Stakeholder co-creation during the innovation process: Identifying capabilities for knowledge creation among multiple stakeholders. *Journal of Business Research*, 69(2), 525–540.

Kanungo, R. N. & Misra, S. (1992). Managerial resourcefulness: A reconceptualization of management skills. *Human Relations*, 45, 1311–1332.

Kempster, S. (2018). *Brexit: A leadership tale*. Retrieved from http://blogs.lse. ac.uk/brexit/2018/12/18/brexit-a-leadership-tale/ (Last accessed 18th December 2018).

Kempster, S. & Carroll, B. (2016). *Responsible leadership: Realism and romanticism*. Abingdon, Oxon: Routledge.

Kempster, S. & Gregory, S. (2017). 'Should I stay or should I go?' Exploring leadership-as-practice in the middle management role. *Leadership*, 13(4), 496–515.

Kempster, S., Guthey, E. & Uhl-Bien, M. (2017). Collaboratory as leadership development. In S. Kempster, A. Turner & G. Edwards (Eds.), *Field guide to leadership development* (pp. 251–271). Cheltenham: Edward Elgar.

Kempster, S., Jackson, B. & Conroy, M. (2011). Leadership as purpose: Exploring the role of purpose in leadership practice. *Leadership*, 7(3), 317–334.

Kingo, L. & Stormer, S. (2011). Dealing with dilemmas and societal expectations: A company's response. In D.J. Bennett & R.C. Jennings (Eds.), *Successful science communication* (pp. 294–311). Cambridge: Cambridge University Press.

Kleindorfer, P.R., Singhal, K. & Van Wassenhowe, L.N. (2005). Sustainable operations management. *Production and Operation Management*, 14(4), 482–492.

KPMG (2014). *A new vision of value: Connecting corporate and societal value creation*. London: KPMG.

KPMG (2015). *Currents of change: The KPMG survey of corporate responsibility reporting 2015*. Retrieved from https://assets.kpmg.com/content/dam/kpmg/pdf/2016/02/kpmg-international-survey-of-corporate-responsibility-reporting-2015.pdf. (Last accessed 14th January 2018).

Laloux, F. (2014). *Reinventing organisations*. Mills, MA: Nelson Parker.

Laplume, A.O., Sonpar, K. & Litz, R.A. (2008). Stakeholder theory: Reviewing a theory that moves us. *Journal of Management*, 34(6), 1152–1189.

Le Breton-Miller, I. & Miller, D. (2006). Why do some family businesses out-compete? Governance, long-term orientations, and sustainable capability. *Entrepreneurship Theory and Practice*, 30(6), 731–746.

Le Breton-Miller, I. & Miller, D. (2015). Family firms and practices of sustainability: A contingency view. *Journal of Family Business Strategy*, 7(1), 26–33.

Le Breton-Miller, I., Miller, D. & Bares, F. (2015). Governance and entrepreneurship in family firms: Agency, behavioral agency and resource-based comparisons. *Journal of Family Business Strategy*, 6(1), 58–62.

Legge, K. (1995). *Human resource management, rhetorics and realities*. London: Macmillan.

Legge, K. (2006). Human resource management. In S. Ackroyd, R. Batt, P. Thompson & P. S. Tolbert (Eds.), *The oxford handbook of work and organization* (pp. 220–241). Oxford: Oxford University Press.

Lev, B. (2000). *Intangibles: Management, measurement, and reporting*. Washington, DC: Brookings Institution Press.

Lev, B. & Gu, F. (2016). *The end of accounting and the path forward for investors and managers*. Hoboken, NJ: John Wiley & Sons.

Levänen, J., Hossain, M., Lyytinen, T., Hyvärinen, A., Numminen, S. & Halme, M. (2016). Implications of frugal innovations on sustainable development: Evaluating water and energy innovations. *Sustainability*, 8(4), doi: 10.3390/su8010004

Liker, J.K. (2004). *The heart of the Toyota production system: Eliminating waste: The Toyota way*. New York: McGraw-Hill.

Lipman-Blumen, J. (2005). *The allure of toxic leaders*. Oxford/New York: Oxford University Press.

Liu, Y., Dietz, T., Carpenter, S.R., Alberti, M., Folke, C., Moran, E., . . . Taylor, W.W. (2007). Complexity of coupled human and natural systems. *Science*, 317, 1513–1516.

Locke, E.A. (1982). The ideas of Frederick W. Taylor: An evaluation. *Academy of Management Review*, 7, 14–24.

Lovelock, J. (1979). *GAIA: A new look at life on earth*. Oxford: Oxford University Press.

Lütge, C., Armbrüster, T. and Müller, J. (2015). Order ethics: bridging the gap between contractarianism and business ethics. *Journal of Business Ethics, 136*(4), 687–697.

Maak, T. & Pless, N.M. (2006a). *Responsible leadership*. London: Routledge.

Maak, T. & Pless, N.M. (2006b). Responsible in a stakeholder society: A relational approach. *Journal of Business Ethics*, 66(1), 99–115.

Maak, T. & Pless, N.M. (2009a). The leader as responsible change agent. In H. Spitzeck, M. Pirson, W. Amann, S. Khan & E. von Kimakowitz (Eds.), *Humanism in business: Perspectives on the development of a responsible business world* (pp. 358–374). Cambridge: Cambridge University Press.

Maak, T. & Pless, N.M. (2009b). Business leaders as citizens of the world: Advancing humanism on a global scale. *Journal of Business Ethics*, 88(3), 537–550.

Maak, T., Pless, N.M. & Voegtlin, C. (2016). Business statesman or shareholder advocate? CEO responsible leadership styles and the micro-foundations of political CSR. *Journal of Management Studies*, 53(3), 463–493.

MacIntyre, A. (1985). *After virtue: A study in moral theory* (2nd ed.). London: Duckworth.

Macpherson, W. (1999). *The Stephen Lawrence inquiry: Report of an inquiry by Sir William Macpherson of Cluny*. London: HMSO.

Majumdar, S.K. & Marcus, A.A. (2001). Rules versus discretion: The productivity consequences of flexible regulation. *Academy of Management Journal*, 44, 170–179.

Margolis, J.D. & Walsh, J.P. (2003). Misery loves companies: Whither social initiatives by business. *Administrative Science Quarterly*, 38(3), 268–305.

Masi, R.J. & Cooke, R.L. (2000). Effects of transformational leadership on subordinate motivation, empowering norms, and organizational productivity. *The International Journal of Organizational Analysis*, 8(1), 16–47.

MacKinnon, D. & Derickson, K.D. (2012). *From resilience to resourcefulness: A critique of resilience policy and activism*. Papers in Evolutionary Economic Geography, no. 12, Utrecht University.

McWilliams, A. & Siegel, D.S. (2001). Corporate social responsibility: A theory of the firm perspective. *Academy of Management Review*, 26, 117–127.

McWilliams, A., Siegel, D.S. & Wright, P.M. (2006). Corporate social responsibility: Strategic implications. *Journal of Management Studies*, 43, 1–18.

Merchant, K.A. & Sandino, T. (2009). Four options for measuring value creation. *Journal of Accountancy*, 208(2), 34.

Meyer, J. (2015). Beyond utility: Providing a moral foundation for capitalism. *The Journal of Private Enterprise*, 30(2), 21–41.

Mikolajek-Gocejna, M. (2016). The relationship between corporate social responsibility and corporate financial performance: Evidence from empirical studies. *Comparative Economic Research*, 19(4), 67–84.

Min Bang, H., Zhou Koval, C. & Wade-Benzoni, K.A. (2017). It's the thought that counts over time: The interplay of intent, outcome, stewardship, and legacy motivations in integenerational reciprocity. *Journal of Experimental Social Psychology*, 73, 197–210.

Moe, K. & Shandy, D. (2010). *Glass ceilings and 100-hour Couples: What the opt-out phenomenon can teach us about work and family.* Athens, GA: University of Georgia Press.

Moore, G. & Beadle, R. (2006). In search of organisational virtue in business: Agents, goods, practices, institutions and environments. *Organisation Studies*, 27(3), 369–389.

Morgan, J.M. & Liker, J.K. (2006). *The Toyota product development system: Integrating people, processes, and technology.* New York: Productivity Press.

Mumford, L. (1967). *The myth of the machine (Vol. I): Technics and human development.* New York: Harcourt, Brace Jovanovich.

Nakao, Y., Nakano, M., Amano, A., Kokubu, K., Matsumura, K. & Gemba, K. (2007). Corporate environmental and financial performances and the effects of information-based instruments of environmental policy in Japan. *International Journal of Environment and Sustainable Development*, 6(1), 95–112.

National Association of Pension Funds (2015). *Where is the workforce in corporate reporting?* London: The National Association of Pension Funds Limited. Retrieved from www.cipd.co.uk/Images/where-is-the-workforce-in-corporate-reporting_tcm18-19910.pdf. (Last accessed 5th April 2018).

The Nielsen Company (2015). *Sustainability imperative: Markets and finances.* Retrieved from www.nielsen.com/us/en/insights/reports/2015/the-sustainability-imperative.html. (Last accessed 29th May 2018).

Nesta (2015). *Pushing boundaries: The 2015 UK alternative finance industry report.* Retrieved from https://www.nesta.org.uk/report/pushing-boundaries-the-2015-uk-alternative-finance-industry-report/ (Last accessed 15th December 2018).

Neumayer, E. (2000). In defence of historical accountability for greenhouse gas emissions. *Ecological Economics*, 33, 185–192.

Newbert, S.L. & Stouder, M.D. (2012). Achieving moral capitalism through entrepreneurial justice. *Review of Social Economy*, 70(2), 233–251.

Nielsen Company (2015). *The sustainability imperative: New insights on consumer expectations.* Retrieved from www.nielsen.com/content/dam/nielsenglobal/dk/docs/global-sustainability-report-oct-2015.pdf. (Last accessed 27th March 2018).

Obolensky, N. (2010). *Complex adaptive leadership.* Farnham: Gower Publishing Limited.

Ocean Tomo. (2016). Intangible asset market value study. Retrieved from http:// www.oceantomo.com/intangible-asset-market-value-study/ (Last accessed 11th July 2018).

Ohno, T. (1988). *The Toyota production system beyond large scale production.* Portland, Oregon: Productivity Press.

Orlitzky, M., Schmidt, F.L. & Rynes, S.L. (2003). Corporate social and financial performance: A meta-analysis. *Organization Studies,* 24, 403–441.

Oxfam (2017). *An economy for the 99%.* Briefing Paper (January). Retrieved from www.oxfam.org/sites/www.oxfam.org/files/file_attachments/bp-econ omy-for-99-percent-160117-en.pdf. (Last accessed 12th February 2018).

Parfitt, D. (2011). *On what matters* (Vol. 2). Oxford/New York: Oxford University Press.

Park, N. & Peterson, C. (2006). Moral competence and character strengths among adolescents: The development and validation of the values in action inventory of strengths for youth. *Journal of Adolescence,* 29, 891–905.

Parry, K.W. (1998). Grounded theory and social process: A new direction for leadership research. *Leadership Quarterly, 9*(1), 85–106.

Penman, S.H. (2009). Accounting for intangible assets: There is also an income statement. *Abacus,* 45(3), 358–371.

Pensions and Lifetime Savings Association (PLSA) (2016). *Understanding the worth of the workforce: A stewardship toolkit for pension funds.* London: PLSA. Retrieved from www.plsa.co.uk/portals/0/Documents/0591-Under standing-the-worth-of-the-workforce-a-stewardship-toolkit-for-pension-funds.pdf. (Last accessed 1st April 2018).

Perl-Vorbach, E., Rauter, R. & Baumgartner, R.J. (2014). *Open innovation in the context of sustainable innovation: Findings based on a literature review.* Proceedings of 9th International Symposium on Sustainable Leadership, 3rd–16th June, Salzburg.

Platt, E., Bullock, N. & Skaggs, A. (2017). US companies transformed into 800lb gorilla in bond market. *Financial Times* (12th September).

Pless, N.M. (2007). Understanding responsible leadership: Roles identity and motivational drivers. *Journal of Business Ethics,* 74(4), 437–456.

Pless, N.M. (2011). Women leading a responsible global business: A study of Dame Anita Roddick, founder of the Body Shop. In P.H. Werhane & M. Painter-Morland (Eds.), *Leadership, gender, and organization* (pp. 245–258). Dordrecht: Springer.

Pless, N.M. & Appel, J. (2012). In pursuit of dignity and social justice: Changing lives through 100 % inclusion: How Gram Vikas fosters sustainable rural development. *Journal of Business Ethics,* 111(3), 389–411.

Pless, N.M. & Maak, T. (2005). Relational intelligence for leading responsibly in a connected world. In K.M. Weaver (Ed.), *Best paper proceedings of the 65th annual meeting of the academy of management,* Honololu.

Pless, N.M. & Maak, T. (2011). Responsible leadership: Pathways to the future. *Journal of Business Ethics,* 98(S1), 3–13.

Pless, N.M., Maak, T. & Harris, H. (2017). Arts, ethics, and the promotion of human dignity. *Journal of Business Ethics,* 144(2), 223–232.

Pless, N.M., Maak, T., & Stahl, G.K. (2011). Developing responsible global leaders through international service-learning programs: The Ulysses experience. *Academy of Management Learning and Education,* 10, 237–260.

Pless, N.M., Maak, T. & Waldman, D.A. (2012). Thinking about doing the right thing: Mapping the responsibility orientations of leaders. *Academy of Management Perspectives* (December), 51–65.

Polman, P. (2017). Paul Polman: In his own words. *Financial Times* (3rd December). Retrieved from www.ft.com/content/2209d63a-d6ae-11e7-8c9a-d9c0a5c8d5c9. (Last accessed 22nd June 2018).

Popadak, J. (2016). *Balancing governance and culture to create sustainable firm value*. Washington, DC: The Brookings Institution.

Porter, M.E. & Kramer, M.R. (2006). Strategy and society: The link between competitive advantage and corporate social responsibility. *Harvard Business Review*, 84(12), 78–92.

Price Waterhouse Coopers (2017). *Working in an SDG economy: Aligning business activity to the global goals*. Retrieved from www.pwc.com/globalgoals. (Last accessed 12th April 2018).

Principles for Responsible Investment (2018). *ESG engagement for fixed-income investors: Managing risks and enhancing returns*. London: Principles of Responsible Investment.

Ramaswamy, V. and Gouillart, F. (2010). Building the co-creative enterprise. *Harvard Business Review*, October, 100–109.

Rand, A. (1967). *Capitalism: The unknown ideal*. New York: The New American Library.

Robeco-SAM (2016). *Annual sustainability yearbook*. Retrieved from https://www.robecosam.com/media/4/a/4/4a4b0ed7c93f685fe53089cb4965ca7f_160120-robecosam-yearbook2016-en-vdef_tcm1011-15961.pdf (Last accessed 12th July 2018.

Reid, W.V., Chen, D., Goldfarb, L., Hackmann, H., Lee, Y.T., Mokhele, K., . . . Whyte, A.V. (2010). Earth system science for global sustainability: Grand challenges. *Science*, 330(6006), 916–917.

Reuters (2010). *BP CEO apologizes*. Retrieved from www.reuters.com/article/us-oil-spill-bp-apology/bp-ceo-apologizes-for-thoughtless-oil-spill-comment-idUSTRE6515NQ20100602. (Last accessed 10th July 2018).

Risse, M. (2012). *On global justice*. Princeton/Oxford: Princeton University Press.

Rittel, H. & Webber, M. (1973). Dilemmas in a general theory of planning. *Policy Sciences*, 4, 155–169.

Robinson Hickman, G. & Sorenson, G. (2014). *The power of invisible leadership: How a compelling common purpose inspires exceptional leadership*. London: Sage.

Roche, O., Freundlich, F., Shipper, F. & Manz, C.C. (2018). Mondragon's amorphous network structure: 'Making the whole truly greater than the sum of its parts'. *Organizational Dynamics*, 47, 155–164.

Ross, L. & Nisbett, R.E. (1991). *The person and the situation: Perspectives of social psychology*. Philadelphia: Temple University Press.

Schaeffer, M., Hare, W., Rahmstorf, S. & Vermeer, M. (2012). Long-term sea-level rise implied by 1.5C and 2C warming levels. *National Climate Change*, 2, 867–870.

Schaubroeck, J., Hannah, S.T., Avolio, B.J., Kozlowski, S.W.J., Lord, R.L., Trevino, L.K., Peng, A.C. & Dimotakas, N. (2012). Embedding ethical leadership within and across organization levels. *Academy of Management Journal*, 55, 1053–1078.

Scherer, A.G. & Palazzo, G. (2011). The new political role of business in a globalized world: A review of a new perspective on CSR and its implications for the firm, governance, and democracy. *Journal of Management Studies*, 48, 899–931.

Schoenherr, T., Power, D., Narasimhan, R. & Samson, D. (2012). Competitive capabilities among manufacturing plants in developing, emerging, and industrialized countries: A comparative analysis. *Decision Sciences*, 43(1), 37–71.

Schumacher, E.F. (1973). *Small is beautiful: Economics as if people mattered*. New York: Harper Row.

Schumpeter, J.A. (1934). *The theory of economic development*. Cambridge, MA: Harvard University Press.

Seelos, C. & Mair, J. (2007). Profitable business models and market creation in the context of peep poverty: A strategic view. *Academy of Management Perspectives*, 21(4), 49–63.

Selsky, J.W. & Parker, B. (2005). Cross-sector partnerships to address social issues: Challenges to theory and practice. *Journal of Management*, 31(6), 849–873.

Senge, P. (1990). *The fifth discipline: The art and science of the learning organization*. New York: Doubleday.

Shah, A. (2013). Poverty facts and stats. *Global Issues* (7th January). Retrieved from www.globalissues.org/article/26/poverty-facts-and-stats. (Last accessed 31st March 2017).

Shand, L., Kalinina, E. & Patel, K. (2017). *Executive pay: Review of FTSE 100 executive pay packages*. CIPD. Retrieved from www.cipd.co.uk/Images/7571-ceo-pay-in-the-ftse100-report-web_tcm18-26441.pdf. (Last accessed 22nd April 2018).

Shao, R., Aquino, K. & Freeman, D. (2008). Beyond moral reasoning: A review of moral identity research and its implications for business ethics. *Business Ethics Quarterly*, 18(4), 513–540.

Shuid, A.N., Kempster, R. & McGuffin, L.J. (2017). ReFOLD: A server for the refinement of 3D protein models guided by accurate quality estimates. *Nucleic Acids Research*, 45, W422–W428.

Slack, N., Brandon-Jones, A. & Johnston, R. (2011). *Essentials of operations management*. London: Pearson Education UK.

Smith, A. (1759). *The theory of moral sentiments*. London: Pantianos Classics.

Smith, A. (1937). *An inquiry into the nature and causes of the wealth of nations*. E. Cannan (Ed.). New York: Random House. [Orig. pub. 1776, London: Methuen & Co.].

Smith, G.A. (1962). *Business, society, and the individual: Problems in responsible leadership of private enterprise organizations operating in a free society*. Homewood, IL: R.D. Irwin.

Sowcik, M., & Allen, S.J. (2013). Getting down to business: A look at leadership education in business schools. *Journal of Leadership Education, 12*(3), 57–75.

Stammer, R. (2016). It pays to become a B-Corporation. *Harvard Business Review* (December). Retrieved from https://hbr.org/2016/12/it-pays-to-become-a-b-corporation. (Last accessed 17th May 2018).

Steffen, W., Richardson, K., Rockström, J., Cornell, S.E., Fetzer, I., Bennett, E.M., Biggs, R., Carpenter, S.R., de Vries, W., de Wit, C.A., Flke, C., Gerten, D., Heinke, J., Mace, G.M., Persson, L.M., Ramanathan, V., Reyers, B. & Sörlin, S. (2015). Planetary boundaries: Guiding human development on a changing planet. *Science, 347*(6223), 1259855. doi: 10.1126/science.1259855

Stoian, C. & Gilman, M. (2017). Corporate social responsibility that 'pays': A strategic approach to CSR for SMEs. *Journal of Small Business Management,* 55(1), 5–31.

Storey, J. (1995). Human resource management: Still marching on or marching out. In J. Storey (Ed.), *Human resource management: A critical text* (pp. 3–32). London: Routledge.

Stork, N.E. (2010). Re-assessing current extinction rates: Biodiversity. *Conservation,* 19, 357–371.

Taghian, M., D'Souza, C. & Polonsky, M.J. (2015). A stakeholder approach to corporate social responsibility, reputation and business performance. *Social Responsibility Journal,* 11(2), 340–363.

Taguchi, G. (1986). *Introduction to quality engineering.* White Plains, NY: UNI-PUB/Kraus International Publications.

Task Force on Human Capital Management (2003). *Accounting for people report.* UK Department for Trade and Industry. Retrieved from http://webar chive.nationalarchives.gov.uk/+/www.berr.gov.uk/bbf/financial-reporting/busi ness-reporting/Accounting%20for%20people/page38836.html. (Last accessed 8th April 2018).

Tata Group (2015). *We dream of a better world: The Tata Group and the SDGs.* Retrieved from www.tata.com/pdf/report-tata-group-and-the-SDGs.pdf. (Last accessed 24th May 2018).

Trevino, L.K., Brown, M. & Hartman, L.P. (2003). A qualitative investigation of perceived executive leadership: Perceptions from inside and outside the executive suite. *Human Relations,* 56(1), 5–37.

Ulrich, P. (2008). *Integrative economic ethics.* Cambridge: Cambridge University Press.

UNICEF (2017). *Fighting famine in a race against time.* Retrieved from www. unicef.org/emergencies/index. (Last accessed 11th June 2018).

Unilever (2017). *Sustainable living plan.* Retrieved from www.unilever.com/ Images/unilever-sustainable-living-plan-2017_tcm244-521742_en.pdf. (Last accessed 26th August 2018).

United Nations (2015). *Adoption of the Paris agreement.* (Draft decision -/CP.21). Paris: Conference of the Parties.

United Nations General Assembly (2014). *Open working group proposal for sustainable development goals (A/68/970).* New York, NY, USA: United Nations.

United Nations Global Compact (2017). *Making global goals local business: New era for responsible business.* New York: United Nations.

Unruh, G., Kiron, D., Kruschwitz, N., Reeves, M., Rubel, H. & Meyer Zum Felde, A. (2016). *Investing for a sustainable future.* Boston, MA: Massachusetts Institute of Technology.

Varghese, E. (2018). *The infinite potential of human resourcefulness, Part I: A new chapter in talent.* Retrieved from https://medium.com/the-future-of-finan cial-services/the-infinite-potential-of-human-resourcefulness-part-i-a-new-chapter-in-talent-72f0eb1b52e0. (Last accessed 22nd July 2018).

Verrecchia, R.E. (1983). Discretionary disclosure. *Journal of Accounting and Economics,* 5 (December), 179–194.

Vickers, G. (1965). *The art of judgement.* London: Chapman Hall (reprinted 1983, London: Harper Row).

Wade-Benzoni, K.A., Hernandez, M., Medvec, V. & Messick, D. (2008). In fairness to future generations: The role of egocentrism, uncertainty, power, and stewardship in judgements of intergenerational allocations. *Journal of Experimental Social Psychology*, 44, 233–245.

Wade-Benzoni, K.A., Sondak, H. & Galinsky, A.D. (2010). Leaving a legacy: Intergenerational allocations of benefits and burdens. *Business Ethics Quarterly*, 20(1), 7–34.

Waldman, D.A. & Balven, R.M. (2014). Responsible leadership: Theoretical issues and research directions. *Academy of Management Perspectives*, 28(3), 224–234.

Waldman, D.A. & Galvin, B.M. (2008). Alternative perspectives of responsible leadership. *Organizational Dynamics*, 37(4), 327–341.

Walker, D. (2009). *A review of corporate governance in UK banks and other financial industry entities*. London: HMSO.

Weber, M. (1910). *The Protestant ethic and the spirit of capitalism*. New York: Charles Scribner's Sons.

Weitzman, M.L. (2009). Some basic economics of climate change. In J.-P. Touffut (Ed.), *Changing climate, changing economy*. Cheltenham: Edward Elgar. Retrieved from https://scholar.harvard.edu/weitzman/publications/some-basic-economics-climate-change. (Last accessed 14th September 2018).

Whiteman, G., Walker, B. & Perego, P. (2013). Planetary boundaries: Ecological foundations for corporate sustainability. *Journal of Management Studies*, 50(2), 307–336.

Wilcox, T., Lowry, D. & Public Interest Enterprises, Inc. (2000). Beyond resourcefulness: Casual workers and the human-centered organisation. *Business and Professional Ethics Journal*, 19(3), 29–53.

Womack, J.P. & Jones, D.T. (1990). *The machine that changed the world*. New York: Rawson Associates.

Womack, J.P. & Jones, D.T. (1996). Beyond Toyota: How to route out waste and pursue perfection. *Harvard Business Review*, 74(5), 140–149.

World Bank (1992). *World Development Report 1992: Development and the environment*. New York/Oxford: Oxford University Press.

World Bank (2016). *People, spaces, deliberation: Exploring the interactions among public opinion, governance and the public sphere*. Retrieved from https://blogs.worldbank.org/publicsphere/world-s-top-100-economies-31-countries-69-corporations. (Last accessed 30th August 2018).

World Business Council for Sustainable Development (2017). *Business and the SDGs: Role, opportunity and responsibility*. Retrieved from www.wbcsd.org/Clusters/Social-Impact/News/Business-and-the-SDGs-Role-opportunity-and-responsibility. (Last accessed 11th June 2018).

World Wildlife Fund (2015). *Ocean assets valued at $24 Trillion, but dwindling fast: New WWF analysis makes the economic case for immediate conservation action*. Retrieved from www.worldwildlife.org/press-releases/ocean-assets-valued-at-24-trillion-but-dwindling-fast. (Last accessed 4th August 2018).

Wren, D.A. (2011). The centennial of Frederick W. Taylor's the principles of scientific management: A retrospective commentary. *Journal of Business and Management*, 17(1), 11–22.

Yang, H. (2010). Moral capitalism. *Journal of International Business Ethics*, 3(2), 80–81.

Yin, H. & Schmeidler, P.J. (2009). Why do standardized ISO 14001 environmental management systems lead to heterogeneous environmental outcomes? *Business Strategy and the Environment*, 18, 469–486.

Young, I.M. (2011). *Responsibility for Justice*. Oxford/New York: Oxford University Press.

Zald, M.N. & Lounsbury, M. (2010). The wizards of Oz: Towards an institutional approach to elites, expertise and command posts. *Organization Studies*, 31(7), 963–996.

Index

Note: Page numbers in italics indicate figures and page numbers in bold indicate tables.

Printed in the United States
by Baker & Taylor Publisher Services